IS CHRIST THE SAVIOUR A PAGAN GOD?

The Revd Dr Gabriel J. Anan, PhD

Paperback: 978-1-964744-14-8
eBook: 978-1-964744-15-5
Library of Congress Control Number: 2024912461

First Edition

Any Scriptural quotations marked KJV are from the Holy Bible, King James
Version (Authorised Version), first published in 1611. Classic Reference Bible,
Copyright © 1983 by The Zondervan Corporation.

And Scripture quotations marked NKJV are taken from the New King James
Version (Authorised Version), used by permission. All rights reserved.

Cover image design by Adom Anan, daughter of the author.

Ordering Information:

Prime Seven Media
518 Landmann St.
Tomah City, WI 54660

Printed in the United States of America

(A)

(**The spccial note:** The author of this book sincerely gives thanks to all the ancient, medieval and contemporary historians. As the experts in your special fields in history, your contribution in this book is vastly appreciated, since the proceeds from the sale of this book would be for the charity).

(B)

The WISDOM OF THE CREATOR of the world is greater than that of a mere COMMON SENSE knowledge of human beings. Thus it's infantile to want to know why if the Creator is Omnipotent should choose to send down Jesus Christ to die for our sins instead of getting rid of Satan once and for all. He is the Creator and can choose to do what is appropriate to Him in His own way.

CONTENTS

PART ONE

What is the Paganism and Tradition?

PART TWO

Why Should Christ be Referred to as God?

PART THREE

Which Gods were being worshipped Before Christianity?

ALSO BY THE AUTHOR

The Organic Church: A Practical Approach to Managing Change (2011).

The Illusive World of Love: Demystifying the Mindset of True Love (2015)

The Truth About Material Wealth: Is it God's Blessing in Disguise? (2015).

Discerning the Prophetic Message: Knowing the Truth (2016)

Baptism: Is the Avowal for Born Again Christian (2017)

The Creator God Blessed the Seventh Day: Keep it Holy (2018)

DYNAMISM OF SUCCESS: Revealing the Managing Strategies for Individuals and Organisations in the World of Uncertainty and Change (2018)

THE EFFECT OF ABSENT PROPHET FOR HAM DESCENDANTS: Ham - Japhet - Shem (2021)

Does the Creator of the World Answer Prayer? If so How? (2023)

Who's the True Creator of the World? (2023)

The Uniqueness of Jesus Christ the Saviour (2024)

STATEMENT OF FAITH
BY THE AUTHOR

In the European Union, the title of *doctor* refers primarily to holders of post- graduate research *doctorates*, such as the *PhD*. With this regards, my attention was drawn to a personal issue regarding ambiguity of professional status in the UK due to the fact that unlike the UK, many European languages have the appropriate term for a medical practitioner. For example the term *Arzt* is in German, *iatros* in Greece, *Lääkäri* in Finnish, *Läkare* in Swedish and others; but in the UK, the term used for a medical practitioner is *doctor (Dr)*, same as the *doctor (Dr)* for the *PhD* holders. For this reason, I was compelled to declare publicly my status as a philosophy *doctor (Dr)*, and not a medical +*doctor (Dr)*, thus necessitated the use of appropriate title the *PhD* after my name on all my books.

It's undeniably fact that a *medical practitioner (or doctor)* in the UK, is a profession well known to many people, especially families and their children for health issues. In this respect, it's necessary to make a clear distinction between the two professions to show mostly parents and their children to know me as *philosophy doctor (PhD)* and not a *medical doctor*. Otherwise, they might be under the assumption that I could be a *medical doctor* who might be able to provide them with medical assistance for their health, especially in the case of emergency. Therefore, making such a distinction of the two professions clarifies any ambiguity or wrong perceptions people might have, especially parents with their children and young people.

The Revd Dr Gabriel J Anan

DEDICATION

*In the loving memory of my late parents especially my mother (Mansah), whose foreknowledge about me to be a priest, shaped my being and illuminated my heart to respond positively to the call of the Living God for the Ministry. I grew up in a Catholic family, both my parents were Catholics. In the pursuance of my faith I joined the Church of England. In the process I was trained and ordained priest. Encouraged to continue searching for the divine truth from the Scriptures led me to have written eight books. My greatest revelation came when I was deeply entrenched preparing a sermon for the Church of England parish church of St George and St Ethelbert, East Ham London for the 24th December 2017. The information l I gathered from my family and friends and the records of Christian History opened a new understanding from what I thought I knew. I also found that most of these New Bibles have removed some of verses and words on the deity of our Lord Jesus Christ from the KING JAMES Version, the most important one is in **Matthew 17:21** for **fasting** and **prayer** recommended by our Lord Jes us Christ Himself, the New Bibles include: NIV, NASV. It has also been compounded by the fact that some of the, The Ten Commandments of God have also been changed or even removed. This is to fulfil the prophecy of Daniel Chapters 2 and 7 about the Four Empires and what the **__Beast__** would do at the end time by changing God's law of the Seventh-Day Sabbath to replace it with the man-made sun-god Sunday Sabbath and other* *rules before the second coming of the Saviour as indicated fully in the book. I thank the Lord for revealing my salvation as He did to the Apostles in Luke 24:45 to open their minds to understand the Scriptures. The living God is worthy of praise, and I thank the Lord Jesus Christ on behalf of my parents and to forgive their lack of knowledge about changes made by the* **Catholicism** *the* **Beast,** *may they rest in His perfect peace.*

The Revd Dr Gabriel J. Anan

ACKNOWLEDGEMENTS

I am indebted for the advice of a number of people both men and women: who are experts in their fields of expertise. They contributed massively to the areas of most needed knowledge during my dialogue with them, with the view to gathering the necessary information for this book. Their willingness to speak out candidly and intellectually resulted in the collection of crucial materials without which this book would not have been in print. I am grateful to my publishers who found the manuscript useful for publication. I am also grateful for my family whose patience allowed me to get on with my loneliness as I continued to compose the message being received and digested for use. I thank my friends and readers of my previous books and the vicar, Revd Canon David Haokip at the Parish of St Georges and St Ethelbert to whom I have worked very closely for a number of years and all the staff of the Church for their morale support.

The Revd Dr Gabriel J Anan

PREFACE

Since human beings are in constant search for quick answers or solutions to many issues they face in this world, the book assesses the importance of **prayer** in the life of believers. Aside from that, the text of the book also highlights the important events and activities in the Bible where prayers on various issues have occurred including miracles, healings, raising up the dead and many more. Further, the text is the investigation of historical backgrounds and the records of **Christian history** for the enrichment of the Christendom. It thus began by looking at the overall Four Empires of Daniel's Prophecies in Chapters 2 and 7 in the King James Bible (KJV) which is the authoritative Word of God. The Four empires include: the Babylonian Empire, the Medo-Persian Empire, the Greek Empire and the Roman Empire. Is the prophecy of Daniel being fulfilled with the false Christ, the Beast occupying the temple of the Most High God and thereby bent on changing the law especially the Ten Commandments written with the finger of God (Exodus 31:18 (KJV), and the introduction of new rules like new moon from Luna to Sola, the Sabbath Day from Saturday to Sunday and some festivals such as Christmas (worship in honour of god of saturn, saturnalia) Easter (the goddess of sex and fertility). These are pagans festivals merged with introduced into Christian beliefs by Rome. Resurrection from the dead, was merged with the pagan celebration, and became known as Easter. The meaning of Easter was also changed to reflect its new Christian orientation. The text therefore is based on extensive primary and particularly secondary research. It extracted from various theological and historical Christian books of different denominations and other religious groups about their stance on the clarity of various important phrases and terms being practised in the churches. It is thus to bring some awareness to the public and even to most of the church members in order to enhance their faiths and belies. The most compelling question engulfing the faith of many believers is whether Christians should observe Seventh Day Sabbath being observed by the Jews before the coming of Jesus Christ when He and His followers also observed. Are Christians under the grace of Christ therefore have no need to observe the law of God which has been affirmed, blessed and summarised as 'Love' by Christ? Has the death of Christ abolished the Commandments in the Old Testament or did He come to die in order to remove the Original Sin brought into the world by one man (Adam)? As the Bible says 'the sin of one man (Adam) brought death into the earth and the Death and Resurrection of one man (Christ) brought life into the world.

If the Deity of Jesus Christ is removed from these new Bibles, do these Bible still retain the holiness and the authoritative Word of our Lord Jesus Christ?

Since Christ is coming for the second time, to judge the living and the death, will He judge people on how much faith and belief they have in Him or will He judge people on how much they have OBEYED His Commands. Jesus said 'If you LOVE me OBEY my commands. The book attempts further, to provide responses to the queries posed for the awareness and thus to instil the importance of salvation and much faith into believers world-wide such as the commands of Jesus Christ in John 3:3-5 to be Born Again to enable believer to enter the Kingdom of heaven. Other prevailing issues for reflection include the fact that: (1) there is a misconception among many Christians that one does not need to be physically Baptised to become Born Again. And that a person just needs to believe and have faith and accept Christ with their mouth as a Personal Saviour thus saved satisfying the specific condition to enter heaven. If this is the case, then: (1) if we claim to have been 'Born Again' Christian, having believed and confessed faith with the mouth that Jesus is the Lord and a personal Saviour, why is Jesus Christ still coming for the second time to judge us of our sin (if so, which sin?), (2) If we all born in sin from birth, which requires forgiveness of this *original sin*, then when should it be reasonable for children raised in believing households reach the age of reason to confess with the mouth that Jesus is Lord, and thus believe in their heart that God raised Him from the dead in order to be saved as a 'Born Again' Christian? (3) Is physical Baptism a Necessity? (4) How true is Predestination? (5) Did Jesus Christ receive training for His Ministry? The prevailing issues raised in this book are paramount importance for our salvation because they give food for spiritual thought to engage us for serious studies of the Scriptures with reflection.

The Revd Dr Gabriel J Anan

INTRODUCTION

Importance of the New Testament

**Whatever has occupied mankind for so long,
it is worth knowing it.
Gabriel Anan**

**The important thing is to not stop questioning
Albert Einstein**

Understanding the Issue of Deitism in the New Testament

This book accesses the reasons why Jesus Christ the Saviour of humanity should not be called or referred to with the pagan word God which was in existence and worshipped in the ancient world before the coming of Jesus 2000 years ago. Jesus Christ must be called the Christ the Saviour or Redeemer. This is because whether the word God is written with small or capital letter it still remains a pagan evil false spirit of Satan. Holding the thoughts has been the main focus of the text of this book which provides my final exegesis of revelation of the true nature of Jesus Christ the Redeemer of humanity which I began investigating and thus highlighting in my previous two books: WHO'S THE TRUE CREATOR

OF THE WORLD and THE UNIQUENESS OF JESUS
CHRIST THE SAVIOUR".

How the Spiritism began or started in the world

Special attention must be drawn here due to the historical
importance of how spiritism began in America and came
into the world and spread like hot fire throughout the world.
The fact is that there were three orphaned Fox sisters who
were possessed by Satan and began communicating with
the spirit in the early years of 1800AD. The phenomena
continued and progressed from there and became a Spiritual
church with their three older sisters Lelah, Marggeretta
and Catherine Fox and other men praying and speaking
in tongues through Satan influence. The church came to
Gold Coast now Ghana in the year 1932 known as Kyire
Bentuo church before some years later it adopted the New
Testament name as Pentecostal Church.

The words to use by Pastors in order to invoke the spirit are
the followings:

1. Ye ma ma ma ma san da lis: is the name for ma me
   water the sea gogddess
2. Mountain top for fasting
3. I am that I am is the another name of the spirit
4. da ka ta ya: is a demon spirit of miracle. This is the
   spirit of demons from shalia oriental
5. And many others…..

The first woman who Satan used to start speaking in the
unknown tongues is Margaret McDonalds.

The church also became a Medium Spiritual Centre in
1846. As indicated earlier the creation of spiritism started
in America by the three Fox sisters who were possessed

by Satan and began speaking with the spirit in the early years of 1800AD. They continued communicating with the spirit in some more years before their elder sisters by name Leah, Margaretta and Catherine Fox and other men were instrumental in promoting the growth of the church with its centre at 312 Azusa street in Los Angeles USA. The church grew very quickly in popularity and spread like fire throughout and reached Gold Coast now Ghana in 1932. It has continued to grow ever since with praying and speaking in tongues or praying in unknown tongues.

Salvation is through Him alone

The true Holy Spirit is exposing many church leaders. It is undeniably fact that many Priests and Pastors are members of the evil secret societies such as Freemasons.

In many churches you can nowadays see many people including the Senior Pastors speaking in demonic tongues through the influence of Satan. Another demonic practice is where a Pastor will openly hold up two Freemasonry swords in his two hands in prayer, whilst in other churches a Pastor will hold up a comb and a magic wand and would lift them up to pray to God for protection. These Pastors would raise the objects up and would ask the church members to also pray for their needs and protection to God as they focus on those idols in the name of Jesus, can the Light and Darkness co-exist?; would the Lord Jesus Christ answer such a prayer (1Peter 3:12-13)? Are they even worshipping Christ in the first place by praying to pagan God which is the false spirit of Satan? Can Jesus Christ who is the True and the Holy Spirit co-exist with the false spirit of Satan which is a pagan God? Of course not..? The word God/Satan was in existence and worshipped before the coming of Jesus Christ 2000 years ago, so Jesus is not a

pagan God and must not be called or referred to as God which is of Satan. How can we justify that the church and members would be saved by the Saviour Jesus Christ? If these large churches are heavily involved in demonic worship instead of our Lord Jesus Christ the Saviour, what is the fate of salvation of those small churches?

Well, Christ came to save everyone who will turn to Him as Jesus Christ whether as an individual or as a group especially families. So salvation is for all regardless of tribe or nation so long as one is adhered to the teachings of the Christ the Saviour.

The main issue is that according to many Bible verses, Satan is God and ruler of this world, before and even after Jesus Christ.

Whereas the mission of Satan is to lead humanity astray, conversely Jesus Christ is for the truth salvation for the humanity. Thus the book attempts to highlight the fact that, the ministry of Jesus Christ is the truth for everyone who would come to Him in truth for salvation. His message of salvation was taken into the world known as the Great Commission by His Apostles. So in order to highlight the truth of Christ's ministry, and to establish the genuineness of His undiluted divine words which His enemies have tried their hardest to dilute them, has been the main reason to highlight the truth. For instance when Jesus said to His disciples "My Father in Heaven", some of them have added the word a God to it to become "my Father God in heaven". Another issue for instance is this, why is it that Jesus Christ who is the True Holy Spirit without sin, would be referred to or being called with the word of the pagan deity as "god/God" which is the false spirit of Satan.

But Jesus Christ has been compared to various historical and mythological traditions within the Mediterranean Basin including Dionysus, Mithras, Sol Invictus, Osiris, Yahweh, Asclepius. Other pagan Gods include: the Greek, Roman, Egyptian, Celtic, Israelites, India and others. These pagan Gods are the false spirits of Satan worshipped by the ancient world before the coming of Jesus Christ 2000 years ago. These false spirits are still being worshipped by many religions and cultures.

These pagan Gods include: Gaia, Gera, Zeus, Junos, Jupiter, Neptune, Venus, Isis, Osiri, Horus, Morrigan, Danu, Lugh, Yahweh, Baal, Tetragrammaton, Brahma, Mazda and many others. But Jesus Christ is not a pagan God because He is NOT a false spirit of Satan but rather the True Holy Spirit Who has no sin.

Another query to highlight is of how these pagan gods/Gods which had been worshipped by the ancient world and still being worshipped by many cultures and religions, could now be claimed to be the true almighty creator of the world. These are the Satan's major spirits such as <u>Yahweh, Brahma, Ahura Mazda and Jupiter</u> who had been deceiving the world claiming to be almighty and monotheistic God who have created the world. And why should Jesus Christ who came to this world 2000 years ago as the true Holy Spirit and the Saviour of humanity through Him that the <u>Father Created the world, (Colossians 1: 16-17)</u> should to be called or referred to as a god/God? Is this not one of the reasons that Jesus refers to it as blasphemy in Mathew 12: 30-32) when Pharisees referred to Him as <u>Beelzebul?</u>

The truth is that if someone or a spirit is called or referred to as god/God, that person or thing is associated with the false spirit of Satan. So, when Jesus was referred to as

Yahweh/God, He rebuked the leadership of Israel when they would not accept Him because He is the Truth and not like their god Yahweh which they wanted Him to be. He rebuked them saying His anointing and being a deity is not of the Kingdom of this world. This is because He is the Truth not a liar like their lying, evil spirit and a murderer like their god Yahweh from the beginning of the world, (John 8: 44-46).

So, to clarify this misconception of how the pagan god/ God of Satan false spirit which had been worshipped by the ancient world and still being worshipped by many cultures and religions before the coming of Jesus Christ, could now be claimed to be the true almighty creator of the world.

The truth is that if someone or a spirit is called or referred to as god/God, that person or thing is associated with the false spirit of Satan. So, when Jesus was referred to as Yahweh/God, He rebuked the leadership of Israel when they would not accept Him because He is the Truth and not like their god Yahweh which they wanted Him to be. He rebuked them saying His anointing and being a deity is not of the Kingdom of this world. This is because He is the Truth not a liar like their lying, evil spirit and a murderer like their god Yahweh from the beginning of the world, (John 8: 44-46).

So, to get some understanding of the issues raised, I resorted in employing primary and secondary research in order to obtain some ideas from people and the experts in their special fields. In so doing, it was revealed in this research that since the pagan god/God is spirit, even though this spirit is false spirit of Satan and whilst Jesus Christ is Holy and True Spirit, many people would not comprehend or see the difference and thus would take a lot of biblical exegesis, hence this book.

However the ministry of Jesus Christ started when He called the disciples. The 12 Apostles were called by Christ and they followed Him till His successful Ministry. He taught us about the truth of salvation on what to do and what not to do with His grace.

Undoubtedly, the Apostles received the true divine message revealed to them by the Holy Spirit of Christ. The issue is did the translators and those who collated the divine message received the same blessing of the Holy Spirit? Probably not because it was revealed that the Greeks and Romans who translated the original bible from Hebrew and Aramaic for the Septuagint, Pentateush and Vulgate, were the worshippers of pagan gods and the false spirit of Satan. The translators of King James Version Bible copied and compiled from the original bibles of the Greeks and the Romans mentioned above.

Aside from the fact that Jesus Christ is the true Creator of the world and everything, He is also Perfect and the true Holy Spirit and the Saviour of humanity. For this reason we need to believe in Him not just having faith in Him but to follow and do what He has taught us about truth, forgiveness, no stealing, no killing, bow down to no idols or worship any gods, known as the Divine Laws.

The Significant of the Last Supper

The Last Supper is what we call the last meal Jesus ate with His disciples before His betrayal and arrest. The Last Supper is recorded in the Synoptic Gospels (Matthew 26:17–30; Mark 14:12–26; Luke 22:7–30). It was more than Jesus' last meal; it was a Passover meal, as well. One of 0the important moments of the Last Supper is Jesus' command to remember what He was about to do on behalf of all mankind: shed His blood on the cross thereby paying the debt of our sins (Luke 22:19).

In addition to predicting His suffering and death for our salvation (Luke 22:15–16), Jesus also used the Last Supper to imbue the Passover with new meaning, institute the New Covenant, establish an ordinance for the church, and foretell Peter's denial of Him (Luke 22:34) and Judas Iscariot's betrayal (Matthew 26:21–24).

It can be argued that, the Last Supper brought the Old Testament observance of the Passover feast to its fulfilment. The Passover was an especially event for the Jewish people in that it commemorated the time when their **Yahweh/God** spared them from the plague of physical death and brought them out of slavery in Egypt (Exodus 11:1—13:16). During the Last Supper with His apostles, Jesus took two symbols associated with Passover and imbued them with **fresh meaning** as a way to **remember His sacrifice, which saves us from spiritual death and delivers us from spiritual bondage:**

> **"After taking the cup, he gave thanks and said, 'Take this and divide it among you. For I tell you I will not drink again from the fruit of the vine until the kingdom of the Father comes.' And he took bread, gave thanks and broke it, and gave it to them, saying, 'This is my body given for you; do this in remembrance of me.' In the same way, after the supper he took the cup, saying, 'This cup is the new covenant in my blood, which is poured out for you'" (Luke 22:17–20).**

Jesus' words during the Last Supper about the unleavened bread and the cup echo what He had said after **He fed the 5,000:** "I am the bread of life. Whoever comes to me will never go hungry, and whoever believes in me will never be thirsty. . . . I am the living bread that came down from heaven. Whoever eats this bread will live forever. This bread is my flesh, which I will give for the life of the world. . . . **Whoever eats my flesh and drinks my blood has eternal life, and I will raise them up at the last day.** For my flesh is real food and my blood is real drink" (John 6:35, 51, 54–55). Salvation comes through Christ and the sacrifice of His physical body on the cross.

Also during the Last Supper, Jesus taught the principles of **servanthood** and **forgiveness** as He washed His disciples' feet: "The greatest among you should be like the youngest, and the one who rules like the one who serves. For who is greater, the one who is at the table or the one who serves? Is it not the one who is at the table? **But I am among you as one who serves**" (Luke 22:26–27; John 13:1–20).

The Last Supper today is remembered during the Lord's Supper, or communion (1 Corinthians 11:23–33). The Bible teaches that Jesus' death was typified in the offering of the Passover sacrifice (John 1:29). John notes that Jesus' death resembles the Passover sacrifice in that His bones were not broken (John 19:36; cf. Exodus 12:46). And Paul said, "Christ, our Passover lamb, has been sacrificed" (1 Corinthians 5:7). Jesus is the fulfilment of the Law, including the feasts of the Lord (Matthew 5:17).

However, at the **Last Supper, the apostles were alone with Jesus** (Luke 22:14), which suggests that this particular meal has specific meaning for the **church, of which the apostles became the foundation** (Ephesians 2:20). While the Last Supper had implications for the Jews, it was designed for the church as well. Today the Lord's Table is one of two ordinances observed by the church.

The Last Supper was rooted in the Old Covenant even as it heralded the New. Jeremiah 31:31 promised a New Covenant between Jesus and Israel, in which H said, "I will put my law in their minds and write it on their hearts. I will be their Lord, and they will be my people" (Jeremiah 31:33). Jesus made a direct reference to this **New Covenant** during the Last Supper: "This cup is the new covenant in my blood" (Luke 22:20). A new dispensation was on the horizon. In His grace, the New Covenant applies to more than Israel; **everyone who has faith in Christ will be saved (see Ephesians 2:12–14).**

The Last Supper was a significant event and proclaimed a turning point in the Fathher's plan for the world. In comparing the crucifixion of Jesus to the feast of Passover, we can readily see the redemptive nature of Christ's death. As symbolised by the original Passover sacrifice in the Old Testament, Christ's death atones for the sins of His people; **His blood rescues us** from death and saves us from slavery. **Today, the Lord's Supper** is when believers reflect upon Christ's perfect sacrifice and know that, through our faith in receiving Him, we will be with Him forever (Luke 22:18; Revelation 3:20)

The History of the New Testament

Understanding the origins of this remarkable book of scripture is very essential for our faith in the Saviour Jesus Christ. Wayment explains further that, each volume of sacred scripture has its own unique history and bears testimony to the gospel of salvation in its own distinct way. The New Testament has the distinction of

being the volume of scripture that preserves the words of individuals who knew Jesus personally or who followed Him shortly after His Resurrection—making t he New Testament an invaluable resource to help us come closer to the Saviour and gain a glimpse of His mortal ministry. An understanding of the history of the New Testament, how it has been passed down to us, and who wrote it can increase our appreciation of this remarkable book of scripture and in turn give us greater spiritual strength as we, like the early followers of Jesus Christ, face our own trials.

What Is the New Testament?

In the years shortly after Jesus died, the term "New Testament" would not have referred to a collection of books about the Lord's life and death but more precisely to something *He said to His disciples on the night of the Last Supper: "This is my blood of the new testament, which is shed for many for the remission of sins" (Matthew 26:28; emphasis added). The Greek words translated as "new testament" actually refer to a covenant, the new covenant the Savior extends to us through the Atonement.* The writings recorded in the Bible and referred to as the New Testament describe, document, and teach about that new covenant between the Lord and His people.

The writings preserved in the New Testament focus upon different aspects of the Saviour's ministry. The New Testament begins with the Gospels, a term that means the "good news," referring to the life, ministry, and divine role of Jesus Christ. The New Testament also contains a history of the first missionary efforts of the Church (the book of Acts); letters from early leaders, such as Peter and Paul, that admonish the early Christians (who were also called Saints) to remain true to the faith; a testimony (Hebrews); and an apocalypse (Revelation) that promises the return of the Lord in the latter days. Each of the writers has a different perspective to offer, and each wrote with a specific audience in mind rather than attempting to fill in perceived gaps in the historical record. In the middle of the fourth century A.D., the 27 books that record the new covenant of the Lordship of Jesus Christ the Saviour, were gathered together and ordered as they appear today.

How Was the New Testament Passed Down to Us?

From the larger group of disciples, Jesus called 12 men as Apostles. Those men followed Him throughout His ministry, suffered with Him, and also enjoyed triumphs and Spirit-filled experiences. After Jesus died, the Apostles, along with other faithful followers, began to record their experiences. Two events may have triggered their desire to preserve their records about the life of Jesus: first, Jerusalem and the temple fell to a Roman army in A.D. 70. Second, the forces of apostasy were already at work (see Acts 20:29–30). Therefore, many of the writings in the New Testament were recorded to help the faithful see their way through the calamity and controversy of their day.

Looking back on their experiences, we can learn how they faced troubling times and how the good news of the gospel became a steadying power in the struggle against the forces of apostasy.

Toward the end of the first century, all of the writings now preserved in the New Testament were completed and circulated widely among the branches of the

Church. Scribes made copies of the texts on papyrus and then later on parchment, but there were relatively few copies available. Church members gathered the books that were available to them and read and studied the words of the Lord and the Apostles. One notable setback to the circulation of the scriptures was the persecution of Christians by the Roman emperor Diocletian in A.D. 303. He ordered that the Christian scriptures be burned and forced Christians to offer sacrifices to pagan gods. Many faithful individuals hid the sacred texts during those years of persecution. Later, when the first Christian emperor, Constantine, ordered new copies of the scriptures to be made, his scholars were able to recover books that had been used in the branches prior to Diocletian's edict. Our modern printed editions of the New Testament trace their ancestry to the copies of the Bible made during Constantine's day and therefore back to those individuals who sacrificed their safety to preserve the new covenant of the Lord.

Not long after Constantine had directed the New Testament to be copied and circulated anew, the books that compose our current Bible came to be organized in their present order. This order follows a pattern set by the Old Testament. The New Testament contains the Law (the Gospels), the history of Christianity (Acts), and the Prophets (Romans through Revelation). Both the Old and New Testaments end with a promise of the Lord's return (Malachi and Revelation). The placement of these prophetic works also emphasises a forward-looking hope of salvation and future revelation.

Who Wrote the New Testament?

Each author of the New Testament wrote with a distinct perspective on the saving mission of Jesus Christ. Two of the Gospels were written by Apostles: Matthew and John. These apostolic witnesses provide an eyewitness testimony to the life of Jesus. Two later followers of the Lord also wrote Gospels: Mark and Luke, who testified to what they had felt and heard. Both of these men were at one time companions of Paul (see Acts 12:25; 2 Timothy 4:11) and reflect in part the interests of the growing number of Saints who lived outside of Judea and who had never known the Lord in His lifetime. Instead, their accounts provide a vivid testimony of Him in whom they believed.

Paul's letters are likely the earliest writings in the New Testament, although they were not all written at the same time. His testimony was borne of experience as a missionary, from several powerful visions (see Acts 9:1–6; 2 Corinthians 12:1–7), and through personal association with Peter and others (see Galatians 1:18–19). He wrote largely to settle disputes within the branches, but at other times he wrote to his personal friends (Timothy and Titus). In one letter Paul asks that a slave owner accept the return of a runaway slave whom Paul had met while they were in prison (Philemon). Traditionally, the book of Hebrews is ascribed to Paul, although the usual introduction wherein he identifies himself as the author is not present. Regardless, the book testifies of how we can boldly come to the Lord through faith. Included in the New Testament after Paul's letters, Hebrews is a treatise on having faith in the face of adversity.

The short Epistle of James was also written quite early and contains references to Jesus's teachings from the

Sermon on the Mount that were transmitted orally and separately from the written Gospel of Matthew (see James 1:13; 4:12; 5:12). James, the Lord's younger brother, is the probable author of this epistle. He was privileged to know and see the resurrected Savior (see 1 Corinthians 15:7) and played an important role in many events in the Church's history (see Acts 15:13–29).

The New Testament also contains two letters by the Apostle Peter and three by the Apostle John. Both urged Christians to be faithful; Peter in particular was concerned about fidelity during times of trial.

Jude is one of the latest books written in the New Testament. Like James, this book was also probably written by one of the Lord's brothers ("Juda" in Mark 6:3). Jude wrote in an attempt to quell growing apostasy in the branches.

Finally, the New Testament ends with the revelation to the Apostle John, who recorded a vision of the Lord's return in glory to usher in His millennial reign. That vision describes in vivid detail the struggle between good and evil. Most of the chapters deal with events that were in the future for John, including events in the latter days our day.

For Whom Was the New Testament Written?

Because the New Testament is properly a new covenant between the Lord and those who have faith in Him, the books are intended for all those who seek to know Him, whether in this dispensation or in previous dispensations. Originally, the authors of the New Testament wrote texts that could be of immediate use in the branches of the Church in their day, with an understanding that they were recording the most important events in the history of humankind. John, for example, viewed his writings as a testimony: "These are written, that ye might believe that Jesus is the Christ, the Son of the Father; and that believing ye might have life through his name" (John 20:31). Others, such as Luke, wrote with the intent to document the history:

> "Forasmuch as many have taken in hand to set forth in order a declaration of those things which are most surely believed among us,
>
> "Even as they delivered them unto us, which from the beginning were eyewitnesses, and ministers of the word;
>
> "It seemed good to me also, having had perfect understanding of all things from the very first, to write unto thee in order" (Luke 1:1–3).

Early Christians were diverse, some coming from Jewish families, while others had been raised in Gentile homes, while still others likely had very little formal religion in their lives prior to being baptized. They were, in effect, a mirror of today's diverse group of Saints. Therefore, their struggles can reveal to us powerful lessons on how to overcome wickedness and remain faithful despite trial and temptation. They also show us how the branches struggled when they were very small and how there was safety in the words of the apostles and prophets.

A Testimony for Today

The New Testament reveals that during uncertain times, when some would not hearken to the call of the gospel, there was safety for those who "continued stedfastly in the apostles' doctrine and fellowship, and in breaking of bread, and in prayers" (Acts 2:42). Other examples teach us how even the righteous are tried (see 1 Corinthians 10:13) and how the heart of the gospel message is as simple today as it was 2,000 years ago: "Pure religion and undefiled before the Father is this, To visit the fatherless and widows in their affliction, and to keep himself unspotted from the world" (James 1:27). Like the Doctrine and Covenants, in which the *Prophet Joseph Smith bore the testimony "that he lives!" (D&C 76:22), the New Testament bears a similar testimony that the tomb was empty on Easter morning: "He is not here: for he is risen"* (Matthew 28:6).

Eyewitness Accounts

> "I love the New Testament's apostolic travels and miracles and the letters of Paul. Most of all, I love its eyewitness accounts of the words and the example and the Atonement of our Saviour Jesus Christ. I love the perspective and peace that come from reading the Bible."

Elder M. Russell Ballard of the Quorum of the Twelve Apostles, "The Miracle of the Holy Bible," *Liahona* and *Ensign,* May 2007, 81.

Many of the writings in the New Testament were recorded to help the faithful.

Apostles in the New Testament

The commissioning of the Twelve Apostles during the ministry of Jesus is described in the Synoptic Gospels.

After his resurrection, Jesus sent eleven of them (as Judas Iscariot by then had died) by the Great Commission to spread his teachings to all nations. This event has been called the dispersion of the Apostles.

In the Pauline epistles, Paul, although not one of the original twelve, described himself as an **apostle**, saying he was called by the resurrected Jesus himself during his road to Damascus event. He later describes himself as "an apostle to the Gentiles". The period and associated events in timeline of early Christianity during the lifetimes of the twelve apostles is called the Apostolic Age.

Names of the 12 disciples of Jesus Christ

1. Simon (also known as Peter)
2. Andrew (Peter's brother)
3. Jacob/James (son of Zebedee and John's brother)
4. John (son of Zebedee and Jacob's brother)
5. Philip (friend of Bartholomew/ Nathanael)
6. Bartholomew (friend of Philip, the Gospel of John refers him as Nathanael)
7. Matthew (the publican, or Levi)
8. Thomas (Thomas (also called Didymus (twin), the translation of his Hebrew name in the Greek Language)
9. Jacob / James (son of Alphaeus to distinguish him from Jacob/James (son of Zebedee))
10. Simon (the Canaanite)
11. Judas Iscariot (son of Simon Iscariot the characterization Iscariot is used to distinguish him from Judas of Jacob)
12. Judas of Jacob (Thaddaeus (or Lebbaeus); called "Judas the Zealot" in some translations).

Apostle and Terminology

The term *apostle* comes from the Greek *apóstolos* – formed from the prefix *apó*- 'from') and root *stéllō*, 'I send, I depart') – originally meaning 'messenger, envoy'. It has, however, a stronger sense than the word *messenger*, and is closer to a 'delegate'.

Biblical narratives

Mark 6:7–13 states that Jesus initially sent out these twelve in pairs (cf. Mt 10:5–42, Lk 9:1–6) to towns in Galilee. The text states that their initial instructions were to heal the sick and drive out demons. They are also instructed to "take nothing for their journey, except a staff only: no bread, no wallet, no money in their purse, but to wear sandals, and not put on two tunics," and that if any town rejects them they ought to shake the dust off their feet as they leave, a gesture which some scholars think was meant as a contemptuous threat.

Later in the Gospel narratives, the Twelve Apostles are described as having been commissioned to preach the Gospel to "all the nations," regardless of whether Jew or Gentile. Paul emphasised the important role of the apostles in the church of God when he said that the household of God is "built upon the foundation of apostles and prophets, Christ Jesus himself being the cornerstone."

Calling by Jesus

Vocation of the Apostles, The Exhortation to the Apostles.

All four canonical Gospels record the circumstances in which some of the disciples were recruited. According to the Gospel of John, Andrew, who was the disciple of John the Baptist, and another unnamed disciple of John the Baptist, traditionally believed to be John, upon hearing the Baptist point out Jesus as the "Lamb of God", followed Jesus and spent the day with him, thus becoming the first two disciples called by Jesus. For this reason the Eastern Orthodox Church honours Andrew with the name *Protokletos*, which means "the first called".

Despite Jesus only briefly requesting that they join him, they are all described as immediately consenting and abandoning their nets to do so. The immediacy of their consent has been viewed as an example of divine power, although this is not stated in the text. Another explanation is that some of the disciples may have heard of Jesus beforehand, as implied by the Gospel of John, which states that Andrew was a disciple of John the Baptist, and that he and his brother started following Jesus as soon as Jesus had been baptised.

Matthew describes Jesus meeting James and John, also fishermen and brothers, very shortly after recruiting Simon and Andrew. Matthew and Mark identify James and John as sons of Zebedee. Luke adds to Matthew and Mark that James and John worked as a team with Simon and Andrew. Matthew states that at the time of the encounter, James and John were repairing their nets, but readily joined Jesus without hesitation.

This parallels the accounts of Mark and Luke, but Matthew implies that the men have also abandoned their father (since he is present in the boat they abandon behind them), and Carter feels this should be interpreted to mean that Matthew's view of Jesus is one of a figure rejecting the traditional patriarchal structure of society, where the father had command over his children; most scholars, however, just interpret it to mean that Matthew intended these two to be seen as even more devoted than the other pair, or that Jesus expected the imminent coming of the kingdom.

The Synoptic Gospels go on to describe that later in Jesus' ministry he noticed a tax collector in his booth. The tax collector, called Matthew in Matthew 9:9, and Levi in Mark 2:14 and Luke 5:27, is asked by Jesus to become one of his disciples. Matthew/Levi is stated to have accepted and then invited Jesus for a meal with his friends. Tax collectors were seen as villains in Jewish society, and the Pharisees are described as asking Jesus why he is having a meal with such disreputable people. The reply Jesus gave is now well known: "it is not the healthy who need a doctor, but the sick. I have not come to call the righteous, but sinners to repentance."

Commissioning of the Twelve Apostles

The commissioning of the Twelve Apostles is an episode in the ministry of Jesus that appears in the three Synoptic Gospels. It relates the initial selection of the Twelve Apostles among the disciples of Jesus.

In the Gospel of Matthew, this event takes place shortly before the miracle of the man with a withered hand. In the gospels of Mark and of Luke, it appears shortly after that miracle.

Then Jesus summoned his twelve disciples and gave them authority over unclean spirits, to cast them out, and to cure every disease and every sickness. These are the names of the twelve apostles: first, Simon, also known as Peter, and his brother Andrew; James son of Zebedee, and his brother John; Philip and Bartholomew; Thomas and Matthew the tax collector; James son of Alphaeus, and Thaddaeus;

Simon the Cananaean, and Judas Iscariot, the one who betrayed him,
Matthew 10:1–4.

He went up the mountain and called to him those whom he wanted, and they came to him. And he appointed twelve, whom he also named apostles, to be with him, and to be sent out to proclaim the message, and to have authority to cast out demons. So he appointed the twelve:[b] Simon (to whom he gave the name Peter); James son of Zebedee and John the brother of James (to whom he gave the name Boanerges, that is, Sons of Thunder); and Andrew, and Philip, and Bartholomew, and Matthew, and Thomas, and James son of Alphaeus, and Thaddaeus, and Simon the Cananaean, and Judas Iscariot, who betrayed him,
Mark 3:13–19.

One of those days Jesus went out to a mountainside to pray, and spent the night praying to God. When morning came, he called his disciples to him and chose twelve of them, whom he also designated apostles: Simon (whom he named Peter), his brother Andrew, James, John, Philip, Bartholomew, Matthew, Thomas, James son of Alphaeus, Simon who was called the Zealot, Judas son of James, and Judas Iscariot, who became a traitor.
Luke 6:12–16

Lists of the Twelve Apostles in the New Testament

Each of the four listings of apostles in the New Testament indicate that all the apostles were men. The canonical gospels and the book of Acts give varyinnames of the Twelve Apostles. The list in the Gospel of Luke differs from Matthew and Mark on one point. It lists "Judas, the son of James" instead of "Thaddaeus". All listings appear in three groupings, always with the same four apostles in each group. Each group is always led by the same apostle, although the order of the remaining three names within the group varies. Thus, Peter is always listed first, Philip is always listed fifth, and James, son of Alphaeus is always listed ninth. Judas Iscariot is always listed last.

Unlike the Synoptic Gospels, the Gospel of John does not offer a formal list of apostles. Although it refers to "the Twelve", the gospel does not present any elaboration of who these twelve actually were, and the author of the Gospel of John does not mention them all by name. There is also no separation of the terms "apostles" and "disciples" in John.

According to the New Testament there were only two pairs of brothers among the Twelve Apostles: Peter and Andrew, the sons of Jonah, as well as James and John, the sons of Zebedee. Since the father of both James, son of Alphaeus and Matthew is named Alphaeus, according to the tradition of the Eastern Orthodox Church the two were brothers as well.[30][31] According to the tradition of the Catholic Church based on the writing of the Apostolic Father Papias of Hierapolis the apostles James, son of Alphaeus, and Thaddaeus were brothers and sons of Alphaeus (named also Clopas) and his wife Mary of Clopas who was the sister of the mother of Jesus. The Golden Legend, compiled by Jacobus de Voragine in the 13th century, adds to **the two apostles also Simon the Zealot.**

Gospel of Matthew	Gospel of Mark	Gospel of Luke	Gospel of John	Acts of the Apostles
Simon ("also known as Peter")	Simon ("to whom he gave the name Peter")	Simon ("whom he named Peter")	Simon Peter / Cephas "which is translated Peter"	Peter
Andrew ("his [Peter's] brother")	Andrew	Andrew ("his [Peter's] brother")	Andrew ("Simon Peter's brother")	Andrew
James ("son of Zebedee")	James ("son of Zebedee") / one of the "Boanerges"	James	one of the "sons of Zebedee"	James
John ("his [James's] brother")	John ("brother of James") / one of the "Boanerges"	John	one of the "sons of Zebedee" / the "disciple whom Jesus loved"[b]	John
Philip	Philip	Philip	Philip	Philip
Bartholomew	Bartholomew	Bartholomew	Nathanael	Bartholomew
Thomas	Thomas	Thomas	Thomas ("also called Didymus")	Thomas
Matthew ("the publican")	Matthew / Levi	Matthew / Levi	not mentioned	Matthew
James ("son of Alphaeus")	James ("son of Alphaeus")	James ("son of Alphaeus")	not mentioned	James ("son of Alphaeus")
Thaddaeus (or "Lebbaeus"); called "Judas the Zealot" in some translations	Thaddaeus	Judas ("son of James," referred to as *brother* in some translations)	Judas ("not Iscariot")	Judas ("son of James," referred to as *brother* in some translations)
Simon ("the Canaanite")	Simon ("the Cananaean")	Simon ("who was called the Zealo	not mentioned	Simon ("the Zealot")
Judas Iscariot	Judas Iscariot	Judas Iscariot	Judas ("son of Simon Iscariot")	(Judas replaced by Matthias)

33

Inner circle among the Twelve Apostles

Peter, James son of Zebedee, and James's brother John formed an informal triumvirate among **the Twelve Apostles in the Gospels. Jesus invited them to be the only apostles present on three notable occasions during his public ministry:** the Raising of Jairus' daughter, the Transfiguration of Jesus, and the Agony in the Garden of Gethsemane.

At the time of the Early Christian Church as a leading trio among the apostles were recognized Peter, John and James, brother of Jesus, known collectively as the three *Pillars of the Church.* According to the tradition of the Catholic Church based on the writing of Jerome this James is identified with the apostle James, son of Alphaeus.

Two of the leading triumvirate, Peter and John, were additionally sent by Jesus into the city to make preparation for the final Passover meal (the **Last Supper),** and were also the only two sent by the collective apostles to visit the newly converted believers in Samaria. If John is to be identified with the disciple whom Jesus loved, then it was also only Peter and John who followed behind Jesus after his capture in the Garden of Gethsemane, and who ran to the empty tomb after Mary Magdalene bore witness to the resurrection of Jesus.

Replacement of Judas Iscariot

After Judas betrayed Jesus (and then in guilt committed suicide before Christ's resurrection, one Gospel recounts), the apostles numbered eleven. The group is referred to as "the eleven" in Mark 16:14 (part of the "longer ending" of Mark) and in Luke 24:9,33. In Acts 1:26 they are "the eleven apostles", in Matthew 28:16 they are "the eleven disciples".

When Jesus had been taken up from them, in preparation for the coming of the Holy Spirit that he had promised them, Peter advised the brethren:

Judas, who was guide to those who took Jesus... For he was numbered with us, and received his portion in this ministry... For it is written in the book of Psalms, "Let his habitation be made desolate, Let no one dwell therein", and, "Let another take his office"... So one of the men who have accompanied us during all the time that the Lord Jesus went in and out among us, beginning from the baptism of John until the day he was taken up from us, must become with us a witness to his resurrection. *Acts 1:15–22*. So, between the Ascension of Jesus and the day of Pentecost, the remaining apostles elected a twelfth apostle by casting lots, a traditional Israelite way to determine the will of God (see Proverbs 16:33). The lot fell upon Matthias.

Paul the Apostle, in his First Epistle to the Corinthians, appears to give the first historical reference to the Twelve Apostles: "For I delivered to you as of first importance what I also received: that Christ died for our sins in accordance with the Scriptures, that he was buried, that he was raised on the third day in accordance with the Scriptures, and that he appeared to Cephas, then to the twelve" (1 Cor 15:3–5). Other apostles mentioned in the New Testament. The **"seventy disciples"** or **"seventy-two disciples"** (known in the **Eastern Christian** traditions as the "Seventy Apostles") were early emissaries of Jesus mentioned in the Gospel of Luke. According to Luke, the only gospel in which they appear, Jesus appointed them and sent them out in pairs on a specific mission which is detailed in the text.

In **Western Christianity**, they are usually referred to as disciples, whereas in Eastern Christianity they are usually referred to as apostles. Using the original Greek words, both titles are descriptive, as an *apostle* is one sent on a mission (the Greek uses the verb form: *apesteilen*) whereas a *disciple* is a student, but the two traditions differ on the scope of the words *apostle* and *disciple*.

Paul, Apostle of the Gentiles

Although not one of the apostles commissioned during the life of Jesus, Paul, a Jew also named **Saul,** claimed a special commission from the post-ascension Jesus as "the apostle of the Gentiles", to spread the gospel message after his conversion. In his writings, the epistles to Christian churches throughout the Levant, Paul did not restrict the term "apostle" to the twelve, and often refers to his mentor Barnabas as an apostle.

In his writings, Paul, although not one of the original twelve, described himself as an *apostle*.[2] He was called by the resurrected Jesus himself during his Road to Damascus event. With Barnabas, he was allotted the role of apostle in the church.

Since Paul claimed to have received a gospel not from teachings of the Twelve Apostles but solely and directly through personal revelations from the post-ascension Jesus, after Jesus' death and resurrection (rather than before like the twelve), Paul was often obliged to defend his apostolic authority (1 Cor. 9:1 "Am I not an apostle?") and proclaim that he had seen and was anointed by Jesus while on the road to Damascus.

Paul considered himself perhaps inferior to the other apostles because he had originally persecuted Christ's followers while thinking he was not in the least inferior to those "super-apostles" and not lacking in "knowledge".

Paul referred to himself as the *apostle of the Gentiles*. According to Paul's account in his Epistle to the Galatians, James, Peter and John in Jerusalem accepted the "grace" given to Paul and agreed that Paul and Barnabas should go to the Gentiles (specifically those not circumcised) and the three apostles who "seemed to be pillars" to the circumcised. Despite the Little Commission of Matthew 10, the Twelve Apostles did not limit their mission to solely Jews as Cornelius the Centurion is widely considered the first Gentile convert and he was converted by Peter, and the Great Commission of the resurrected Jesus is specifically to "all nations".

As the *Catholic Encyclopedia* states, "It is at once evident that in a Christian sense, everyone who had received a mission from the Father, or Christ, to man could be called 'Apostle'"; thus extending the original sense beyond the twelve.

Deaths

Of the Twelve Apostles to hold the title after Matthias' selection, Christian tradition has generally passed down that all of the Twelve Apostles except John were martyred. It is traditionally believed that John survived all of them, living to old age and dying of natural causes at Ephesus sometime after AD 98, during the reign of Trajan. However, only the death of his brother James who became the first Apostle to die in c. AD 44 is described in the New Testament. (Acts 12:1–2)

Matthew 27:5 says that Judas Iscariot threw the silver he received for betraying Jesus down in the Temple, then went and hanged himself. Acts 1:18 says that he purchased a field, then "falling headlong he burst open in the middle and all his bowels gushed out".

According to the 18th-century historian Edward Gibbon, early Christians (second half of the second century and first half of the third century) believed that only Peter, Paul, and James, son of Zebedee, were martyred. The remainder, or even all, of the claims of martyred apostles do not rely upon historical or biblical evidence, but only on late legends.

PART ONE

WHAT IS THE PAGANISM AND TRADITION?

CHAPTER 1

Paganism is a term that refers to diverse religious movements and traditions sharing certain characteristics. Many scholars of religion classify Pagan traditions as alternative and emergent religions. Pagan traditions are alternative in the sense of being misaligned to dominant socio-cultural and religious narratives. In other words, they are "fringe" religions that appeal to atypical members of a population. Further, they are emergent in the sense of being symbolically and organizationally new. Although scholars do not agree on how old a religion must be in order to be considered "new", we are usually dealing with religions that emerged in the latter half of the twentieth century.

Although these are helpful ways to conceptualise Paganism, many Pagan devotees object to their beliefs and practices being called a "religion" and often prefer the term "spirituality" as a signifier. Many of them are distrustful of organized religions and institutional hierarchies wishing to distance themselves from these. Moreover, although various Paganisms are emergent in having only recently become established in the West during the twentieth century, many Pagans wish to see their tradition as having ancient routes in **"pre-Christian"** Europe. We will revisit these claims shortly.

It is important to acknowledge the historical use of the term "pagan". According to Pearson, *"By the second and third centuries, the pagani were those who had not enlisted as part of God's 'army', as militia Christi (soldiers of Christ) against the forces of Satan" (ibid: 18-19). By the fifth century CE, Christian writers used the term "pagani" to refer to urban nobility and academics who fore fronted Pagan resistance to Christianity"* (1).

In recent popular culture, the term "Pagan" has come to refer to any person who is a non-Christian or even anti-Christian. This is only partly accurate given the religiosity of some Pagans is indeed a backlash to Christianity or is because of a disenchantment with the Christian faith. However, many other Pagans previously embraced worldviews other than Christianity and are not particularly hostile to the Christian religion. In its academic use, the Pagan is an individual who embraces a legitimate form of religion, such as <u>Wicca</u>.

There are a number of Pagan traditions, the most common being Wicca, <u>Druidry,</u> <u>Goddess</u> traditions, and the New Age. Dale Wallace identifies the following five characteristics to be most common to contemporary Pagan traditions (2):

[1] Paganism is a Nature Religion, where the Earth may be seen as Mother, or, for many, as Goddess.
[2] Paganism can be polytheistic, pantheistic, duotheistic, panentheistic and/or <u>animistic</u>.
[3] Paganism is anti-hierarchical and opposed to any form of external domination. It is likewise resistant to central authority, and to dominant religious traditions that are seen to desacralise Nature through dualisms that separate spirit from matter.

[4] Paganism resists patriarchal religious traditions through its assertion of the feminine aspect to divine reality.

[5] Paganism is illustrative of the magical worldview that there are unseen relations between all elements of the cosmos, and that an individual can, through various technologies, participate with, and engage in, these relations.

Collectively these traits suggest an incredibly diverse tradition. There is a certain femininity to contemporary forms of Paganism as, for example, most proponents of the Goddess movement and Wicca are female and celebrate female spirituality. The Earth and celestial bodies are often feminised and various female goddesses are embraced. This is often in response to perceived dominant patriarchal religions that undermine or relegate to secondary status the role of women in spiritual life. In line with [2], Pagans hold to various conceptions of Deity. The Druids are pantheistic because they believe the world and God not to be separate but connected. Some, like the New Agers, are panetheistic holding God to be both infused with the world as well as transcendent above it. Wiccans often embrace various gods and goddesses (polytheism), or duotheism by worshiping a God and Goddess. In light of [3], Pagans are anti-hierarchical and they generally do not perceive religious institutional hierarchies in a positive light. Hierarchy provides certain persons power over others, which can come to undermine spiritual autonomy that Pagans cherish. Pagan religions often encourage devotees to create their own spiritual realities by selecting preferred deities to worship, selecting what paths to venture down to attain enlightenment or union with God, decide what rituals to perform, with whom they are performed, and so on. Because of this autonomy and eclecticism, there is usually no central spokesperson to represent or speak for the tradition. There are also no prescribed prayers, creeds, clergy, or <u>holy texts</u>, which suggests a lack of any centralized control of religious life and practice.

The reverence of and respect for nature are perhaps the most common threads running through all the Pagan traditions. Pagan gatherings in covens, circles, and groves often take place in nature where various rituals purposed for channeling the Earth's energy are performed. Ecological sensitivity is of paramount importance and Pagans often get behind initiatives attempting to spread awareness of the environment, environmental exploitation, and the need for preservation. The Druids oppose violence against animals, some of which on their view possess special powers (healing, vitality, and inner knowledge) that can be used by humans. Pagan holidays and festivities often centre on the natural world, such as Sabbaths and Esbats honouring the gods.

Finally, Pagans engage in various methods to communicate with the spirit world. The New Ager often consumes hallucinogenic herbs or plants as this is believed to provide her access to the spirit world. Entities from the spirit world, including angels and guides, can be interacted with to provide the devotee with knowledge or counsel.

Pagan traditions and expressions vary widely and can involve communal outdoor rituals, solitary meditation or contemplation, or the use of symbols, talismans, or altars. Pagan magic is a spiritual practice aimed at creating change in an individual and in the world through prayer and physical actions.

Pagan traditions have a strong focus on ritual, and practitioners may draw from multiple sources or follow a single contemporary Pagan tradition. The largest of the latter is Wicca, a form of religious witchcraft that includes dozens of lineages, paths, and styles. Other traditions include Druidry, non-Wiccan forms of religious witchcraft, Heathenry and Ásatrú (Northern European Paganisms), feminist Goddess worship, and a variety of reconstructionisms including Greek, Egyptian, Celtic, Roman, Canaanite as well as other historical religions. Some practitioners of Afro-Caribbean religions also may consider themselves to be Pagan, while others do not.

Pagan rituals commonly focus on honouring a deity or deities; observing natural cycles, such as seasonal changes or the waxing and waning of the moon; or celebrating rites of passage, such as birth, transitioning into adulthood, marriage, and death. Although the form of ritual varies by tradition, Pagan rituals tend to engage the participants physically. Rituals often include drumming, chanting, and dancing. Some Pagans offer food or drink to their gods or ancestors; these offerings may be shared by the participants as part of a feast, or sometimes disposed of ritually. Representations of earth, air, fire, and water may also be employed for cleansing and consecration; for instance, participants might anoint themselves with salt water (earth and water) and burn incense (air and fire) as part of ritual preparation.

Pagans generally do not proselytize and, while classes and retreats may introduce people to the path, the initiative to practice is with each individual. Some Pagans also participate in other religious communities such as churches or synagogues. From the 1970s through the early 1990s, the source of growth in Paganism was through small groups variously called groves, nests, covens, or circles. After the mid-1990s, the availability of the internet and communications technology increased access to religious material for geographically isolated Pagans, who slowly grew into a majority in the movement.

Although some Pagans still practise regularly in either small private or large public groups, many are "solitaries," meaning they practice alone and may only gather with a group for special occasions. Sociologist Helen Berger reports that as many as 79% of American Pagans today may identify as solitary. Most do not celebrate within a specific temple or building, though there are a few Pagan temple buildings in the United States. On the whole, Pagans prefer to worship out of doors, or else in private homes and rented halls.

Building an altar a place for divinity, and a sacred workplace for performing rituals is one of the first ways many Pagans begin spiritual practice. Pagans often have altars in their homes, sometimes tucked in a corner of the bedroom. Pagans with yards, or those who live in rural settings, may build altars outdoors. The altar may contain natural objects, photographs of the beloved dead, ritual tools, and objects of beauty or personal power. At the altar, one might leave an offering for a deity, enter into meditation, create an herbal charm, or undertake a personal cleansing or healing ritual. Gazing at an altar is a reminder of one's spiritual life, and meditating there can lead to spiritual insight.

Pagans might perform a wide variety of spiritual exercises on a daily basis, though probably no two Pagans practise their faith exactly the same way. Pagan personal practice can be as simple as lighting a candle at the dark of the moon and meditating on the flame, or pouring a fresh cup of water for one's ancestors and saying a prayer. Spoken intention is thought to be very powerful: Pagans often believe that verbalising their desires is the first step toward bringing change into their lives. Respect for this principle leads many Pagans to choose their words carefully, lest a habit of self-deprecation or pessimism interfere with achieving life goals.

One important form of daily practice for many Pagans is "grounding" meditation, which connects the individual with the energy of the Earth and helps to maintain physical and emotional balance. Another is the practice of divination, which may take the simple form of asking about the day ahead, or inquiring about a specific question. Some Pagans consult astrology, while others use Tarot cards, runes, or pendulums to access sources of spiritual knowledge. Others look to movements in the natural world interactions with animals, plants, wind, and water to gain intuitions about patterns in the local environment. The sense of connection gained through these practices helps Pagans live out their belief that divinity is present in the world around them.

Some Pagans choose to wear sacred jewelry. <u>Pagan symbols include the pentacle,</u> an interlaced five-pointed star that is often worn by Wiccans. The star is pointed up to align with an upright human body, with one point up for the head and outward- and downward-facing points for the arms and legs. **The pentacle is a symbol of life** and the union of the elements **(earth, air, water, and fire) with spirit**, though it has often been misrepresented as a **symbol of evil** in popular horror films. Not all Pagans use the pentacle as a religious symbol, however. Pagans who follow a Northern European path may wear Mjölnir, Thor's hammer, a traditional religious pendant worn by those resisting Christian conversion in medieval Scandinavia. Images of natural objects, such as trees, or abstract Goddess figures are also popular among Pagans. In 2007, the Department of Veterans Affairs added the pentacle as an approved religious symbol for veterans' headstones, a decision that delighted Wiccans. Druids and Heathens are in the process of petitioning to have their symbols of choice approved.

Many Pagans practice magick (often spelled with a 'k' to differentiate it from stage magic and the fanciful magic of fantasy novels). In Paganism, magic is a spiritual practice aimed at creating change in the individual and in the world. Magick functions somewhat like prayer in other traditions, but it tends to have more of a physical component than prayer usually does in the West. When Pagans do magick, they begin by stating a clear intention and then raise energy to support that intention. This might be done, for instance, through chanting and dancing, breath exercises, or concentration. The energy is then released, either out into the world or sometimes into an object that will serve as a focus for the intention. The latter could be a candle, a piece of jewelry, or an altar object. Pagans often feel that magick cannot be successful without practical component. Successful job magick, for instance, involves filling out job applications, not just setting intention and raising energy.

The Germanic peoples were converted to Christianity in different periods: many of the Goths in the 4th century, the English in the 6th and 7th centuries, the Saxons, under force of Frankish arms, in the late 8th century, and the Danes, under German pressure, in the course of the 10th century. The pagan religion held out longest in the most northerly lands, Iceland, Norway, and Sweden.

The story of the conversion of Iceland is known best because of the wealth of historical documents written in that country during the Middle Ages. Icelanders were, in many ways, the most international of northern Scandinavians. Among those who settled in Iceland in the late 9th century were men and women partly of Norse stock from Christian

Ireland. Some of these were Christians; some were mixed in their beliefs, worshiping Christ and <u>Thor</u> at once. There were others who believed in no gods at all. Lack of faith in the <u>heathen</u> gods seems to have grown during the 10th century. Influence of Christian thought on some Icelandic poets is noticeable. Occasional missions to Iceland in the later 10th century are recorded, but little progress was made until **Olaf I Tryggvason, king of Norway**, sent out the German priest Thangbrand about 997. **Thangbrand was a ruthless, brutal man; he was outlawed and returned to Norway about 999**. But in the year after Thangbrand left (c. 1000), the Icelandic parliament (Althingi) resolved, at the instigation of King Olaf, that all should be baptised, although <u>concessions</u> were made to those who wished to practice heathen rites in private. Many of those who had been hereditary pagan chieftains became leaders of the church and, largely for this reason, tradition survived in Iceland as in no other Scandinavian land.

The conversion of <u>Norway</u> was far less peaceful. Much is known about it, chiefly from highly colourful Icelandic records. **Olaf Tryggvason, who had come to Norway from England about 995,** quickly **overcame the arch-pagan ruler <u>Haakon Sigurdsson</u>. Paganism was deeply rooted** in the minds of hereditary landowners, as the whole social system was largely founded upon its principles. Using fire and sword rather than persuasion, <u>Olaf</u> <u>converted</u> the whole of Norway in his short reign of five years. When he died in a naval battle, about 1000, many of Olaf's subjects were Christians in name only.

By the time <u>Olaf II Haraldsson</u> (later <u>St. Olaf</u>) came to the throne about 15 years later, some of the Norwegians had been baptized and some not, and one believed whatever one chose. Olaf II set out to complete the work of his predecessor, resorting to the same methods. He was such a tyrant that his own subjects, Christian though they were, drove him into exile in Russia. When he returned with a motley army, about 1030, he met his death and was soon regarded as a saint. **For all his faults, Olaf had established Christianity firmly in Norway.**

Very little is known about the conversion of <u>Sweden</u>. It was a slow and complicated process. The people of West Gautland were, apparently, converted earlier than the rest, but public pagan <u>sacrifice</u> persisted in the temple of <u>Uppsala</u> until late in the 11th century. Kings who professed to be Christian were driven out, presumably because of their religious activities. Sweden was hardly a Christian country before about 1100.

The picture that Scandinavian sources provide of Germanic religion is to a large extent lopsided, since many of the documents date to the period when waning paganism was threatened with doom by the growing impact of Christianity. This may account for the pessimistic worldview that pervades some aspects of Eddic poetry, as well as for some rather <u>derogatory</u> descriptions of the behaviour of the gods. The rigorous <u>ethics</u> of early Germanic society, based on trust, loyalty, and courage, and the perhaps somewhat idealised picture of the <u>moral</u> code given by <u>Tacitus,</u> had a divine sanction, but, when Christianity arrived in the north, the message had apparently been dimmed by the gods' disrespect of their most solemn oaths. Paganism no longer had the stamina and inner drive to resist the pressure of Christianity, with its strong, well-organised church and its positive monotheistic creed, <u>encompassing</u> faith and ethics.

The Siegfried is figure from the heroic literature of the ancient Germanic people. He appears in both German and Old Norse literature, although the versions of his stories told by these two branches of the Germanic tradition do not always agree. He plays a part in the story of <u>Brunhild</u>, in which he meets his death, but in other stories he is the leading character and triumphs. A feature common to all versions is his outstanding strength and courage.

One story tells of Siegfried's fight with a <u>dragon</u>, and another of how he acquired a treasure from two brothers who quarrelled over their inheritance. These two stories are combined into one in the Norse *Poetic Edda* and told in detail, whereas in <u>German literature</u>, where they are kept entirely separate, the information is scant and largely contained in <u>allusions</u>.

Siegfried plays a major part in the *<u>Nibelungenlied</u>*, where this old material is used but is much overlaid with more recent additions. *Das Lied vom hürnen Seyfrid,* not attested before about 1500, also retains the old material in identifiable form, although the poem's central theme is the release of a maiden from a dragon; and an *Edda* poem tells how Sigurd awakened a <u>Valkyrie</u> maiden from a charmed sleep. Here, too, many critics have tried to establish a connection between German and Norse; but besides important differences, there is doubt about the antiquity of both poems.

In the original stories Siegfried was presented as a boy of noble <u>lineage</u> who grew up without parental care; this background shows through clearly, although in the full accounts in both Norse and German it is overlaid with elaborate accounts of his courtly upbringing. It is still disputed, as with Brunhild, whether the figure of Siegfried is of mythical or historical (Merovingian) origin.

Idun

Idun, in <u>Norse mythology</u>, the goddess of spring or rejuvenation and the wife of <u>Bragi</u>, the god of poetry. She was the keeper of the magic apples of immortality, which the gods must eat to preserve their <u>youth</u>. When, through the cunning of <u>Loki</u>, the trickster god, she and her apples were seized by the giant Thiassi and taken to the realm of the giants, the gods quickly began to grow old. They then forced Loki to rescue Idun, which he did by taking the form of a <u>falcon</u>, changing Idun into a <u>nut</u> (in some

Griffin, <u>composite</u> mythological creature with a <u>lion's</u> body (winged or wingless) and a <u>bird's</u> head, usually that of an <u>eagle</u>. The griffin was a favourite decorative motif in the ancient Middle Eastern and Mediterranean lands. Probably originating in the Levant in the 2nd millennium BCE, the griffin had spread throughout western Asia and into <u>Greece</u> by the 14th century BCE. The Asiatic griffin had a crested head, whereas the Minoan and Greek griffin usually had a mane of spiral curls. It was shown either recumbent or seated on its haunches, often paired with the <u>sphinx</u>; its function may have been protective.

griffin

In the <u>Iron Age</u> the griffin was again prominent in both Asia and Greece. Greek metalworkers evolved a handsome stylised rendering, the beak open to show a curling tongue and the head provided with horses' ears and a large knob on top. Apparently the griffin was in some sense sacred, appearing frequently in <u>sanctuary</u> and tomb furnishings. Its precise nature or its place in cult and <u>legend</u> remains unknown.

Atli

Lay of Atli, heroic poem in the Norse *Poetic Edda* (*see* Edda), an older variant of the tale of slaughter and revenge that is the subject of the German epic *Nibelungenlied,* from which it differs in several respects. In the Norse poem, Atli (the Hunnish king Attila) is the villain, who is slain by his **wife,** Gudrun, to avenge her brothers.

Gudrun.

In the *Lay of Atli,* Gudrun's brothers Gunnar and Hogni are lured to Atli's court so that Atli can learn the secret of their treasure. Gunnar and Hogni refuse to tell. Atli has Hogni's heart cut out while Gunnar laughs in scorn. Gunnar is thrown into a **snake pit, then put to death**. Gudrun, "the sweet-faced delight of the shield-folk," takes her revenge by serving the murderers dainties that are actually the roasted hearts of Atli's sons. Then she stabs the wine-weary Atli and burns down his hall, allowing only the dogs to escape. In the German epic the characters of Atli, Gudrun, Gunnar, and Hogni are represented, respectively, by Etzel, Kriemhild, Gunther, and Hagen.

Svadilfari, in Norse mythology, an unusually swift and intelligent horse belonging to a giant who offered to build a great wall around Asgard (the kingdom of the gods) to keep invaders away. The gods stipulated that, if the builder completed the wall in one winter's time, his reward would be the goddess Freyja and possession of the sun and the moon. Svadilfari gave his owner such assistance that the wall was almost completed a few days before the end of winter. **The gods,** however, were able to prevent the giant from winning his payment by the aid of the trickster god Loki, who changed himself into a mare and attracted

Svadilfari away from his work. From their union Loki bore Odin's magical horse, Sleipnir.

Norn, in Germanic mythology, any of a group of supernatural beings who corresponded to the Greek Moirai; they were usually represented as three maidens who spun or wove the fate of men. Some sources name them Urd, Verdandi, and Skuld, perhaps meaning "past," "present," and "future." They were depicted as living by Yggdrasill, the world tree, under Urd's well and were linked with both good and evil. Being frequently attendant at births, they were sometimes associated with midwifery. The name Norn appears only in Scandinavian sources, but the cult of Nornlike beings occurs in several European folklores. In Norse literature the Norns are sometimes called *disir*.

Loch Ness monster, large marine creature believed by some people to inhabit Loch Ness, Scotland. However, much of the alleged evidence supporting its existence has been discredited, and it is widely thought that the monster is a myth.

Reports of a monster inhabiting Loch Ness date back to ancient times. Notably, local stone carvings by the Pict depict a mysterious beast with flippers. The first written account appears in a 7th-century biography of St. Columba. According to that work, in 565 AD the monster bit a swimmer and was prepared to attack another man when Columba intervened, ordering the beast to "go back." It obeyed, and over the centuries only occasional sightings were reported. Many of these allege encounters seemed inspired by Scottish folklore, which abounds with mythical water creatures.

Loch Ness, Scotland

In 1933 the Loch Ness monster's legend began to grow. At the time, a road adjacent to Loch Ness was finished, offering an unobstructed view of the lake. In April a couple saw an enormous animal which they compared to a "dragon or prehistoric monster" and after it crossed their car's path, it disappeared into the water. The incident was reported in a Scottish newspaper, and numerous sightings followed. In December 1933 the _Daily Mail_ commissioned Marmaduke Wetherell, a big-game hunter, to locate the sea serpent. Along the lake's shores, he found large footprints that he believed belonged to "a very powerful soft-footed animal about 20 feet [6 metres] long." However, upon closer inspection, zoologists at the Natural History Museum determined that the tracks were identical and made with an umbrella stand or ashtray that had a hippopotamus leg as a base; Wetherell's role in the hoax was unclear.

The news only seemed to spur efforts to prove the monster's existence. In 1934 English physician Robert Kenneth Wilson photographed the alleged creature. The iconic image known as the "surgeon's photograph" appeared to show the monster's small head and neck. The _Daily Mail_ printed the photograph, sparking an international sensation. Many speculated that the creature was a plesiosaur, a marine reptile that went extinct some 65.5 million years ago.

The Loch Ness area attracted numerous monster hunters. Over the years, several sonar explorations (notably in 1987 and 2003) were undertaken to locate the creature, but none were successful. In addition, numerous photographs allegedly showed the beast, but most were discredited as fakes or as depicting other animals or objects. Notably, in 1994 it was revealed that Wilson's photograph was a hoax spearheaded by a revenge-seeking Wetherell; the "monster" was actually a plastic-and-wooden head attached to a toy submarine. In 2018 researchers conducted a DNA survey of Loch Ness to determine what organisms live in the waters. No signs of a plesiosaur or other such large animal were found, though the results indicated the presence of numerous eels. This finding left open the possibility that the monster is an oversized eel. Despite the lack of conclusive evidence, the Loch Ness monster remained popular and profitable. In the early 21st century it was thought that it contributed nearly $80 million annually to Scotland's economy.

Hel, in <u>Norse mythology</u>, originally the name of the world of the dead; it later came to mean the goddess of death. Hel was one of the children of the trickster god <u>Loki</u>, and her kingdom was said to lie downward and northward. It was called <u>Niflheim</u>, or the World of Darkness, and appears to have been divided into several sections, one of which was Náströnd, the shore of <u>corpses</u>. There stood a castle facing north; it was filled with the venom of serpents, in which murderers, adulterers, and perjurers suffered torment, while the dragon <u>Nidhogg</u> sucked the blood from their bodies. Mention is made in an early poem of the nine worlds of Niflheim. It was said that those who fell in battle did not go to Hel but to the god <u>Odin</u>, in <u>Valhalla</u>, the hall of the slain.

Skadi, in <u>Norse mythology</u>, the <u>giant</u> wife of **the sea god** Njörd. In order to <u>avenge</u> the death of her father, the giant Thiazi, Skadi took up arms and went to attack the rival tribe of the **<u>gods</u>** (the <u>Aesir</u>) in <u>Asgard</u>, home of the **gods.** The Aesir, wanting to appease her anger, offered her the choice of one of their number for a husband, with the stipulation that she choose a **god** by his legs (or feet) alone. She chose <u>Njörd</u>, thinking that he was the fair **god Balder**; their marriage failed because Njörd preferred to live by the sea, and Skadi was happier in her father's home in the mountains

(Thrymheim). In some sources, Skadi was known as **the goddess** of snowshoes. Another tradition relates that Skadi later married the **god** Odin and bore him sons.

Some contemporary evangelical scholars suggest that Matthew's use of the Old Testament is like the way rabbis of that period used it. For example the Qumran community contemporised the **Old Testament (a.k.a. *pesher*)** by holding that Old Testament scriptures were predictive of their own situation. Many modern scholars would argue that Matthew also interprets the Old Testament using *pesher* when, for example, he applies Hosea 11:1 to Christ's sojourn in Egypt. If it is true that **New Testament authors interpreted the Old Testament** this way, then it is a little unsettling. The most pressing concern is that *pesher*, *peshat* and many later *misrash* techniques are fundamentally eisegetical. That is, these hermeneutical approaches are hostile to the notion of objective interpretation. If this is the case, then **it brings into question the legitimacy of many critical NT uses of the OT. Ultimately, if NT authors** did use rabbinical hermeneutics, then one must question the very authority of the New Testament in critical matters of faith.

A second, if lesser, concern is the contribution New Testament authors make to the study of scripture interpretation. Even if Matthew was not using *pesher* techniques, what interpretive approach was he taking? Can modern scholarship use his methods or was he exercising the insights of a prophet when he interpreted the Old Testament? If so, then contemporary interpreters can gain little assistance in their own hermeneutical tasks from Matthew. The purposes of this paper are twofold: to investigate whether Matthew was using *pesher* techniques in his use of Old Testament and, if not, to identify what interpretive approach to the Old Testament he was taking in his gospel.

What is Pesher?

Several approaches to scripture analysis may be discovered in first century Hebrew documents including literalistic, allegorical, *midras* and *pesher*. Longman doubts that these methods were distinguished from one another in the first century. Of these methods, *pesher* is of the greatest interest to this study, principally because Matthew does not lie under the accusation that he interprets the OT literalistically or allegorically but rather through *pesher*. Perhaps Matthew uses *midrashic* techniques, as many contend, but it can be argued that first century *midrash* could be very much akin to the manner in which Psalmists interpreted the Pentateuch. Early *midrash*, as defined by Hillel, is a fairly objective hermeneutical approach. It is the claim that Matthew is using *pesher* contemporisation of the OT, particularly in 'fulfilment' citations, that provides the most serious challenge to those holding to verbal, plenary inspiration.

The term *pesher* means, "to explain." In fact, however, *pesher* is an application of OT scripture with little to no concern for the context of the passage applied. *Pesher* may refer either to commentaries on the OT found amongst the Dead Sea scrolls or to the interpretive technique typical of these commentaries. *Pesher* interpreters assume that OT authors were speaking to the contemporary audience. This form of interpretation is tied to a word, text or OT allusion, which is then related to a present person, place or thing. The interpretations are generally aloof from the source context and appear to lack any coherent methodology. According to Lundberg, "This kind of commentary (*pesher*) is not an attempt to explain what the Bible meant when it was originally written, but rather what it means in the day and age of the commentator, particularly for his own community."

For instance, in the *pesher* Habakkuk the writers simply take Habakkuk's references to the Chaledeans and apply them to the Romans without any effort to justify the application. The context of Habakkuk seems to hold little interest for such interpreters. In the same commentary all the destructive activities described by Habakkuk are attributed to the 'wicked priest' while all the good things are attributed to the 'righteous teacher' the antagonist and protagonist typical of Qumran *pesher* writing. Again, the interpreter shows little inclination to justify the wholesale substitution of the authorial intent for that of his community.

Was Matthew Using Pesher?

Clearly, Matthew is not a *pesher* commentary. Such texts are line-by-line analyses of an OT text and Matthew's gospel does not conform to this format. Rather, Matthew applies OT citations to his narrative of the life of Christ. While Matthew cannot be construed as a *pesher* commentary, it could still be true that Matthew is using the *pesher* devise of OT contemporisation. Matthew's use of Hosea 11:1 seems so disinterested in its plain meaning that a cursory comparison of Hosea 11:1 with Matthew 2:15 certainly leaves the impression he is using this approach. However, there are several reasons to doubt that Matthew is using *pesher* techniques: While both Matthew and *pesher* commentaries use citations from a variety of sources, it appears that many of Matthew's translations are his own and Matthew's citations do not show interpretive or selection bias typical of *pesher*.

The formal features of OT quotes in Matthew do not correspond to any such features in Qumran text. Qumran applications were treated as identical to interpretations without regard to historic context - few such tendencies are found in NT use of the OT. Matthew did not use many OT passages that conform to a fulfilment motif which is unexpected if he was simply grabbing proof-texts from the OT.

Many fulfilment passages used by Matthew do not conform to known messianic prophecy material advanced in Jewish circles. If Matthew wanted to make a case about Jesus claim to be messiah he should have taken better advantage of accepted messiah texts.

Some citations are so surprising that it is unreasonable to expect the NT author would have bent them to conform to the life of Christ (e.g. Jeremiah 31:15 for Matthew 2:16,18) Even in the most radical examples of *pesher* used by the Qumran community, the authors do not modify their history to conform to an OT passage. Yet this is what a proponent of *pesher* Matthew must claim for him.

OT quotations in NT fall under a limited set of themes. This is much different than the piecemeal treatment in the DSS and in rabbinical writings. **Motifs of NT citations of OT include the following:**

1. **Jesus acts as YHWH**
2. Jesus is the predicted messiah
3. Jesus is the predicted servant of the Lord
4. **Jesus is the son of man**
5. Jesus culminates the prophetic line
6. Jesus is in a succession of OT righteous sufferers
7. Jesus fulfils the Davidic dynasty
8. **Jesus reverses the Adamic curse**

9. Jesus fulfils the Abrahamic covenant of universal blessing
10. Jesus recapitulates the history of Israel
11. The priesthood of Melchizedek & Aaron...the latter sometimes contrastingly anticipate the priesthood of Jesus
12. The Passover lamb and other sacrifices prefigure the substitutionary atonement of Christ and Christian service
13. Jesus and manna
14. The rock/living water
15. The serpent
16. The tabernacle/temple
17. John the Baptist & Elijah
18. The new covenant prophecy
19. Judas Iscariot
20. The law of Moses prefigured grace positively and negatively
21. The flood - last judgment/baptism
22. Red Sea/circumcision - baptism
23. Jerusalem - eternal city of Yahweh/God
24. Taking Canaan - spiritual rest

There are many reasons **for doubting that Matthew is writing like an author** of Qumran-*pesher* materials but particular OT citations do seem as careless of context as *pesher*. This requires an explanation of which Stendahl's failed *pesher* conclusion was an attempt to respond.

How was Matthew Interpreting the Old Testament?

Given that Matthew does not use *pesher* hermeneutics, what kind of interpretive approach is he applying and is it useful for contemporary interpreters?

It is important to realize that most of the time Matthew's use of the OT is so straightforward that it is not susceptible to the charge of OT misuse or misinterpretation. For instance, at times Christ utters language from the OT in ways that suggest he is calling forth the mood of the text he cites. This is entirely unsurprising for one steeped in the language and tone of the OT. At other times the OT is used by way of application. For example, Christ is recorded as using the OT for training when he frames OT narratives into question and answer sessions (e.g. 15:4; 19:4-7, 18-19). In other ways Christ draws particular applications out of OT narratives (e.g. Matthew 12:3-8, citing Isaiah 21:6; Leviticus 24:5,9; Numbers 28:9 to condemn Sabbath legalism). In these cases, however, Christ is generally using the OT the way OT authors used antecedent text. The psalmists often cited **Pentateuchal** narratives in order to draw out salient spiritual principles or theology. Even in those cases where Christ's application of the OT differs from the approach of OT authors, his use still is not at all like the approach seen in first century *midrash* because unlike much rabbinical *midrash*, Jesus works within the context of the citations he uses. When Jesus applies the OT differently from the psalmist application hermeneutic, he is speaking prophetically (e.g. "You've heard it said, but I say…"). In these ways he adds to earlier revelation, not in a way that disregards but rather extends the earlier revelation. This too is an interpretive role played by OT prophets in their use of antecedent and new revelation. In these uses of the Old Testament Christ, or Matthew as his biographer, are not guilty of interpreting the scripture in ways alien to how Old Testament authors interpreted the Old Testament.

Many of Matthew's citations are apologetic in nature, that is, Matthew cites the OT to show how Christ fulfilled OT scripture. It is because of this that Matthew is often charged with deriving from the OT meanings no competent OT scholar could ever develop independently. As a result of some of the more extraordinary examples of fulfilment citations Matthew is often held to be using *pesher* approaches to the OT. How is Matthew using the OT in these cases? How can modern interpreters make use of this approach?

As we saw earlier, a fairly common solution to this dilemma is to suggest that **everybody was using the OT this way during the first century (i.e. *midrash pesher*).** This not only appears unlikely but unsafe for the veracity of much of Matthew's gospel, to say nothing of the rest of the New Testament. Other scholars recognize the problem but suggest that careful analysis of the relevant OT citations would vindicate Matthew's interpretation. Some suggest that God's intent when he inspired the OT author was much more profound than the OT author himself realized. Still others say that Matthew was simply noting historically analogous situations for his audience with the suggestion that Christ completed the earlier motifs. Each of these attempted solutions to the problem of OT usage in NT fulfilment passages have provided some important insights into NT use of the OT but each also serves to raise critical questions about the appropriate use of the Old Testament. A few points must be considered before the question of Matthew's OT use can be fully addressed.

First, as many scholars have noted, Matthew's terminology pertaining to fulfilment is much richer than such words suggest to most readers. Matthew indicates 15 times that Christ fulfilled an OT scripture. The term *pleroo* and related terms have wider semantic range than simple predictive realization. These words can communicate the idea of 'completing', 'establishing' or 'filling up' as well as prediction-outcome. For Matthew to suggest that some aspect of the life of Christ fulfils some antecedent scripture could mean that an OT passage made a prediction and Christ expressed that precise prediction. But, fulfilment can also mean that Christ "filled to overflowing" or "completed" the antecedent scripture. This second sense is the way a reader can comprehend Christ's claim that he fulfilled the Law & Prophets in Matthew 5:17. Fulfilment quotations are infused with the concept of God's redemptive purpose in human history and so Matthew quotes texts that directly predict but also passages that have thematic significance that exceeds the OT author immediate meaning. This is different than *sensus plenior* because the NT author is not uncovering meaning hidden to the OT author. Instead, he is using the OT passage as an example of a broad theme of which the OT author was aware. Thus, some concerns over Matthew's use of the OT may be tempered by a better sense of what Matthew intended when he said **Christ fulfilled a scripture.**

Second, C. H. Dodd has shown that the NT use of the OT is not haphazard proof-texting but the use of a few text plots in the OT. For instance Isaiah 53 is cited 34 times in the NT. For the early church, it is likely that a limited citation served as a pointer to an entire theme of which the audience was well apprised:

Given this, it is possible to look, not merely to a limited citation used by Matthew, but to the whole theme of which Matthew's citation is simply a pointer.

Case Study: Matthew 2:15

In this citation, Matthew takes the MT approach of literally translating "son" rather than "His children." It is possible that Matthew may have intended to allude to the entire section through the use of a single citation (c.f. Hosea 11:1-11). It is difficult to concede that Matthew is using midrashic interpretive approaches for the reasons articulated above. On the other hand, efforts to find ways to argue that Matthew's use is an appropriate analysis of a prediction are also hard to concede.

Howard sees Matthew's use of Hosea as retrospective analogical correspondence rather than an effort on God's part to embed a projective type or prophecy about Christ in Hosea's words. That is, Matthew noted that Jesus was like Israel in that he also went to Egypt but that, unlike Israel, he was the son obedient to the covenant. When Israel left Egypt they dropped the ball. Whereas, **when Christ left Egypt he was the son, in whom God was very pleased.** In this way, **Christ fulfilled (i.e. competed) all that God intended for Israel.**

An alternative view is that the Exodus event was a prototype that was subsequently echoed when it was recalled for the purpose of instruction and that was repeated in the coming of Joshua to Palestine & Judah from the Babylonian exile.

The approach taken to the interpretation of this passage will include the following stages:

1. Analysis of the context of Matthew's citation of Hosea;
2. Analysis of the context of Hosea 11:1;
3. Assessment of the retrospective and projective function of Hosea's citation and
4. Assessment of Matthew's use of Hosea as an example of fulfilment.

Analysis of the context of Matthew 2:13-15

The narrative passages before and after Matthew 2:13-15 appear to be arguments from the Torah that Jesus was the messiah and the fulfillment of the Abrahamic and Davidic covenants. The genealogy of chapter 1:1-17 is framed at the beginning and end with the claim that Jesus was the messiah. Chapter 1:18-25 is a reference to a passage that culminates in the promise of a **God/king** who would rule from the throne of David (Isaiah 7:14-9:7). Chapter 2:1-12 contain a reference to a messianic scripture that contains allusions to **both the Davidic and Abrahamic covenants.** After 2:13-15 Matthew cites Jeremiah 31:15 which is a clear reference to the mourning associated with the **Babylonian captivity** but is at the beginning of a long prediction of the restoration of b that will result in the laws of God being internalised by his people (c.f Isaiah 31:31-34). It is difficult to make definitive statements about Matthew 2:19-23 but many scholars believe it refers to prophecies concerning the 'branch' found in Isaiah 4:2, Zechariah 3:8,9 & 6:12. Finally, Matthew's citation of Isaiah 40:3 appears to be a pointer to a lengthy passage concerned with God's redemption of Israel through Cyrus and through the Servant of YHWH (Isa. 42:1-7).

The context of Matthew 2:13-15 is the correlation of Jesus with significant OT scriptures that address God's redemptive activity toward Israel and toward Gentiles - scriptures that identify Jesus as messiah and the fulfilment of the covenants of Abraham and David. It would be expected, therefore, that Matthew's citation of Hosea 11:1 would also anticipate his role as redeemer or sovereign.

Analysis of the context of Hosea 11:1

Hosea is citing the exodus in Hosea 11:1. This event was a critical one in the OT because it demonstrated **God's** remembrance and redemption of Israel. The expression "out of Egypt" appears several times in Hosea 11:1 is in the context of **God's** love for Israel speaks of **God's** discipline. Chapter 12:13 talks of how **God** used a prophet to redeem an ungrateful people. Hosea 13:4 uses the exodus to promise God will assert his sovereign rights over Israel once again. These passages and the core narrative of Hosea's redemption of Gomer make it clear that Hosea 11:1 is intensely **focused on God's** once and future redemption of Israel (c.f. Hosea 2:14 - 3:4). Assessment of the retrospective and projective function of Hosea 11:1

The exodus account is a deferred hope in critical respects. Israel could have been a nation of **priests** (e.g. Exodus 19:4-6) but it chose not to satisfy the terms of the covenant. In this sense the exodus was incomplete. Hosea addresses the exodus to remind Israel of **God's** love, power and sovereignty and to anchor his promise for future redemption both from Assyria and ultimately from their own rebelliousness.

When Matthew cites Hosea 11:1 he is citing the entire redemptive context, not only of Hosea but of the rest of the Old Testament. Citation of Hosea 11:1 reminds Israel of their double redemption from Egypt & Assyria/Babylon but also anticipates their final redemption from themselves.

Assessment of Matthew 2:15's use of Hosea 11:1 as fulfilment

When Hosea records, *Out of Egypt I have called my son*, he is tapping into an exodus motif that was expressed in the original event; reiterated and extended to "the king" of

Israel by Balaam (Nu.24:8); reiterated when Joshua entered Palestine; reiterated when the principle of redemption was applied repeatedly in OT didactic material; that would be reiterated later when Israel was restored after her impending discipline (Hosea 6:1-3; 8:1-10:5) and again **when Yahweh/ God would permanently redeem his people.** Matthew was simply noting something implicit in Hosea, namely, Christ was the ultimate fulfilment of **God's** promised redemption of Israel (Hosea 11:1-14:5). Hosea certainly understood that his recollection of the Exodus was anchored in **God's** past redemptive history as well as his future promise of final redemption. And, this is exactly what Matthew did by pointing to its manifestation in **Christ. Christ** returned to Israel from Egypt, as an obedient **son and also as God coming again** to dwell in the tents of Shem. The resonance with the exodus motif is so remarkable that Matthew could say **Christ 'filled up** to overflowing' the entire theme. If we were contemporaries of Matthew we too could have anticipated a final redemption of Israel and rejoiced when we saw its penultimate fulfilment in the first **advent of Christ** and hoped in its ultimate fulfilment in his second advent. And, in this sense, Hosea's recall of the exodus has a projective role because it is connected both to the past **Exodus event and to God's redemptive** commitment to Israel yet unrealised. When Matthew considers the words of Hosea he is not merely saying, "Gee, isn't this interesting how **both Israel and Christ returned to the land from Egypt."** What he is communicating must not merely be analogical correspondence. Isn't Matthew also saying, "What Hosea hoped for, the redemption of Israel from sin, was fully realised in Christ?"

Conclusion

What is clear from this preliminary study is that Matthew was not using *pesher*-like eisegetical techniques, when **he used the Old Testament in his gospel. He apparently often used his own translations of Greek, Hebrew and Aramaic sources** rather than isolating extant translations that fit an interpretive agenda. Significantly, his putative interpretations are not self-serving but correspond to interpretations found in **Septuigental, Masoretic, Syrian and rabbinical materials from the same era.** Similarly, his applications of the Old Testament to New Testament events do not have the tortured appearance of those found in the Dead Sea Scrolls. Even in some of the more challenging 'fulfilment' materials Matthew's use of the Old Testament does not correspond with *pesher* techniques used by the Qumran community.

What Matthew's fulfilment citations often appear to do is often show points of resonance with well developed redemptive themes in the OT of which Christ is the consummation. If this is true, Matthew may show us how to interpret the OT by indicating that earlier scriptures have both projective and retrojective functions as they reiterate the theology of an earlier motif or prototype and yet anticipate complete realisation in some **future act of God.**

Interestingly, quoting from the **Old Testament Mathew** affirms that, **Christ's** *exodus* not only recapitulated the return of Israel to the land but also the **advent of God dwelling** with his people. For **Christ's return** to Israel was also the **return of God** dwelling in the tents of Shem. In these ways **Christ** *filled to overflowing* **the exodus.**

PART TWO

WHY SHOULD CHRIST BE REFERRED TO AS GOD?

CHAPTER 2

Why should Christianity accept the Pagan word God be added to the name Christ and His Father in Heaven, such as the Son of God or God the Father? Are these changes necessary and if so why and who does it benefit? Does it benefit the pagan world or those pagans and Gentiles who wish to come to Christ for salvation without being followed with demonic influence? Unless many Christians are not aware the meaning of God/god is the pagan demonic false spirit which had been worshipped by the ancient world before the coming of Immanuel Jesus Christ the Saviour.

So, this chapter accesses the logic behind the spiritual revelation and the understanding to further ask the reasons why Jesus Christ should be called and referred to with the pagan word God. Unless the Christians are unaware, the Pagan word God is the false spirit. So, to change or to give additional name to Christ such as God or the Son of God is blasphemous just as He told the Pharisees who referred to Him as chief Demon after He had healed the dumb person. This is not safe because Jesus Christ is the Holy Spirit without sin but True Divine whilst the pagan God is evil and a false spirit.

It is no wonder when the theologian Dan Birchfield queried thus: as a Christian, if you have a pagan name should you change it? He added, I have a pagan name Ulf. If I become Christian, could I keep the name or change or will I have to change it to e.g. David? So why should Christians replace the existing pagan God with Christ the True Divine? <u>Lack of knowledge people perish indeed.</u> The Israelites pagan God/Yahweh has claimed to be the head-God over the numerous gods they worshipped and still worshipping. Yahweh is their national god still leading them in their wars fighting their enemies. He claimed to have created the world. How can a Demon God of Yahweh and other gods such as Brahma, Mazda, Jupiter and other head-Gods claiming to have created the world? Although this is deception, unfortunately many people do follow their lies blindly?

Bierchfield stated further that, becoming a Christian doesn't necessitate a name change. "Ulf" is a cool name, derived from the old Norse word for "wolf". Should you decide to become a Christian, keep your pagan name.

The Christian perspective is that our relationship with Christ helps us to do those good and noble works while also attaining a kind of peace, joy, love and hope we formerly didn't have. Christ will change your heart for the better, Ulf.

Another example is this, the word <u>Amen</u> comes from the same root as the word for the <u>pagan god Amun-Ra.</u> Whenever a supplicant would finish his prayers to this pagan god, he would upturn his hands and call out the name of his god and say....Amun. Does that mean you should stop saying Amen?

To avoid invoking anything pagan in origin, such as the names of the days, the months and the weeks, you would almost need to invent an entirely new language

that had no etymological roots in any previous language. For instance we might say "gosh darnit" instead of "God dammit" even though it means the same thing. Or…. instead of saying "Jesus!" we might say "geez" or even "gee whiz". Therefore referring to or calling Jesus Christ as God or the Son of God instead of the "Father" in Heaven that He Himself gave the world is tantamount to blasphemy.

As already queried, why should Jesus be referred to as a God? Can the Light and the Darkness co-exist? This chapter argues the fact that Jesus should not be referred to as God or the Son of God for the reason that the word God/god is a pagan initiative. And this pagan-god had been in existence and worshipped by the pagan world especially the Romans, Greeks, Israelites, India, Egypt and many European countries before the coming of Jesus to **save** mankind from the clutches of Satan? So, why has it ended up by calling the Saviour the Jesus Christ with the same pagan name God/god? This is the God/god of Satan the false spirit, whilst Jesus Christ is the True Holy Spirit. Importantly, if Jesus never called Himself God, how and why did He become One? This is the question being seriously put to the world to ponder by Prosser Bart D. Ehrmann. As many are not aware, it is necessary to take note that the early bible translators such as the Septuagint, Pentateuch and Vulgate were the works of Greeks and the Romans who are the agents of Satan and worshipped the false evil Spirit of Satan. With their liking of Satan they were compelled to vicissitude or alter and add the words of Jesus Christ after His death. When Jesus Christ said my 'Father in heaven the translators were compelled to add Father God to it even calling the Son of God or a God. In order to continue worshipping their **sun/god the Sol Invictus they replaced it with Jesus Christ.** And how could they continue celebrating their yearly pagan-gods anniversary if the name Christ could not be enmeshed as His birthday to be celebrated in December 25th? According to historian Bart Ehrman, "If Jesus had not been declared God by his followers, his followers would've remained a sect within Judaism, a small Jewish sect". **So, when Bart Ehrman was a young Evangelical Christian, he wanted to know how God became a man, but now, as an agnostic and historian of early Christianity, he wants to know how a man became God.**

When and why did Jesus' followers start saying "Jesus as God" and what did they mean by that? His new book is called *How Jesus Became God: The Exaltation of a Jewish Preacher from Galilee.*

In order to benefit from the full story and experience of Ehrman, he was interviewed by Terry Gross with regards to how Jesus was referred to as God.

"In this book I actually do not take a stand on either the question of whether Jesus was God, or whether he was actually raised from the dead,". "I leave open both questions because those are theological questions based on religious beliefs and I'm writing the book as a historian."

Ehrman is the author of several books about early Christianity, including *Misquoting Jesus* **and** *Jesus Interrupted.*

The Interview Highlights on three gospel writers

On a major difference between the first three gospels Matthew, Mark and Luke and the last gospel, John

During his lifetime, <u>Jesus himself didn't call himself God</u> and didn't consider himself God, and … none of his disciples had any inkling at all that he was God. …

During his lifetime, Jesus himself didn't call himself God and didn't consider himself God, and … none of his disciples had any inkling at all that he was God.

Historian Bart Ehrman

You do not find *Jesus calling himself God in the Gospel of John, or the last Gospel. Jesus says things like, "Before Abraham was, I am." And, "I and the Father are one," and, "If you've seen me, you've seen the Father." These are all statements you find only in the Gospel of John, and that's striking because* we have earlier gospels and we have the writings *of Paul, and in <u>none of them is there any indication that Jesus said such things.</u> … even if Jesus said them He did not use the <u>pagan word God. He is not God because He is the true Holy Spirit</u>*

I think it's completely implausible that Matthew, Mark and Luke would not mention that Jesus called himself God if that's what he was declaring about himself. That would be a rather important point to make. This is not an unusual view amongst scholars; it's simply the view that the Gospel of John is providing a theological understanding of Jesus <u>that is not what was historically accurate.</u>

How Jesus Became God

According to Ehrman, Jesus was referred to as God similar to how Roman emperors who were called "God". Right at the same time that Christians were calling Jesus "God" is exactly when Romans wer calling their emperors "God." So these Christians were not doing this in a vacuum; they were actually doing it in a context. I don't think this could be an accident that this is a point at which the emperors are being called "God." So by calling Jesus "God," in fact, it was a <u>competition between your God, the emperor, and our God, Jesus.</u>

When Constantine, the emperor, then converted to Christianity, it changed everything because now rather than the emperor being God, the emperor was the worshipper of the God, Jesus. That was quite a forceful change, and one could argue that it changed the understanding of religion and politics for all time.

On the Emergence of the Trinity

Christians had a dilemma as soon as they declared that Christ was God. *If Christ is God and God the Father is God, doesn't that make two gods? And when you throw the Holy Spirit into the mix, doesn't that make three gods? So aren't Christians polytheists? Christians wanted to* insist, no, they're monotheists. Well, if they're monotheists, how can all three be God?

So there are various ways of trying to explain this, and one of the most popular ways ... was called modalism. It's called modalism because it insisted that God existed in three modes just as I myself at the same time am a son, and a brother and a father, but there's only one of me well these theologians said: That's what God is like. He's manifest in three persons, but there's only one of him, so he's at the same time father, son and spirit. So he's in three modes of existence, so there's only one of him.

On the difference between history and the past

What I try to teach my students is that history is not the past. ... There are a lot of things in the past that we cannot show historically. For example ... you simply cannot show what my grandfather ate on March 23, 1956. I mean, he ate *something* for lunch that day, I'm sure, but there's no way we have access to it. So it's in the past, but it's not part of history. History is what we can show to have happened in the past.

Historians acting as historians whether they're believers or nonbelievers acting as historians, they simply cannot say Jesus was probably raised by God from the dead.

One of the things that historians cannot show as having happened in the past is anything that's miraculous. Because to believe that a miracle has happened, to believe that God has done something in our world, requires a person to believe in God. It requires a theological belief, but historians can't require theological beliefs to do their work.

Historians in most cases, don't invoke miracle because it's beyond what historians can prove. Miracles may have happened in the past, but they're not part of history. So that applies to the resurrection of Jesus. Historians acting as historians, whether they're believers or nonbelievers, acting as historians, they simply cannot say Jesus was probably raised by the Lord God the dead. But historians can look at other aspects of the resurrection traditions and see whether they bear up, historically.

Bart Ehrman is also the author of *Misquoting Jesus, God's Problem* and *Jesus, Interrupted.* He's a professor of religious studies at the University of North Carolina, Chapel Hill. *Dan Sears/Haper One*

On the empty tomb and the resurrection

Was Jesus put in a tomb and three days later that tomb was found empty? Well, that's a historical question. And to answer it, it doesn't require any set of religious beliefs; you can simply look at the sources and draw some historical conclusions.

Before I wrote this book and did the research on it, I was convinced, as many people are, that Jesus was given a decent burial, and on the third day the women went to the tomb, found it empty, and that started the belief in the resurrection.

Apart from the fact that I don't think Jesus was given a decent burial that he was probably thrown into a common grave of some kind apart from that, I was struck in doing my research by the fact that the New Testament never indicates that people came to believe in the resurrection because of the empty tomb. This was a striking find because it's just commonly said that that's what led to the resurrection belief.

But if you think about it for a second, it makes sense that the empty tomb wouldn't make anybody believe. If you put somebody in a tomb and three days later you go back and the body's not in the tomb, your first thought isn't, "Oh, he's been exalted to heaven and made the son of God." Your first thought is, "Somebody stole the body." Or, "Somebody moved the body." Or, "Hey, I'm at the wrong tomb." You don't think he's been exalted to heaven. In the New Testament it's striking that in the Gospels the empty tomb leads to confusion but it doesn't lead to belief. What leads to belief is that some of the followers of Jesus have visions of him afterward.

If Jesus had not been declared God by his followers, his followers would've remained a sect within Judaism a small Jewish sect, and if that was the case it would not have attracted a large number of gentiles. If they hadn't attracted a large number of gentiles, there wouldn't have been this steady rate of conversion over the first three centuries to Christianity; it would've been a small Jewish sect.

If Christianity had not become a sizable minority in the empire, the Roman emperor Constantine almost certainly would not have converted, but then there wouldn't have been the masses of conversions after Constantine, and Christianity would not have become the state religion of Rome. If that hadn't happened, it would never have become the dominant religious, cultural, political, social, economic force that it became so that we wouldn't have even had the Middle Ages, the Renaissance, the Reformation or modernity as we know it. ... It all hinges on this claim the early Christians had that Jesus was God.

In the words of Bart Willruth, historically, many rulers have assumed titles such as the **son of God**, the **son of a god** or the **son of heaven**.

The term "son of God" is used in the Hebrew Bible as another way to refer to humans who have a special relationship with God. *In Exodus, the nation of Israel is called God's firstborn son.* **Solomon is also called "son of God".** Angels, just and pious men, and the kings of Israel are all called "sons of pagan God.

In the New Testament of the Christian Bible, "Son of God" is applied to Jesus Christ copied from the Greek Septuagint Bible. On two occasions, Jesus is recognised as the Son of God by a voice which speaks from Heaven. Jesus Himself did not explicitly and implicitly describes himself as the Son of God and he is also described as the Son of God by various individuals who appear in the New Testament. Jesus is called the "son of God," by Paul's converted "Christians and not Christ's own followers the Apostles." As applied to Jesus, the term is a reference to his role as the Messiah, or Christ. The contexts and ways in which Jesus' title, Son of God, means something more or something other than the title Messiah remain the subject of ongoing scholarly study and discussion.

The term "Son of God" should not be confused with the term "God the Son" (Greek: Θεός ὁ υἱός), the second Person of the Trinity in Christian theology. The doctrine of the Trinity identifies Jesus as God the Son, identical in essence but distinct in person with regard to God the Father and God the Holy Spirit (the first and third Persons of the Trinity). Nontrinitarian Christians accept the application to Jesus of the term "Son of God", which is found in the New Testament quoted from the Old Testament.

Throughout history, emperors and rulers ranging from the Western Zhou dynasty (c. 1000 BC) in China to Alexander the Great (c. 360 BC) to the Emperor of Japan (c. 600 AD) have assumed titles that reflect a filial relationship with deities

The title "Son of Heaven" i.e. meaning sky/heaven/god and meaning child) was first used in the Western Zhou dynasty (c. 1000 BC). It is mentioned in the Shijing book of songs, and reflected the Zhou belief that as Son of Heaven (and as its delegate) the Emperor of China was responsible for the well-being of the whole world by the Mandate of Heaven. This title may also be translated as "son of God" given that the word *Tiān* in Chinese may either mean sky or god. The Emperor of Japan was also called the Son of Heaven starting in the early 7th century.

Among the Eurasian nomads, there was also a widespread use of "Son of God/Son of Heaven" for instance, in the third century BC, the ruler was called Chanyü and similar titles were used as late as the 13th century by Genghis Khan.

Examples of kings being considered the son of god are found throughout the Ancient Near East. Egypt in particular developed a long lasting tradition. Egyptian pharaohs are known to have been referred to as the son of a particular god and their begetting in some cases is even given in sexually explicit detail. Egyptian pharaohs did not have full parity with their divine fathers but rather were subordinate. Nevertheless, in the first four dynasties, the pharaoh was considered to be the embodiment of a god. Thus, Egypt was ruled by direct theocracy, wherein "God himself is recognized as the head" of the state. During the later Amarna Period, King Amenhotep IV/Akhenaten redefined the pharaoh's godship. He taught "there was only one god and only one person who now knew the god: Akhenaten himself" and assumed position of the ḥm ntr tpy (first servant of god). He eventually eliminated all representation on his behalf by the priests of Amun as he also eliminated the god Amun, to solely lead worship identifying as the Son of the God he called Father, the latter which he recognized through the aten (sun), the vehicle through which the power of the God manifested to him. Within a few years of his first epiphany and becoming king, King Akhenaten had dropped the priestly title, but remained serving as the sole cleric and son of the Father in his rule of the Two Lands.

Later still, the closest Egypt came to the Jewish variant of theocracy was during the reign of <u>Herihor</u>. He took on the role of ruler not as a god but rather as a high-priest and king.

According to the Bible, several kings of Damascus took the title son of Hadad. From the archaeological record a stela erected by Bar-Rakib for his father Panammuwa II contains similar language. The son of Panammuwa II a king of Sam'al referred to himself as a son of Rakib. Rakib-El is a god who appears in Phoenician and Aramaic inscriptions. Panammuwa II died unexpectedly while in Damascus. However, his son the king Bar-Rakib was not a native of Damascus but rather the ruler of Sam'al it is unknown if other rules of Sam'al used similar language.

In Greek mythology, Heracles (son of Zeus) and many other figures were considered to be sons of gods through union with mortal women. From around 360 BC onwards Alexander the Great may have implied he was a demigod by using the title "Son of Ammon–Zeus".

A denarius minted circa 18 BC. Obverse: CAESAR AVGVSTVS; reverse: DIVVS IVLIV(S)

In 42 BC, Julius Caesar was formally deified as "the divine Julius" (*divus Iulius*) after his assassination. His adopted son, Octavian (better known as Augustus, a title given to him 15 years later, in 27 BC) thus became known as *divi Iuli filius* (son of the divine Julius) or simply *divi filius* (son of the god). As a daring and unprecedented move, Augustus used this title to advance his political position in the Second Triumvirate, finally overcoming all rivals for power within the Roman state.

The word which was applied to Julius Caesar when he was deified was *divus*, not the distinct word *deus*. Thus, Augustus called himself. The line between been god and god-like was at times less than clear to the population at large, and Augustus seems to have been aware of the necessity of keeping the ambiguity. As a purely semantic mechanism, and to maintain ambiguity, the court of Augustus sustained the concept that any worship given to an emperor was paid to the "position of emperor" rather than the person of the emperor. However, the subtle semantic distinction was lost outside Rome, where Augustus began to be worshiped as a deity. The inscription DF thus came to be used for Augustus, at times unclear which meaning was intended. The assumption of the title *Divi filius* by Augustus meshed with a larger campaign by him to exercise the power of his image. Official portraits of Augustus made even towards the end of his life continued to portray him as a handsome youth, implying that miraculously, he never aged. Given that few people had ever seen the emperor, these images sent a distinct message.

Later, Tiberius (emperor from 14 to 37 AD) came to be accepson of *divus Augustus* and Hadrian as the son of *divus Trajan*. By the end of the 1st century, the emperor Domitian was being called *dominus et deus* (i.e. *master and god*).

Outside the Roman Empire, the 2nd-century Kushan King Kanishka I used the title *devaputra* meaning **"son of God"**.

Adulteration to the New Testament

The accuracy of the New Testament is in doubt because of the credibility of Mark and Paul as stressed by Bart Willruth. Bart stated thus: As a New Testament scholar, I can speak with a solid background in the field. I have studied the issue for many years. So.....I think the Christ Myth is the most probable explanation for the rise of Christianity, but not because it was based on pagan myths. Dying and rising saviour gods were ubiquitous in the **Roman world**. Jesus shares many similarities with some of them and could be a type of that genre, but with a Jewish twist. Yet, this isn't the reason to doubt his historicity. That comes from other places. Willruth pointed to the credibility of the earliest Christian writers like this: the earliest Christian writings, those of Paul and the book of Hebrews speak as though no recently living Jewish man was in mind. **<u>Paul knows nothing</u>** of a so-called and theoretical oral tradition **<u>about Jesus</u>** and specifically denies knowledge of anything of the sort in Galatians. He mentioned no details of that which we think was part of the biography of Jesus. No genealogy, no mother and father, no birth narrative, no disciples, no preaching, no miracles, no triumphal entry, not trial before Pilate, nothing about Galilee, no crucifixion in Jerusalem, etc. **<u>Nothing.</u> This is inconceivable that <u>the first Christian writer addressing new converts</u> <u>was so lacking</u> in curiosity of this amazing man, not to mention the new Christians having no interest in him**...unless he wasn't writing about a recently living man, and there is no evidence that he was. **The <u>book of Hebrews even places the sacrifice of Jesus in heaven, not on earth</u>** It wasn't until decades later that an anonymous writer who we refer to as **<u>Mark</u> wrote a story about Jesus placed in Galilee/ Judea ca 30 CE. We don't know his purpose in writing. Was it history, or allegory, or a large parable?** We don't know his intent. We don't know when he wrote. It could have been **anywhere between the 70's to the 130's**. We don't know who he was other than being a diaspora Jew writing to other diaspora Jews **(living in Greece and present day Turkey), whose language was Greek.** He never tells how he knows his information; no sources no criteria for sorting true from false, **nothing.** But we do know something of his sources. As a literate Greek, he would have studied Homer's epics, and there is evidence that some of his stories were patterned after Odysseus, especially from the Odyssey (Dennis MacDonald). **But his main source of material was from the Old Testament; not in prophecies fulfilled, but in finding hidden meanings in verses taken completely out of context.** As Paul said that he found his information about long held mysteries in the prophets via revelation and a new method of interpretation (midrash) **Rom 16:25–27 and elsewhere, so Mark played on this theme of secret information with his Jesus character telling people to keep his messiahship secret. Mark essentially constructed every event of his narrative out of OT verses, grabbing phras...**

On the obverse side of this coin dating from 327 CE, Constantine is seen facing right, wearing a diadem of three bands of pearls, with most importantly his eyes raised to the sky. This is markedly different from any other portrayals of Roman emperors on coinage and directly relates to the legend associated with his conversion to Christianity. According to his self-appointed biographer Eusebius, Bishop of Caesara, in the year 312 CE, Constantine was on campaign when around midday he saw a shining cross made of light over the sun with the text "by this conquer" (Flower 2012). This image, a combination of the Greek letters, chi (X) and ro (P), became one of the most widely used symbols for Christianity

Christian Constantine? Despite common belief that Constantine was strictly Christian, some evidence suggests "superstitious" would be a more appropriate term (Madden 1877). In fact, Constantine used pagan gods and goddesses such as Victory and Sol on his coins like emperors prior to him. This coin minted a year after his vision depicts the busts of both Constantine curiassed and wreathed with laurel and pagan god Sol Invictius. His shield also displays a galloping sun quadriga, further reinforcing his association with the sun god.

Following Constantine's vision and the legalization of Christianity, the emperors to follow, like Magnentius, seen on the coin above, started including Christograms on their coins. Magnentius, who was actually very tolerant of and sympathized with pagans, best exemplifies this as seen on the reverse of this coin from around 352 CE. The Christogram takes up the majority of the composition on the reverse, almost as large as his bust on the obverse, making it the "greatest numismatic affirmation of Christianity in antiquity" (Rubin 1998). The Greek letters A and Ω are also seen in the horizontal cross field, a direct reference to Revelation 1:8 from the Christian Bible: "'I am the Alpha and Omega–the beginning and the end,' says the Lord God. The Legalization of Christianity Not too long after, in 380 CE, the emperor Theodosius signed the Edict of Thessalonica, making Nicene Christianity the official religion of the state, which confirmed and solidified the influence of Christianity not only on the Roman world at the time but also for the rest of world history. Theodosius was also the last emperor to rule before Rome was once again split between West and East, meaning his legalization reached all territories.

Lord showing the emperor to be the supreme ruler, Theodosius, dutiful and wise Augustus." Theodosius was the Roman emperor who made Christianity the official religion of the Roman world. History credits him as the one presiding over the beginning of the end of paganism and the champion of Christian orthodoxy (Errington 1997).

The reverse of this coin portrays the pagan goddess Victory advancing left, carrying a trophy and dragging a captive, with the inscription SALVIS REIPVBLICAE, meaning "Salvation of the Republic." There is also what appears to be a Christogram in the middle of the composition just to the left of Victory. While Theodosius is commonly portrayed in history as ridding the **empire of traces of paganism, this coin raises an important juxtaposition regarding the continuation of images of Victory in early Christian art, until she is eventually replaced by images of angels.**

Justinian II Solidus (692-695 CE)

Justinian II set the precedent of moving the image of the emperor to the reverse and placing the image of Christ on the obverse, as seen in this coin from 692-695 CE (Kazhdan 1991). On the obverse, Jesus Christ is depicted raising his right hand in benediction and holding the Gospel, while the edges of the cross project from behind his head. The inscription reads, "Jesus Christ, King of Kings." On the reverse, "Justinian, servant of Christ" is inscribed while he stands wearing a crown with a cross and holding a cross potent. This important stylistic shift represents the full evolution of Christianity within the Roman world, from the subject of persecution to gradual acceptance and representation to eventually becoming the forefront of subject matter and dethroning designated spots for the rulers that were first standardized even prior to the birth of Jesus Christ.

Paul was not one of the 12 Apostles

Although St. Paul was not one of the original 12 Apostles of Jesus, he was one of the most prolific contributors to the New Testament. Of the 27 books in the New Testament,

13 or 14 are traditionally attributed to Paul, though only 7 of these Pauline epistles are accepted as being entirely authentic and dictated by St. Paul himself. The authorship of the others is debated, and they are commonly thought to have come from contemporary or later followers writing in Paul's name. These authors likely used material from his surviving letters and may have even had access to letters written by him that no longer survive. Read on to learn which Biblical books St. Paul is known to have authored and which ones he probably did not write himself.

Letter of Paul to the Romans

The sixth book of the New Testament, the Letter of Paul to the Romans, was written by St. Paul while he was in Corinth about 57 CE. It was addressed to the Christian church at Rome, whose congregation he hoped to visit for the first time on his way to Spain. The epistle is the longest and doctrinally most significant of St. Paul's writings and is more of a theological treatise than a letter. In it he acknowledges the unique religious heritage of the Jews (prior to his conversion, Paul was a Jewish Pharisee) but asserts that righteousness no longer comes through the Mosaic Law but through Christ.

First and Second Letter of Paul to the Corinthians

The First Letter of Paul to the Corinthians and the Second Letter of Paul to the Corinthians were both written by St. Paul. The first letter was probably written about 53–54 CE at Ephesus and addresses some of the problems that arose in the new Christian community that he had established in Corinth during his initial missionary visit (c. 50–51). The second letter was written from Macedonia about 55 CE and applauds the Corinthians' response to his first letter and reaffirms his apostolic authority. The letters deal with a church of Gentile Christians and are therefore the best evidence of how St. Paul operated on Gentile territory.

Letter of Paul to the Galatians

The Letter of Paul to the Galatians, the ninth book of the New Testament, was authored by St. Paul. The letter was likely written between 53–54 CE and addresses division within the Christian community about whether new converts needed to be underlined circumcised and follow the prescriptions of the Mosaic Law. He reaffirms his teaching that Jewish law is no longer the exclusive path to righteousness and argues that Christians have a new freedom in Christ. The letter is very forceful and specific in dealing with the problems concerned and is the only epistle without kindly ingression, thanksgiving, or personal greetings appended to the final blessings.

Letter of Paul to the Ephesians

Although the Letter of Paul to the Ephesians has been attributed to St. Paul, it is more likely the work of one of his disciples. Scholars think the letter was probably written before 90 CE and that the author consulted St. Paul's letter to the Colossians as a reference. Of the 155 verses in Ephesians, 73 have verbal parallels with Colossians. When parallels to genuine Pauline letters are added, 85 percent of Ephesians is duplicated elsewhere. This and several other contested letters are usually designated as "deuter-Pauline epistles" to indicate that they were probably written by St. Paul's followers after his death.

Letter of Paul to the Philippians

The Letter of Paul to the Philippians is believed to have been written by St. Paul while he was in prison, probably at Rome about 62 CE. According to several scholars, the canonical work is likely a later collection of fragments of Paul's correspondence with the congregation in Philippi. Apprehensive that his execution was close at hand, yet hoping somehow to visit the Philippians again, St. Paul explains that he welcomes death for Jesus' sake but is equally concerned to continue his apostolate.

Letter of Paul to the Colossian

The authorship of the <u>Letter of Paul to the Colossians</u> is debated. For some scholars, the developed <u>theology</u> of the letter indicates that it was composed by St. Paul during his imprisonment in Rome about 62 CE. Others question Pauline authorship on the basis of the distinctive vocabulary and suggest that it is a deuter-Pauline epistle, written by Paul's followers after his death. Given its similarities to the <u>Letter of Paul to Philemon</u>, some have suggested that a later Paulinist simply changed details to meet a different situation.

First and Second Letter of Paul to the Thessalonians

The first <u>L</u>etter of Paul to the Thessalonians was likely written by St. Paul from Corinth about 50 CE. However, the second letter is possibly deuter-Pauline in origin, though this is debated. Second Thessalonians is obviously an imitation of the style of First Thessalonians but seems to reflect a later time. Additionally, given that there is notable ambiguity about the proximity of Christ's <u>Second Coming</u>, its authorship by St. Paul is doubted.

First and Second Letter of Paul to Timothy

Neither of the two Letters of Paul to Timothy are thought to have been written by St. Paul. Linguistic facts—such as short connectives, particles and other syntactical peculiarities; use of different words for the same things; and repeated unusual phrases otherwise not used by Paul— offer fairly conclusive evidence against Pauline authorship and authenticity. Both epistles are usually considered "trito-Pauline," meaning that they were probably written by members of the Pauline school a generation after his death, likely between 80 and 100 CE.

Letter of Paul to Titus

The authorship of the Letter of Paul to Titus is disputed. Given many of the similarities in content and style to the two Letters of Paul to Timothy, it is possible that this work is also a trito-Pauline epistle, written a generation after the death of St. Paul. In fact, the three letters together are often called Pastoral Letters, as they were written to instruct and admonish the recipients in their pastoral office rather than to address the specific problems of congregations like many of the other Pauline epistles.

Letter of Paul to Philemon

The Letter of Paul to Philemon was probably composed by St. Paul in a Roman prison about 61 CE, though some sources date it earlier. The brief epistle was written to Philemon, a wealthy Christian of Colossae, on behalf of Onesimus, Philemon's former slave. While passing no judgment on slavery itself, Paul exhorts Philemon to manifest true Christian love that removes barriers between slaves and free people.

Letter to the Hebrews

While the <u>Letter to the Hebrews</u> has traditionally been ascribed to St. Paul, the work does not contain a salutation with the name of the author. The book is still included in the Pauline corpus in the East but not in the West. Given that the thoughts, metaphors, and ideas of Hebrews are distinct from the rest of the <u>New Testament</u>, most scholars doubt that it was **written by St. Paul or his followers.** Various authors have been suggested over the ages, and it is possible that the work was composed by a Jewish convert among the second generation of **Christians suffering persecution.**

PART THREE

WHICH GODS WERE BEING WORSHIPPED BEFORE CHRISTIANITY?

CHAPTER 3

This chapter examines the existence of the gods being worshipped by individuals and many religious organisations in the pagan world before the advent of Christ and the establishment of Christianity. According to Quisi H, the first Christians were Jewish, so they still worshiped the **same god** that Christians worship (although Christians worship that god in two additional forms Jesus Christ and the Holy Spirit.

The next wave of Christians were the Romans and Hellenised Jews (Jews who had assimilated to Greek culture). They would have had particular gods in the Greek/Roman pantheon they paid particular homage to. That would have depended on their location and family tradition.

After that, the Romans adopted and adapted Christianity and spread it as they spread their empire. By the time the Roman empire collapsed, Christianity had already spread as far as Ireland. Various other states and shorter-lived empires emerged, continuing to enforce Christianity across Europe as they conquered the peoples that unfortunately are usually just labelled "pagan." Someone else can tell you more about pre-Christian groups in Africa and the Middle East.

In English, people may write the words "god" and "gods" in lowercase letters. People that believe in only one god (monotheists) like to write *God* **with a <u>capital letter</u>.** Some people that believe in more than one god (polytheists) also like to use capital letters when writing about their gods. Most people that **believe in God or gods d**o not believe in the gods of other religions.

Does God exist?

Many people have asked themselves if God exists. Philosophers, theologians, and others have tried to prove that it exists. Others have tried to disprove the hypothesis. In philosophical terminology, such arguments are about the epistemology of the ontology of God. The debate exists mainly in philosophy, because science does not address whether or not supernatural things exist.

There are many philosophical issues with the existence of God. Some definitions of God are not specific. Arguments for the existence of God typically include metaphysical, empirical, inductive, and subjective types. Some theories try to explain order and complexity in the world without evolution or scientific method. Arguments against the existence of God typically include empirical, deductive and inductive arguments. Conclusions sometimes include: "God does not exist" (strong atheism); "God almost certainly does not exist" (*de facto* atheism); "no one knows whether God exists" (agnosticism); "God exists, but this cannot be proven or disproven" (deism or theism); and "God exists and this can be proven" (theism). There are many variations on these positions, and sometimes different names for some of them. For example, the position "God exists and this can be proven" and sometimes called "gnostic theism" or "strong theism".

Believing in God [change | change source]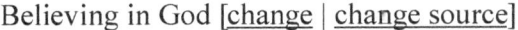

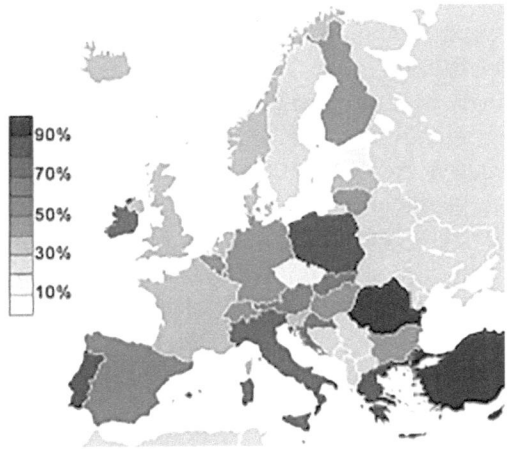

The percentage of people in European countries who said in 2005 that they "believe there is a God". Countries with Eastern Orthodox (i.e.: Greece, Romania, etc.) or Muslim (Turkey) majorities tend to poll highest.

By the year 2000, approximately 53% of the world's population were part of one of the three main Abrahamic religions (33% Christian, 20% Islam, less than 1% Judaism), 6% with Buddhism, 13% with Hinduism, 6% with traditional Chinese religion, 7% with various other religions, and less than 15% as non-religious. Most of these religious beliefs involve God or gods. Some religions do not believe in a god or do not include the concept of gods.

In monotheistic belief systems, **God** is usually viewed as the supreme being, creator, and principal object of faith. In polytheistic belief systems, a god is "a spirit or being believed to have created, or for controlling some part of the universe or life, for which such a deity is often worshipped". Belief in the existence of at least one god is called theism.

Views regarding God vary considerably. Many notable theologians and philosophers have developed arguments for and against the existence of God. Atheism rejects the belief in any deity. Agnosticism is the belief that the existence of God is unknown or unknowable. Some theists view knowledge concerning God as derived from faith. God is often conceived as the greatest entity in existence.[1] God is often believed to be the cause of all things and so is seen as the creator, sustainer, and ruler of the universe. Pagan God is often thought of as incorporeal and independent of the material creation, while pantheism holds that the pagan God is the universe itself. Pagan God is sometimes seen as omnibenevolent, while deism holds that pagan God is not involved with humanity apart from creation.

Some traditions attach spiritual significance to maintaining some form of relationship with God, often involving acts such as worship and prayer, and see God as the source of all moral obligation. **God is sometimes described without reference to gender,** while others use terminology that is gender-specific. Pagan God is referred to be different names depending on the language and cultural tradition, sometimes with different titles of pagan God used in reference to pagan God's various attributes.

The meaning of pagan God

The Mesha Stele bears the earliest known reference (840 BCE) to the Israelite God Yahweh.

The earliest written form of the Germanic word *God* comes from the 6th-century Christian *Codex Argenteus*. The English word itself is derived from the Proto-Germanic *ǥuđan. The reconstructed Proto-Indo-European form *ǵhu-tó-m was likely based on the root *ǵhau(ə)-, which meant either "to call" or "to invoke". The Germanic words for *God* were originally neuter, but during the process of the Christianization of the Germanic peoples from their indigenous Germanic paganism, the words became a masculine syntactic form In the English language, capitalization is used when the word is used as a proper noun, as well as for other names by which a god is known. Consequently, the capitalized form of *god* is not used for multiple gods or when used to refer to the generic idea of a deity.

The English word *God* and its counterparts in other languages are normally used for any and all conceptions and, in spite of significant differences between religions, the term remains an English translation common to all.

El means *God* in Hebrew, but in Judaism and in Christianity, God is also given a personal name, the tetragrammaton **YHWH,** in origin possibly the name of an Edomite or Midianite deity, **Yahweh.** In many English translations of the Bible, when the word *LORD* is in all capitals, it signifies that the word represents the tetragrammaton. Jah or Yah is an abbreviation of Jahweh/Yahweh, and often sees usage by Jews and Christians in the interjection "Hallelujah", meaning "Praise Jah", which is used to give God glory. In Judaism some of the Hebrew titles of God are considered holy names.

Allāh is the Arabic term with no plural used by Muslims and Arabic speaking Christians and Jews meaning "The God", is the term used for a deity or a god in general. Muslims also use a multitude of other titles for God.

In Hinduism, Brahman is often considered a monistic concept of God. God may also be given a proper name in monotheistic currents of Hinduism which emphasize the personal nature of God, with early references to his name as Krishna-Vasudeva in Bhagavata or later Vishnu and Hari. Sang Hyang Widhi Wasa is the term used in Balinese Hinduism.

In Chinese religion, Shangdi is conceived as the progenitor (first ancestor) of the universe, intrinsic to it and constantly bringing order to it.

Ahura Mazda is the name for God used in Zoroastrianism. "Mazda", or rather the Avestan stem-form *Mazdā-*, nominative *Mazdå*, reflects Proto-Iranian **Mazdāh (female)*. It is generally taken to be the proper name of the spirit, and like its Sanskrit cognate *medhā*, means "intelligence" or "wisdom". Both the Avestan and Sanskrit words reflect Proto-Indo-Iranian **mazdhā-*, from Proto-Indo-European mn̩sdʰeh₁, literally meaning "placing (*dʰeh₁*) one's mind (**mn̩-s*)", hence "wise". Meanwhile 101 other names are also in use.

Waheguru (*Punjabi: vāhigurū*) is a term most often used in Sikhism to refer to God. It means "Wonderful Teacher" in the Punjabi language. *Vāhi* (a Middle Persian borrowing) means "wonderful" and *guru* (*Sanskrit: guru*) is a term denoting "teacher". Waheguru is also described by some as an experience of ecstasy which is beyond all description. The most common usage of the word "Waheguru" is in the greeting Sikhs use with each other – *Waheguru Ji Ka Khalsa, Waheguru Ji Ki Fateh* "Wonderful Lord's Khalsa, Victory is to the Wonderful Lord."

Baha, the "greatest" name for God in the Bahá'í Faith, is Arabic for "All-Glorious".

Other names for God include Aten in ancient Egyptian Atenism where Aten was proclaimed to be the one "true" supreme being and creator of the universe, Chukwu in Igbo, and Hayyi Rabbi in Mandaeism.

Isaac Newton saw the existence of a Creator necessary in the movement of astronomical objects (painting by Godfrey Kneller, 1689).

The existence of God is a subject of debate in theology, philosophy of religion and popular culture. In philosophical terms, the question of the existence of God involves the disciplines of epistemology (the nature and scope of knowledge) and ontology (study of the nature of being or existence) and the theory of value (since some definitions of God include "perfection").

Ontological arguments refer to any argument for the existence of God that is based on *a priori* reasoning. Notable ontological arguments were formulated by Anselm and René Descartes. Cosmological arguments, such as those described below, use concepts around the origin of the universe to argue for the existence of God.

The *Teleological argument*, also called the "argument from design", uses the complexity within the universe as a proof of the existence of God. It is countered that the fine tuning required for a stable universe with life on earth is illusionary, as humans are only able to observe the small part of this universe that succeeded in making such observation possible, called the anthropic principle, and so would not learn of, for example, life on other planets or of universes that did not occur because of different laws of physics. Non-theists have argued that complex processes that have natural explanations yet to be discovered are referred to the supernatural, called god of the gaps. Other theists, such as John Henry Newman who believed theistic evolution was acceptable, have also argued against versions of the teleological argument and held that it is limiting of God to view him having to only intervene specially in some instances rather than having complex processes designed to create order.

The *Argument from beauty* states that this universe happens to contain special beauty in it and that there would be no particular reason for this over aesthetically neutrality other than God. This has been countered by pointing to the existence of ugliness in the universe. This has also been countered by arguing that beauty has no objective reality and so the universe could be seen as ugly or that humans have made what is more beautiful than nature.

The *Argument from morality* argues for the existence of God given the assumption of the objective existence of morals. While prominent non-theistic philosophers such as the atheist J. L. Mackie agreed that the argument is valid, they disagreed with its premises. David Hume argued that there is no basis to believe in objective moral truths while biologist E. O. Wilson theorized that the feelings of morality are a by-product of natural selection in humans and would not exist independent of the mind. Philosopher Michael Lou Martin argued that a subjective account for morality can be acceptable. Similar to the argument from morality is the *argument from conscience* which argues for the existence of God given the existence of a conscience that informs of right and wrong, even against prevailing moral codes. Philosopher John Locke instead argued that conscience is a social construct and thus could lead to contradicting morals.

Atheism is, in a broad sense, the rejection of belief in the existence of deities. Agnosticism is the view that the truth values of certain claims—especially metaphysical and religious claims such as whether God, the divine or the supernatural exist—are unknown and perhaps unknowable. Theism generally holds that God exists objectively and independently of human thought and is sometimes used to refer to any belief in God or gods.

Some view the existence of God as an empirical question. Richard Dawkins states that "a universe with a god would be a completely different kind of universe from one without, and it would be a scientific difference." Carl Sagan argued that the doctrine of a Creator of the Universe was difficult to prove or disprove and that the only conceivable scientific discovery that could disprove the existence of a Creator (not necessarily a God) would be the discovery that the universe is infinitely old. Some theologians, such as Alister McGrath, argue that the existence of God is not a question that can be answered using the scientific method.

Agnostic Stephen Jay Gould argued that science and religion are not in conflict and proposed an approach dividing the world of philosophy into what he called "non-overlapping magisteria" (NOMA). In this view, questions of the supernatural, such as those relating to the existence and nature of God, are non-empirical and are the proper domain of theology. The methods of science should then be used to answer any empirical question about the natural world, and theology should be used to answer questions about ultimate meaning and moral value. In this view, the perceived lack of any empirical footprint from the magisterium of the supernatural onto natural events makes science the sole player in the natural world. Stephen Hawking and co-author Leonard Mlodinow state in their 2010 book, *The Grand Design*, that it is reasonable to ask who or what created the universe, but if the answer is God, then the question has merely been deflected to that of who created God. Both authors claim, however, that it is possible to answer these questions purely within the realm of science and without invoking divine beings.

Is YHWH a pagan god and how does it affect Christianity?

It is a belief **that Yahweh has been one of the pagan gods being worshipped by the Jews** before He was elevated by the Jews as their head-god and also became their national god. Ian accepts and said yes to the the concept to be true. He adds thus, it's astonishing how many Christians and Jews appear to be unaware of the pagan mythological origin of their god, claiming he's eternal and is "The Creator and Lord of the Universe" or some other similar description.

You should know, since it's quite explicit in the Bible itself, that your god **God, Jehovah, or Yahweh** was once called **YHWH** in Hebrew and has pagan origins as the god of metallurgy of itinerant copper miners from Midian and Edom.

This god was brought to the early Nation of Israel not long after it was formed by Canaanite migrants moving inland during the 15th and 14th centuries BCE at a time when that nation was still polytheistic, worshipping gods like Baal, El and Asherah, all of whom are mentioned in the Bible. YHWH was just another of these early polytheistic gods.

The Bible says explicitly that God "*came from Teman*" (Habakkuk 3:3), that he "*went out of Seir*" and he "*marched out of Edom*" (Judges 5:4-5) — all toponyms associated with the area ranging from Sinai to the Negev and northern Arabia, an area which was extensively mined for copper by the **YHWH-worshipping** Midianite and Edomite copper miners.

There are several further references to the metallurgical **origin of YHWH in the Bible**, with passages describing **YHWH** as dwelling in "*mountains of copper*" (Zech 6:1-5), "*a land whose stones are iron, and out of whose hills you may dig copper*" (Deut 8:9), "*Oh, that you would rend the heavens and come down, with the mountains quaking before you*" (Isaiah 63:19b), and "*Bow your heavens, YHWH, and come down! Touch the mountains so that they smoke!*" (Psalms 144:5). This is a likely reference to a metal-smelting furnace, perhaps confirmed in Psalm 18:8 where **Yahweh** is depicted as an anthropomorphised furnace: "*smoke rose* *from his nostrils; consuming fire came from his mouth, burning coals blazed out of it".*

The Judahites were still polytheistic right through the time of the Babylonian Exile in the 6th century BCE during which time the Torah, or the first 5 books of the Old Testament, were written by unknown scribes however there was a move towards monolatry during this time, and a complete move to monotheism with, for reasons unknown, Yahweh becoming the sole god, during the 4th and 5th centuries BCE.

The Christian god, adopted from Judaism, isn't who most people think he is. Far from being eternal and this imaginary "Creator and Lord of the Universe", he's just another adopted pagan god with very human origins and a series of changed names; **YHWH → Yahweh → Jehovah → God...**

As is so often the case, it takes an atheist, someone who's read the Bible and understands it in the context of time, place, and primitive beliefs of the authors of its texts, to point them out to those theists who just cherry-pick at the bits they like and nod away at the other bits their religion tells them are true.

Why Jesus is Compared to various Various Figures?

Jesus has been compared to a broad variety of figures from various mythological traditions within the Mediterranean Basin, including (in rows from left to right) Dionysus, Mithras, Sol Invictus, Osiris, Asclepius, Attis, and Adonis. The study of **Jesus in comparative mythology** is the examination of the narratives of the life of Jesus in the Christiangospels, traditions and theology, as they relate to Christianity and other religions. Although the vast majority of New Testament scholars and historians of the ancient Near East agree that Jesus existed as a historical figure, most secular historians also agree that the gospels contain large quantities of a historical legendary details mixed in with historical information about Jesus's life. The Synoptic Gospels of Mark, Matthew, and Luke are heavily shaped by Jewish tradition, with the Gospel of Matthew deliberately portraying Jesus as a "new Moses". Although it is highly unlikely that the authors of the Synoptic Gospels directly based any of their accounts on pagan mythology, it is possible that they may have subtly shaped their accounts of Jesus's healing miracles to resemble familiar Greek stories about miracles associated with Asclepius, the god of healing and medicine. The birth narratives of Matthew and Luke are usually seen by secular historians as legends designed to fulfil Jewish expectations about the Messiah.

The Gospel of John bears indirect influences from Platonism, via earlier Jewish deuterocanonical texts, and may also have been influenced in less obvious ways by the cult of Dionysus, the Greek god of wine, though this possibility is still disputed. Later Christian traditions about Jesus were probably influenced by Greco-Roman religion and mythology. Much of Jesus's traditional iconography is apparently derived from Mediterranean deities such as Hermes, Asclepius, Serapis, and **Zeus and his traditional birthdate on 25 December,** which was not declared as such until the fifth century, was at one point named a **holiday in honour of the Roman sun god Sol Invictus.** At around the same time Christianity was expanding in the second and third centuries, th was also flourishing. Though the relationship between the two religions is still under dispute, Christian apologists at the time noted similarities between them, which some scholars have taken as evidence of borrowing, but which are more likely a result of shared cultural environment. More general comparisons have also been made between the accounts about Jesus's birth and resurrection and stories of other divine or heroic figures from across the Mediterranean world, including supposed "dying-and-rising gods" such as Tammuz, Adonis, Attis, and Osiris, although the concept of "dying-and-rising gods" itself has received scholarly criticism.

Synoptic Gospels

The Sermon on the Mount from the Gospel of Matthew, depicted in this nineteenth-century painting by Carl Bloch, is an example of an instance in which one of the gospel-writers shapes his account in light of Jewish tradition. Although the sermon itself may contain some authentic sayings of the historical Jesus, the context of the sermon is a literary invention to make Jesus seem like a "new Moses".

Jesus, Historicity of Jesus, and Historical Jesus

The majority of New Testament scholars and historians of the ancient Near East agree that Jesus existed as a historical figure. While some scholars have criticized Jesus scholarship for religious bias and lack of methodological soundness, with very few exceptions such critics generally do support the historicity of Jesus and reject the Christ myth theory that Jesus never existed. There is widespread disagreement among scholars about the accuracy of details of Jesus' life as it is described in the gospel narratives, and on the meaning of his teachings, and the only two events subject to "almost universal assent" are that Jesus was baptised by John the Baptist and that he was crucified under the orders of the Roman prefect Pontius Pilate. It is also generally, although not universally, accepted that Jesus was a Galilean Jew who called disciples and whose activities were confined to Galilee and Judea, that he had a controversy in the Temple, and that, after his crucifixion, his ministry was continued by a group of his disciples, several of whom were persecuted.

Nonetheless, most secular scholars generally agree that the gospels contain large amounts of material that is not historically accurate and is better categorized as legend. In a discussion of genuinely legendary episodes from the gospels, New Testament scholar Bart Ehrman mentions the birth narratives in the Gospels of Matthew and Luke and the release of Barabbas. He points out, however, that, just because these accounts are not true does not mean that Jesus himself did not exist. **According to theologians Paul R. Eddy and Gregory A. Boyd, there is no evidence that the portrayal of Jesus in the Synoptic Gospels (the three earliest gospels of Mark, Matthew, and Luke) was directly influenced by pagan mythology in any significant way. <u>The earliest followers of Jesus were devout Palestinian Jews who abhorred paganism and would have therefore been extremely unlikely to model accounts about their founder on pagan myths.</u>**

Despite this, several scholars have noticed that some of the healing miracles of Jesus recorded in the Synoptic Gospels bear similarities to Greek stories of miracles associated with Asclepius, the god of healing and medicine. Brennan R. Hill states that Jesus's miracles are, for the most part, clearly told in the context of the **<u>Jewish belief in the healing power of Yahweh,</u>** but notes that **the authors of the Synoptic Gospels may have subtly borrowed from Greek literary models**. He states that Jesus' healing miracles chiefly differ from those of Asclepius by the fact that Jesus' are attributed to a human being on earth; whereas Asclepius's miracles are performed by a distant god. According to classical historians Emma J. Edelstein and Ludwig Edelstein, the most obvious difference between Jesus and Asclepius is that Jesus extended his healing to "sinners and publicans"; whereas Asclepius, as a god, refused to heal those who were ritually impure and confined his healing solely to those who thought pure thoughts. Scholars disagree whether the parable of the rich man and Lazarus recorded in Luke 16:19–31 originates with Jesus or if it is a later Christian invention, but the story bears strong resemblances to various folktales told throughout the Near East. Modern secular historians regard the birth narrative in the Luke 1:26–2:52 as a legend invented by early Christians based on Old Testament predecessors.

It is, however, widely agreed that the portrayal of Jesus in the gospels is deeply influenced by Jewish tradition. According to E. P. Sanders, a leading scholar on the historical Jesus, the Synoptic Gospels contain many episodes in which Jesus's described actions clearly emulate those of the prophets in the Hebrew Bible. Sanders states that, in some of these cases, it is impossible to know for certain whether these parallels originate from the historical Jesus himself having deliberately imitated the **Hebrew prophets, or from later Christians inventing mythological stories in order to portray Jesus as one of them, but, in many other instances, the parallels are clearly the work of the gospel-writers.** The author of the Gospel of Matthew in particular intentionally seeks to portray Jesus as a "new Moses". Matthew's account of Herod's attempt to kill the infant Jesus, Jesus' family's flight into Egypt, and their subsequent return to Judaea is a mythical narrative based on the account of the Exodus in the Torah. In the Gospel of Matthew, Jesus delivers his first public sermon on a mountain in imitation of the giving of the Law of Moses atop Mount Sinai. According to New Testament scholars

Gerd Theissen and Annette Merz, the teachings preserved in the sermon are statements that Jesus himself really said on different occasions that were originally recorded without context, but the author of the Gospel of Matthew compiled them into an organised lecture and invented context for them in order to fit his portrayal of Jesus as a "new Moses".

According to Sanders, the birth narratives in Matthew and Luke are the clearest examples of legends in the Synoptic Gospels.[15] Both accounts have Jesus born in Bethlehem, in accordance with Jewish salvation history, and both have him growing up in Nazareth, but they present two different explanations for how that happened. The accounts of the Annunciation of Jesus's conception found in Matthew 1:18–22 and Luke 1:26–38 are both modelled on the accounts of the annunciations of Ishmael, Isaac, and Samson in the Old Testament. Matthew quotes from the Septuagint translation of Isaiah 7:14 to support his account of the virgin birth of Jesus.[57] The Hebrew text of this verse states "Behold, the young woman [ha'almāh] is with child and about to bear a son and she will call him Immanuel." The Septuagint, however, translates the Hebrew word 'almāh, which literally means "young woman", as the Greek word παρθένος (parthenos), which means "virgin". Most secular historians therefore generally see the two separate accounts of the virgin birth from the Gospels of Matthew and Luke as independent legendary inventions designed to fulfill the mistranslated passage from Isaiah. Sanders clarifies that the birth narratives are "an extreme case" resulting from the gospel authors' lack of knowledge about Jesus's birth and childhood; no other part of the gospels relies so heavily on Old Testament parallels. Sanders also notes that, despite the clearly intentional parallels, the "striking differences" between Jesus and the prophets of the Old Testament are also highly significant and the gospels' accounts of Jesus' life on the whole do not closely resemble the lives of any of the figures in the Hebrew Bible.

Greek relief carving from Aphrodisias showing Heracles unchaining Prometheus from the Caucasus Mountains. Martin Hengel notes that the only apparent instance from classical literature of a god being crucified is a satirical retelling of the binding of Prometheus from the late second century. Although Jesus' crucifixion is one of the few events in his life that virtually all scholars of all different backgrounds agree really happened, historians of religion have also compared it to Greek and Roman stories in order to gain a better understanding of how non-Christians would have perceived accounts of Jesus's crucifixion. The German historian of religion Martin Hengel notes that the Hellenized Syrian satirist Lucian of Samosata ("the Voltaire of antiquity"), in his comic dialogue *Prometheus*, written in the second century AD (about two hundred years after Jesus), describes the god Prometheus being fastened to two rocks in the Caucasus Mountains using all the terminology of a Roman crucifixion: he is nailed through the hands in such a manner as to produce "a most serviceable cross". The gods Hermes and Hephaestus, who perform the binding, are shown as slaves whose brutal master Zeus threatens with the same punishment if they weaken. Unlike the crucifixion of Jesus in the Synoptic Gospels, Lucian's crucifixion of Prometheus is a deliberate, angry mockery of the gods, intended to show Zeus as a cruel and capricious tyrant undeserving of praise or adoration. This is the only instance from all of classical literature in which a god is apparently crucified and the fact that the Greeks and Romans could only conceive of a god being crucified as a form of "malicious parody" demonstrates the kind of horror with which they would have regarded Christian accounts of Jesus' crucifixion.

American theologian Dennis R. MacDonald has argued that the Gospel of Mark is, in fact, a Jewish retelling of the *Odyssey*, with its ending derived from the *Iliad*, that uses Jesus as its central character in the place of Odysseus. According to MacDonald, the gospels are primarily intended to show Jesus as superior to Greek heroes and, although Jesus himself was a real historical figure, the gospels should be read as works of historical fiction centered on a real protagonist, not as accurate accounts of Jesus's life. MacDonald's thesis that the gospels are modelled on the Homeric Epics has been met with intense scepticism in scholarly circles due to its almost complete reliance on extremely vague and subjective parallels. Other scholars state that his argument is also undermined by the fact that the Gospel of Mark never directly quotes from either of the Homeric Epics and uses completely dissimilar language. Pheme Perkins also notes that many of the incidents in the Gospel of Mark that MacDonald claims are derived from the *Odyssey* have much closer parallels in the Old Testament. MacDonald's argument, in a misunderstood form, has nonetheless become popular in non-scholarly circles, mostly on the internet, where it is used to support the Christ Myth theory. MacDonald himself rejects this interpretation as too drastic.

Gospel of John

Late sixth-century BC black-figure painting showing Dionysus extending a *kantharos*, a kind of drinking cup. Some scholars have argued that the portrayal of Jesus in the Gospel of John may have been influenced by Dionysian symbolism.

The Gospel of John, the latest of the four canonical gospels, possesses ideas that originated in Platonism and Greek philosophy, where the "Logos" described in John's prologue was devised by the Pre-Socratic philosopher Heraclitus and adapted to Judaism by the Jewish Middle Platonist Philo of Alexandria. However, the author of the Gospel of John was not personally familiar with any Greek philosophy and probably did not borrow the Logos theology from Platonic texts directly; instead, this philosophy probably influenced earlier Jewish deuterocanonical texts, which John inherited and expanded his own Logos theology from. In Platonic terminology, Logos was a universal force that represented the rationality and intelligibility of the world. On the other hand, as adapted into Judaism, Logos becomes a mediating divine figure between God and man and mostly owed influence from Wisdom literature and biblical traditions, and by the time it was transmitted into Judaism, seems to have only retained the concept of the universality of the Platonic logos. Davies and Finkelstein write "This primeval and universal Wisdom had, at God's command, found itself a home on Mount Zion in Jerusalem. This mediatorial figure, which in its universality can be compared with the Platonic 'world-soul' or the Stoic 'logos', is here exclusively connected with Israel, God's chosen people, and with his sanctuary."

Scholars have long suspected that the Gospel of John may have also been influenced by symbolism associated with the cult of Dionysus, the Greek god of wine. The issue of whether the Gospel of John was truly influenced by the cult of Dionysus is hotly disputed, with reputable scholars passionately defending both sides of the argument. Dionysus was one of the best-known Greek deities; he was worshipped throughout most of the Greco-Roman world and his cult is attested in Palestine, Asia Minor, and Italy. At the same time, other scholars have argued that it is highly implausible that the devout Christian author of the Gospel of John would have deliberately incorporated Dionysian imagery into his account and instead argue that the symbolism of wine in the Gospel of John is much more likely to be based on the many references to wine found throughout the Old Testament. In response to this objection, proponents of Dionysian influence have argued that it is possible that the author of the Gospel of John may have used Dionysian imagery in effort to show Jesus as "superior" to Dionysus.

The first instance of possible Dionysian influence is Jesus's miracle of turning water into wine at the Marriage at Cana in John 2:1–11. The account bears some resemblance to a number of stories that were told about Dionysus. Dionysus's close associations with wine are attested as early as the writings of Plato and the second-century AD Greek geographer Pausanias describes a ritual in which Dionysus was said to fill empty barrels that had been left locked inside a temple overnight with wine. In the Greek novel *Leucippe and Clitophon* by Achilles Tatius, written in the first or second century AD, a herdsman takes Dionysus into his home and offers him a meal, but he can only offer him the same thing to drink as his oxen. Miraculously, Dionysus turns the drink into wine. The account of turning water into wine does not occur in any of the Synoptic Gospels and is only found in the Gospel of John, indicating that the author of the fourth gospel may have invented it. A second occurrence of possible Dionysian influence is the allegory found in John 15:1–17, in which Jesus declares himself to be the "True Vine", a title reminiscent of Dionysus, who was said to have discovered the first grape vine.

First-century AD Roman wall painting from the House of the Vettii in Pompeii showing Dionysus's enemy Pentheus being torn to pieces by the *maenads*, Dionysus's female followers, the climactic scene of Euripides's *Bacchae*

Mark W. G. Stibbe has argued that the Gospel of John also contains parallels with *The Bacchae*, a tragedy written by the Athenian playwright Euripides that was first performed in 405 BC and involves Dionysus as a central character. In both works, the central figure is portrayed as an incarnate deity who arrives in a country where he should be known and worshipped, but, because he is disguised as a mortal, the deity is not recognized and is instead persecuted by the ruling party. In the Gospel of John, Jesus is portrayed as elusive, intentionally making ambiguous statements to evade capture, much like Dionysus in Euripides's *Bacchae*. In both works, the deity is supported by a group of female followers. Both works end with the violent death of one of the central figures; in John's gospel it is Jesus himself, but in *The Bacchae* it is Dionysus's cousin and adversary Pentheus, the king of Thebes.

Stibbe emphasizes that two accounts are also radically different, but states that they share similar themes. One of the most obvious differences is that, in *The Bacchae*, Dionysus has come to advocate a philosophy of wine and hedonism; whereas Jesus in the Gospel of John has come to offer his followers salvation from sin. Euripides portrays Dionysus as aggressive and violent; whereas the Gospel of John shows Jesus as peaceful and full of mercy. Furthermore, *The Bacchae* is set within an explicitly polytheistic world, but the Gospel of John admits the existence of only two gods: **Jesus Himself and His Father in Heaven.**

Infancy Gospel of Thomas

The Infancy Gospel of Thomas is a short apocryphal gospel, probably written in the second century AD, describing Jesus's childhood. It is unique as the only purported account of Jesus's childhood to survive from early Christian times.

It describes a variety of miracles attributed to the young Jesus. It remained continuously in popular use throughout the Middle Ages up until the time of the Reformation. Reidar Aasgaard has argued that the Infancy Gospel may have been partially intended for children and discusses how the accounts in the gospel fit the genre of Greco-Roman fairy tales. J. R. C. Cousland argues that the Infancy Gospel may have been originally written for a primarily pagan audience, noting that the Greeks and Romans told stories about their gods' miraculous doings as children and that miracle stories were often instrumental in converting pagans to Christianity.

Mithraism

Ancient Roman *tauroctony*, dating to the third century AD, depicting Mithras slaying the bull, the most important story of the Mithraic Cult. Around the same time that Christianity was expanding, the cult of the god Mithras was also spreading throughout the Roman Empire. Very little is known for certain about the Mithraic cult because it was a "Mystery Cult", meaning its members were forbidden from disclosing the cult's beliefs to outsiders. No Mithraic sacred texts have survived, if any such writings ever existed. Consequently, it is disputed how much influence Christianity and Mithraism may have had on each other. Michael Patella states that the similarities between Christianity and Mithraism are more likely a result of their shared cultural environment rather than direct borrowing from one to the other. Christianity and Mithraism were both of Oriental origin and their practices and respective saviour figures were both shaped by the social conditions in the Roman Empire during the time period.

Most of what is known about the legendary life of Mithras comes from archaeological excavation of Mithraea, underground Mithraic sanctuaries of worship, which were found all across the Roman world. Like Jesus, Mithras was seen as a divine saviour, but, unlike Jesus, Mithras was not believed to have brought his salvation by suffering and dying. Mithras was believed to have been born fully-grown from a rock, a belief which is confirmed by a vast number of surviving sculptures showing him rising from the rock nude except for a Phrygian cap, clutching a sword in his right hand and a torch in his left. In many depictions, the rock is also encircled by a snake. In Mithraic cults primarily from the Rhine-Danube region, there are also representations of a myth in which Mithras shoots an arrow at a rock face, causing water to gush forth. This myth is one of the closest parallels between Mithras and Jesus. Both Christians and Mithraists used water as a symbol for their respective saviours. In the New Testament, Jesus is referred to as the "water of life" and a votive altar to Mithras from Poetovio proclaims him as the *fons perennis* ("the ever-flowing stream").

In the center of every Mithraeum was a *tauroctony*, a painting or sculpture showing Mithras as a young man, usually wearing a cape and Phrygian cap, plunging a knife into the neck or shoulder of a bull as he turns its head towards him, simultaneously turning his own head away. A dog laps up the blood pouring from the bull's wound, from which emerges an ear of corn, as a scorpion stings the bull's scrotum. Human torchbearers stand on either side of the scene, one holding his torch upright and other upside-down. A serpent is also present. The exact interpretation of this scene is unclear, but the image certainly depicts a narrative central to Mithraism and the figures in it appear to correspond to the signs of the zodiac. The closest parallel between Jesus and Mithras is the use of a ritual mea. After slaying the bull, Mithras was believed to have shared the bull's meat with the sun-god Sol Invictus, a meal which is shown in Mithraic iconography and which was ritually reenacted by Mithraists as part of their liturgy. Manfred Clauss, a scholar of the Mithraic cult, speculates that the similarities between Christianity and Mithraism may have made it easier for members of the Mithraic cult to convert to Christianity without having to give up their ritual meal, sun-imagery, candles, incense, or bells, a trend which might explain why, as late as the sixth century, the Christian Church was still trying to stamp out the *stulti homines* who still paid obeisance to the sun every morning on the steps of the church itself.

Mithras rising from the rock

Mithras born from the rock (c. 186 AD; Baths of Diocletian)

A few Christian apologists from the second and third centuries, who had neverbeen members of the Mithraic cult and had never spoken to its members, claimed that the practices of the Mithraic cult were copied off Christianity. The second-century Christian apologist Justin Martyr writes in his *First Apology*, after describing the Christian Eucharist, that "...the wicked devils have imitated [this] in the mysteries of Mithras, commanding the same thing to be done. For, that bread and a cup of water are placed with certain incantations in the mystic rites of one who is being initiated, you either know or can learn." The later apologist Tertullian writes in his *De praescriptione haereticorum* that, the devil (is the inspirer of the heretics) whose work it is to pervert the truth, who with idolatrous mysteries endeavours to imitate the realities of the divine sacraments. Some he himself sprinkles as though in token of faith and loyalty; he promises forgiveness of sins through baptism; and if my memory does not fail me marks his own soldiers with the sign of Mithra on their foreheads, commemorates an offering of bread, introduces a mock resurrection, and with the sword opens the way to the crown. Moreover has he not forbidden a second marriage to the supreme priest? He maintains also his virgins and his celibates.

According to Ehrman, these writers were ideologically motivated to portray Christianity and Mithraism as similar because they wanted to persuade pagan officials that Christianity was not so different from other religious traditions, so that these officials would realise that there was no reason to single Christians out for persecution. These apologists therefore intentionally exaggerated similarities between Christianity and Mithraism to support their arguments. Scholars are generally wary of trusting anything these sources have to say about the Mithraic cult's alleged practices.

Late Roman copy of a fifth-century BC Greek statue showing Hermes, the god of travellers, carrying a ram over his shoulders in his role as Kriophoros (the "Ram-Bearer")

In late antiquity, early Christians frequently adapted pagan iconography to suit Christian purposes. This does not in any way indicate that Christianity itself was derived from paganism, only that early Christians made use of the pre-existing symbols that were readily available in their society. Sometimes Christians deliberately used pagan iconography in conscious effort to show Jesus as superior to the pagan gods. In classical iconography, the god Hermes was sometimes shown as a *kriophoros*, a handsome, beardless youth bearing a ram or sheep over his shoulders. In late antiquity, this image developed a generic association with philanthropy. Early Christians adapted images of this kind as representations of Jesus in his role of as the "Good Shepherd".

Early Christians also identified Jesus with the Greek hero Orpheus, who was said to have tamed wild beasts with the music of his lyre. The Church Father Clement of Alexandria writes that Orpheus and Jesus are similar in that they have both been subject to admiration on account of their "songs", but insists that Orpheus misused his gift of eloquence by persuading people to worship idols and "tie themselves to temporal things"; whereas Jesus, the singer of the "New Song" brings peace to men and frees them from the bonds of the flesh. The later Christian historian Eusebius, drawing on Clement, also compares Orpheus to Jesus for having both brought peace to men. One unusual possible instance of identification between Jesus and Orpheus is a hematite gem inscribed with the image of a crucified man identified. The gem has long been suspected to be a forgery created in the late seventeenth or early eighteenth century, but, if authentic, it may date to the late second or early third century AD. If authentic, the gem would represent a remarkable instance of pagans adopting Christian iconography, rather than *vice versa* as is generally more common. The gem was formerly housed at the Altes Museum in Berlin, but was lost or destroyed during World War II.

Early Christians found it hard to criticise Asclepius because, while their usual tactics were to denounce the absurdity of believing in gods who were merely personifications of nature and to accuse pagan gods of being immoral, neither of these could be applied to Asclepius, who was never portrayed as a personification of nature and whose stories were inscrutably moral. The early Christian apologist Justin Martyr argued that believing in Jesus' divinity should not be hard for pagans, since it was no different from believing in the divinity of Asclepius. Eventually, Christians adapted much of the iconography of Asclepius to suit the miracles of Jesus. Images of Jesus as a healer replaced images of Asclepius and Hippocrates as the ideal physician. Jesus, who was originally shown as clean-shaven, may have first been shown as bearded as a result of this syncretism with Asclepius, as well as other bearded **deities such as Zeus and Serapis**. A second-century AD head of Asclepius was discovered underneath a fourth-century AD Christian church in Gerasa, Jordan.

In some depictions from late antiquity, Jesus was shown with the halo of the **sun god Sol Invictus**. Images of "Christ in Majesty" seated upon a throne were inspired by classical depictions of Zeus and other chief deities. By the fourth century AD, the recognizable image of Jesus as long-haired, bearded, and clad in long, baggy-sleeved clothing had fully emerged. This widespread adaptation of pagan iconography to suit Jesus did not sit well with many Christians A fragment of a lost work by Theodor Lector preserves a miracle story dated to around 465 AD in which the bishop Gennadius of Constantinople was said to have healed an artist who had lost all strength in his hand after painting an image of Christ showing him with long, curly hair, parted in the same manner as traditional representations of Zeus.

Christians also may have adapted the iconography of the Egyptian goddess Isis nursing her son Horus and applied it to the Virgin Mary nursing her son Jesus. Some Christians also may have conflated stories about the Egyptian god Osiris with the resurrection of Jesus. The title of *kosmokrateros* ("Ruler of the Cosmos"), which was eventually applied to Jesus, had previously been borne by Serapis. The Church Father Jerome records in a letter dated to the year 395 AD that "Bethlehem... belonging now to us... was overshadowed by a grove of Tammuz, that is to say, Adonis, and in the cave where once the infant Christ cried, the lover of Venus was lamented." This same cave later became the site of the Church of the Nativity. The church historian Eusebius, however, does not mention pagans having ever worshipped in the cave, nor do any other early Christian writers Peter Welten has argued that the cave was never dedicated to Tammuz and that Jerome misinterpreted Christian mourning over the Massacre of the Innocents as a pagan ritual over Tammuz's death. Joan E. Taylor has countered this argument by arguing that Jerome, as an educated man, could not have been so naïve as to mistake Christian mourning over the Massacre of the Innocents as a pagan ritual for Tammuz. During the sixth century AD, some Christians in the Middle East borrowed elements from poems of Tammuz's wife Ishtar mourning over her husband's death into their own retellings of the Virgin Mary mourning over the death of her son Jesus. The Syrian writers Jacob of Serugh and Romanos the Melodist both wrote laments in which the Virgin Mary describes her compassion for her son at the foot of the cross in deeply personal terms closely resembling Ishtar's laments over the death of Tammuz.

PART FOUR

THE EARLY CHRISTIANITY

CHAPTER 4

Early Christianity: otherwise called the Early Church or Paleo-Christianity, describes the historical era of the Christian religion up to the First Council of Nicaea in 325. Christianity spread from the Levant, across the Roman Empire, and beyond. Originally, this progression was closely connected to already established Jewish centres in the Holy Land and the Jewish diaspora throughout the Eastern Mediterranean. **The first followers of Christianity were Jews who had converted to the faith, i.e. Jewish Christians**. Early Christianity contains the Apostolic Age and is followed by, and substantially overlaps with, the Patristic era.

The Apostolic sees claim to have been founded by one or more of the apostles of Jesus, who are said to have dispersed from Jerusalem sometime **after the crucifixion of Jesus, c. 26–33, perhaps following the Great Commission. Early Christians gathered in small private homes,[1] known as house churches,** but a city's whole Christian community would also be called a "church"—the Greek noun ἐκκλησία (*ekklesia*) literally means "assembly", "gathering", or "congregation" but is translated as "church" in most English translations of the New Testament.

Many early Christians were merchants and others who had practical reasons for travelling to Asia Minor, Arabia, the

Balkans, the Middle East, North Africa, and other regions. Over 40 such communities were established by the year 100, many in Anatolia, also known as Asia Minor, such as the Seven churches of Asia. By the end of the first century, Christianity had already spread to Rome, Armenia, Greece, and Syria, serving as foundations for the expansive spread of Christianity, eventually throughout the world.

Christianity originated as a minor sect within Second Temple Judaism. The Second Temple in Jerusalem was built c. 516 BC after the Babylonian captivity. The central tenets of Judaism in this period revolved around monotheism and the belief that Jews were a chosen people. As part of their covenant with God, Jews were obligated to obey the Torah. In return, they were given the land of Israel and the city of Jerusalem where God dwelled in the Temple. Apocalyptic and wisdom literature had a major influence on Second Temple Judaism.

While the Persian Empire permitted Jews to return to Judea, there was no longer a native monarchy. Instead, political power devolved to the high priest, who served as an intermediary between the Jewish people and the empire. This arrangement continued after the region was conquered by Alexander the Great (356–323 BC).

Alexander's conquests initiated the Hellenistic period when the Ancient Near East underwent Hellenization (the spread of Greek culture). Judaism was thereafter both culturally and politically part of the Hellenistic world; however, Hellenistic Judaism was stronger among diaspora Jews than among those living in the land of Israel. Diaspora Jews spoke Koine Greek, and the Jews of Alexandria produced a Greek translation of the Hebrew Bible called the Septuagint. The Septuagint was the translation of the Old Testament used by early Christians. Diaspora Jews continued to make pilgrimage to the Temple, but they started forming local religious institutions called synagogues as early as the 3rd century BC.

After Alexander's death, the region was ruled by Ptolemaic Egypt (c. 301 – c. 200 BC) and then the Seleucid Empire (c. 200 – c. 142 BC). The anti-Jewish policies of Antiochus IV Epiphanes (r. 175 – 164 BC) sparked the Maccabean Revolt in 167 BC, which culminated in the establishment of an independent Judea under the Hasmoneans, who ruled as kings and high priests. This independence would last until 63 BC when Judea became a client state of the Roman Empire.

The Maccabean Revolt caused Judaism to divide into competing sects with different theological and political goals, each adopting different stances towards Hellenization. The main sects were the Sadducees, Pharisees, and Essenes. The Sadducees were mainly Jerusalem aristocrats intent on maintaining control over Jewish politics and religion. Sadducee religion was focused on the Temple and its rituals. The Pharisees emphasized personal piety and interpreted the Torah in ways that provided religious guidance for daily life. Unlike Sadducees, the Pharisees believed in the resurrection of the dead and an afterlife. The Essenes rejected Temple worship, which they believed was defiled by wicked priests. They were part of a broader apocalyptic movement in Judaism, which believed the end times were at hand when Yahweh/God would restore Israel. Roman rule exacerbated these religious tensions and led the radical Zealots to separate from the Pharisees. The territories of Roman Judea and Galilee were frequently troubled by insurrection and messianic claimants.

Messiah (Hebrew: *meshiach*) means "anointed" and is used in the Old Testament to designate Jewish kings and in some cases priests and prophets whose status was symbolised by being anointed with holy anointing oil. The term is most associated with King David, to whom Yahweh/God promised an eternal kingdom (2 Samuel 7:11–17). After the destruction of David's kingdom and lineage, this promise was reaffirmed by the prophets Isaiah, Jeremiah, and Ezekiel, who foresaw a future king from the House of David who would establish and reign over an idealised kingdom.

In the Second Temple period, there was no consensus on who the messiah would be or what he would do. Most commonly, he was imagined to be an end times son of David going about the business of "executing judgment, defeating the enemies of God, reigning over a restored Israel, [and] establishing unending peace". Yet, there were other kinds of messianic figures proposed as well—the perfect priest or the celestial Son of Man who brings about the resurrection of the dead and the final judgment.

Christianity centres on the life and ministry of Jesus of Nazareth, who lived c. 4 BC – c. AD 33. **Jesus left no writings of his own, and most information about him comes from early Christian writings that now form part of the New Testament.** The earliest of these are the Pauline epistles, letters written to various Christian congregations by Paul the Apostle in the 50s AD. The four canonical gospels of Matthew (c. AD 80 – c. AD 90), Mark (c. AD 70), Luke (c. AD 80 – c. AD 90), and John (written at the end of the 1st century) are ancient biographies of Jesus' life.

Jesus grew up in Nazareth, a city in Galilee. He was baptised in the Jordan River by John the Baptist. Jesus began his own ministry when he was around 30 years old around the time of the Baptist's arrest and execution. **Jesus' message** centred on the coming of the Kingdom of the Lord (in Jewish eschatology a future when the Lord would actively rule over the world in justice, mercy, and peace). *Jesus urged his followers to repent in preparation for the kingdom's coming. His ethical teachings included loving one's enemies (Matthew 5:44; Luke 6:28–35), giving alms and fasting in secret (Matthew 6:4–18), not serving both the Lord and Mammon (Matthew 6:24; Luke 16:13), and not judging others (Matthew 7:1–2; Luke 6:37–38). These teachings are highlighted in the Sermon on the Mount and the Lord's Prayer. Jesus chose 12 Disciples who represented the 12 tribes of Israel (10 of which were "lost" by this time) to symbolize the full restoration of Israel that would be accomplished through him.*

Christ with the Two Thieves by Fra Angelico c. 1437 – c. 1446

*The gos*pel accounts provide insight into what early Christians believed about Jesus. As the Christ or "Anointed One" (Greek: *Christos*), Jesus is identified as the fulfilment of messianic prophecies in the Hebrew scriptures. Through the accounts of his miraculous virgin birth, the gospels present Jesus as the Son of the Father. The gospels describe the miracles of Jesus which served to authenticate his message and reveal a foretaste of the coming kingdom. The gospel accounts conclude with a description of the crucifixion and resurrection of Jesus, ultimately leading to his Ascension into Heaven. Jesus' victory over death became the central belief of Christianity. In the words of historian Diarmaid MacCulloch:

Whether through some mass delusion, some colossal act of wishful thinking, or through witness to a power or force beyond any definition known to Western historical analysis, those who had known Jesus in life and had felt the shattering disappointment of his death proclaimed that he lived still, that he loved them still, and that he was to return to earth from the Heaven which he had now entered, to love and save from destruction all who acknowledged him as Lord.

Christianity in the 1st century

The decades after the crucifixion of Jesus are known as the Apostolic Age because the Disciples (also known as Apostles) were still alive. Important Christian sources for this period are the Pauline epistles and the Acts of the Apostles. **After the death of Jesus, his followers established Christian groups in cities, such as Jerusalem. The movement quickly spread to Damascus and Antioch, capital of Roman Syria and one of the most important cities in the empire. Early Christians referred to themselves as brethren, *disciples* or *saints*, but it was in Antioch, according to Acts 11:26, that they were first called Christians** (Greek: *Christianoi*).

According to the New Testament, Paul the apostle established Christian communities throughout the Mediterranean world. He is known to have also spent some time in Arabia. After preaching in Syria, he turned his attention to the cities of Asia Minor. By the early 50s, he had moved on to Europe where he stopped in Philippi and then traveled to Thessalonica in Roman Macedonia. He then moved into mainland Greece, spending time in Athens and Corinth. While in Corinth, Paul wrote his Epistle to the Romans, indicating that there were already Christian groups in Rome. Some of these groups had been started by Paul's missionary associates Priscilla and Aquila and Epainetus.

Social and professional networks played an important part in spreading the religion as members invited interested outsiders to secret Christian assemblies (Greek: *ekklēsia*) that met in private homes (see house church). Commerce and trade also played a role in Christianity's spread as Christian merchants travelled for business. Christianity appealed to marginalized groups (women, slaves) with its message that "in Christ there is neither Jew nor Greek, neither male nor female, neither slave nor free" (Galatians 3:28). Christians also provided social services to the poor, sick, and widows.

Historian Keith Hopkins estimated that by AD 100 there were around 7,000 Christians (about 0.01 percent of the Roman Empire's population of 60 million). Separate Christian groups maintained contact with each other through letters, visits from itinerant preachers, and the sharing of common texts, some of which were later collected in the New Testament.

Jerusalem church

The Cenacle on Mount Zion, claimed to be the location of the Last Supper and Pentecost. Bargil Pixner **claims the original Church of the Apostles is located under the current structure**.

Jerusalem in Christianity

Jerusalem was the first center of the Christian Church according to the Book of Acts. The apostles lived and taught there for some time after Pentecost According to Acts, the early church was led by the Apostles, foremost among them Peter and John. When Peter left Jerusalem after Herod Agrippa I tried to kill him, James, brother of Jesus appears as the leader of the Jerusalem church.[44]

Clement of Alexandria (c. 150–215 AD) called him Bishop of Jerusalem. Peter, John and James were collectively recognized as the three pillars of the church (Galatians 2:9).

At this early date, Christianity was still a Jewish sect. Christians in Jerusalem kept the Jewish Sabbath and continued to worship at the Temple. In commemoration of Jesus' resurrection, they gathered on Sunday for a communion meal. Initially, Christians kept the Jewish custom of fasting on Mondays and Thursdays. Later, the Christian fast days shifted to Wednesdays and Fridays (see Friday fast) in remembrance of Judas' betrayal and the crucifixion.

James was killed on the order of the high priest in AD 62. He was succeeded as leader of the Jerusalem church by Simeon, another relative of Jesus. During the First Jewish-Roman War (AD 66–73), Jerusalem and the Temple were destroyed after a brutal siege in AD 70. Prophecies of the Second Temple's destruction are found in the synoptic gospels, specifically in the Olivet Discourse.

According to a tradition recorded by Eusebius and Epiphanius of Salamis, the Jerusalem church fled to Pella at the outbreak of the First Jewish Revolt. The church had returned to Jerusalem by AD 135, but the disruptions severely weakened the Jerusalem church's influence over the wider Christian church.

Gentile Christians

Jerusalem was the first centre of the Christian Church according to the Book of Acts. The apostles lived and taught there for some time after Pentecost. James the Just, brother of Jesus was leader of the early Christian community in Jerusalem, and his other kinsmen likely held leadership positions in the surrounding area after the destruction of the city until its rebuilding as *Aelia Capitolina* in c. 130 AD, when all Jews were banished from Jerusalem.

The first Gentiles to become Christians were Lord-fearers, people who believed in the truth of Judaism but had not become prosel ytesbecome proselytes (see Cornelius the Centurion). As Gentiles joined the young Christian movement, the question of whether they should convert to Judaism and observe the Torah (such as food laws, male circumcision, and Sabbath observance) gave rise to various answers. Some Christians demanded full observance of the Torah and required Gentile converts to become Jews. Others, such as Paul, believed that the Torah was no longer binding because of Jesus' death and resurrection. In the middle were Christians who believed Gentiles should follow some of the Torah but not all of it.

In c. 48–50 AD, Barnabas and Paul went to Jerusalem to meet with the three *Pillars of the Church*: James the Just, Peter, and John. Later called the Council of Jerusalem, according to Pauline Christians, this meeting (among other things) confirmed the legitimacy of the evangelising mission of Barnabas and Paul to the Gentiles. It also confirmed that Gentile converts were not obligated to follow the Mosaic Law, especially the practice of male circumcision, which was condemned as execrable and repulsive in the Greco-Roman world during the period of Hellenization of the Eastern Mediterranean, and was especially adversed in Classical civilization from ancient Greeks and Romans, who valued the foreskin positively. The resulting Apostolic Decree in Acts 15 is theorized to parallel the seven Noahide laws found in the Old Testament. However, modern scholars dispute the connection between Acts 15 and the seven Noahide laws. In roughly the same time period, rabbinic Jewish legal authorities made their circumcision requirement for Jewish boys even stricter

The primary issue which was addressed related to the requirement of circumcision, as the author of Acts relates, but other important matters arose as well, as the Apostolic Decree indicates. The dispute was between those, such as the followers of the "Pillars of the Church", led by James, who believed, following his interpretation of the Great Commission, that the church must observe the Torah, i.e. the rules of traditional Judaism, and Paul the Apostle, who called himself "Apostle to the Gentiles", who believed there was no such necessity. The main concern for the Apostle Paul, which he subsequently expressed in greater detail with his letters directed to the early Christian communities in Asia Minor, was the inclusion of Gentiles into God's New Covenant, sending the message that faith in Christ is sufficient for salvation.

The Council of Jerusalem did not end the dispute, however. There are indications that James still believed the Torah was binding on Jewish Christians. Galatians 2:11-14 describe "people from James" causing Peter and other Jewish Christians in Antioch to break table fellowship with Gentiles. Joel Marcus, professor of Christian origins, suggests that Peter's position may have lain somewhere between James and Paul, but that he probably leaned more toward James. This is the start of a split between Jewish Christianity and Gentile (or Pauline) Christianity. While Jewish Christianity would remain important through the next few centuries, it would ultimately be pushed to the margins as Gentile Christianity became dominant. Jewish Christianity was also opposed by early Rabbinic Judaism, the successor to the Pharisees. When Peter left Jerusalem after Herod Agrippa I tried to kill him, James appears as the principal authority of the early Christian church. Clement of Alexandria (c. 150–215 AD) called him Bishop of Jerusalem. A 2nd-century church historian, Hegesippus, wrote that the Sanhedrin martyred him in 62 AD.

In 66 AD, the Jews revolted against Rome. After a brutal siege, Jerusalem fell in 70 AD. The city, including the Jewish Temple, was destroyed and the population was mostly killed or removed. According to a tradition recorded by Eusebius and Epiphanius of Salamis, the Jerusalem church fled to Pella at the outbreak of the First Jewish Revolt. According to Epiphanius of Salamis, the Cenacle survived at least to Hadrian's visit in 130 AD. A scattered population survived. The Sanhedrin relocated to Jamnia. Prophecies of the Second Temple's destruction are found in the Synoptic Gospels, specifically in Jesus' Olivet Discourse.

1st century persecution

Romans had a negative perception of early Christians. The Roman historian Tacitus wrote that Christians were despised for their "abominations" and "hatred of humankind". The belief that Christians hated humankind could refer to their refusal to participate in social activities connected to **pagan worship**—these included most social activities such as the theater, the army, sports, and classical literature. They also refused to worship the Roman emperor, like Jews. Nonetheless, Romans were more lenient to Jews compared to Gentile Christians. Some anti-Christian Romans further distinguished between Jews and Christians by claiming that Christianity was "apostasy" from Judaism. Celsus, for example, considered Jewish Christians to be hypocrites for claiming that they embraced their Jewish heritage.

Emperor Nero persecuted Christians in Rome, whom he blamed for starting the Great Fire of AD 64. It is possible that Peter and Paul were in Rome and were martyred at this time. Nero was deposed in AD 68, and the persecution of Christians ceased. Under the emperors Vespasian (r. 69–79) and Titus (r. 79–81), Christians were largely ignored by the Roman government. The Emperor Domitian (r. 81–96) authorized a new persecution against the Christians. It was at this time that the Book of Revelation was written

In the 2nd century, Roman Emperor Hadrian rebuilt Jerusalem as a Pagan city and renamed it *Aelia Capitolina*,[83] erecting statues of Jupiter and himself on the site of the former Jewish Temple, the Temple Mount. In the years AD 132–136, Bar Kokhba led an unsuccessful revolt as a Jewish Messiah claimant, but Christians refused to acknowledge him as such. When Bar Kokhba was defeated, Hadrian barred Jews from the city, except for the day of Tisha B'Av, thus the subsequent Jerusalem bishops were Gentiles ("uncircumcised") for the first time.

The general significance of Jerusalem to Christians entered a period of decline during the persecution of Christians in the Roman Empire. According to Eusebius, Jerusalem Christians escaped to Pella, in Perea (Transjordan), at the beginning of the First Jewish–Roman War in AD 66. Jerusalem's bishops became suffragans (subordinates) of the Metropolitan bishop in nearby Caesarea, Interest in Jerusalem resumed with the pilgrimage of the Roman Empress Helena to the Holy Land (c. 326–328 AD). According to the church historian Socrates of Constantinople, Helena (with the assistance of Bishop Macarius of Jerusalem) claimed to have found the *cross of Christ*, after removing a Temple to Venus (attributed to Hadrian) that had been built over the site. Jerusalem had received special recognition in Canon VII of the First Council of Nicaea in 325 AD. The traditional founding date for the Brotherhood of the Holy Sepulchre (which guards the Christian Holy places in the Holy Land) is 313, which corresponds with the date of the Edict of Milan promulgated by the Roman Emperor Constantine the Great, which legalized Christianity in the Roman Empire. Jerusalem was later named as one of the Pentarchy, but this was never accepted by the Church of Rome.

Antioch

The Church of St Peter near Antakya, Turkey, said to be the spot where Saint Peter first preached the Gospel. In Roman Antioch, *School of Antioch, Patriarch of Antioch, and Antiochene Rite*. Antioch, a major centre of Hellenistic Greece, and the third-most important city of the Roman Empire, then part of Syria Province, today a ruin near Antakya, Turkey, was where Christians were first called Christians and also the location of the Incident at Antioch. It was the site of an early church, traditionally said to be founded by Peter who is considered the first bishop. The Gospel of Matthew and the Apostolic Constitutions may have been written there. The church father Ignatius of Antioch was its third bishop. The School of Antioch, founded in 270, was one of two major centres of early church learning. The Curetonian Gospels and the Syriac Sinaiticus are two early (pre-Peshitta) New Testament text types associated with Syriac Christianity. It was one of the three whose bishops were recognized at the First Council of Nicaea (325) as exercising jurisdiction over the adjoining territories.

Alexandria

Alexandrian school, Catechetical School of Alexandria, Bishop of Alexandria, Egypt (Roman province) § Christian Egypt, and Alexandrian Rite. Alexandria, in the Nile delta, was established by Alexander the Great. Its famous libraries were a center of Hellenistic learning. The Septuagint translation of the Old Testament began there and the Alexandrian text-type is recognized by scholars as one of the earliest New Testament types. It had a significant Jewish population, of which Philo of Alexandria is probably its most known author. It produced superior scripture and notable church fathers, such as Clement, Origen, and Athanasius; also noteworthy were the nearby Desert Fathers. By the end of the era, Alexandria, Rome, and Antioch were accorded authority over nearby metropolitans. The Council of Nicaea in canon VI affirmed Alexandria's traditional authority over Egypt, Libya, and Pentapolis (North Africa) (the Diocese of Egypt) and probably granted Alexandria the right to declare a universal date for the observance of Easter (see also Easter controversy). Some postulate, however, that Alexandria was not only a centre of Christianity, but was also a centre for Christian-based Gnostic sects.

Asia Minor

The "Seven Churches of Asia" and the Greek island of Patmos, *History of Anatolia and Christianity in Turkey.* The tradition of John the Apostle was strong in Anatolia (the *near-east*, part of modern Turkey, the western part was called the Roman province of Asia). The authorship of the Johannine works traditionally and plausibly occurred in Ephesus, *c.* 90–110, although some scholars argue for an origin in Syria. This includes the Book of Revelation, although modern Bible scholars believe that it to be authored by a different John, John of Patmos (a Greek island about 30 miles off the Anatolian coast), that mentions Seven churches of Asia. According to the New Testament, the Apostle Paul was from Tarsus (in south-central Anatolia) and his missionary journeys were primarily in Anatolia. **The First Epistle of Peter (1:1–2) is addressed to Anatolian regions.** On the southeast shore of the Black Sea, Pontus was a Greek colony mentioned three times in the New Testament. Inhabitants of Pontus were some of the very first converts to Christianity. Pliny, governor in 110, in his letters, addressed Christians in Pontus. Of the extant letters of Ignatius of Antioch considered authentic, five of seven are to Anatolian cities, the sixth is to Polycarp. Smyrna was home to Polycarp, the bishop who reportedly knew the Apostle John personally and probably also to his student Irenaeus. Papias of Hierapolis is also believed to have been a student of John the Apostle. In the 2nd century, Anatolia was home to Quartodecimanism, Montanism, Marcion of Sinope and Melito of Sardis who recorded an early Christian Biblical canon. After the Crisis of the Third Century, Nicomedia became the capital of the Eastern Roman Empire in 286. The Synod of Ancyra was held in 314. In 325 the emperor Constantine convoked the first Christian ecumenical council in Nicaea and in 330 moved the capital of the reunified empire to Byzantium (also an early Christian centre and just across the Bosphorus from *Anatolia*, later called Constantinople), referred to as the Byzantine Empire, which lasted till 1453. The First seven Ecumenical Councils were held either in Western Anatolia or across the Bosphorus in Constantinople.

Caesarea Maritima and Early Christian centre, and Bishop of Caesarea. Caesarea, on the seacoast just northwest of Jerusalem, at first *Caesarea Maritima*, then after 133 *Caesarea Palaestina*, was built by Herod the Great, c.

25–13 BC, and was the capital of Iudaea Province (6–132) and later *Palaestina Prima*. It was there that Peter baptized the centurion Cornelius, considered the first gentile convert. Paul sought refuge there, once staying at the house of Philip the Evangelist, and later being imprisoned there for two years (estimated to be 57–59). The Apostolic Constitutions (7.46) state that the first Bishop of Caesarea was Zacchaeus the Publican.

After Hadrian's siege of Jerusalem (c. 133), Caesarea became the metropolitan see with the bishop of Jerusalem as one of its *"suffragans"* (subordinates). Origen (d. 254) compiled his Hexapla there and it held a famous library and theological school, St. Pamphilus (d. 309) was a noted scholar-priest. St. Gregory the Wonder-Worker (d. 270), St. Basil the Great (d. 379), and St. Jerome (d. 420) visited and studied at the library which was later destroyed, probably by the Persians in 614 or the Saracens around 637. The first major church historian, Eusebius of Caesarea, was a bishop, c. 314–339. F. J. A. Hort and Adolf von Harnack have argued that the Nicene Creed originated in Caesarea. The Caesarean text-type is recognized by many textual scholars as one of the earliest New Testament types.

Paphos was the capital of the island of Cyprus during the Roman years and seat of a Roman commander. In 45 AD, the apostles Paul and Barnabas, who according to Acts 4:36 was "a native of Cyprus", came to Cyprus and reached Paphos preaching the message of Jesus, see also Acts 13:4–13. According to Acts, the apostles were persecuted by the Romans but eventually succeeded in convincing the Roman commander Sergius Paulus to renounce his old religion in favour of Christianity. Barnabas is traditionally identified as the founder of the Cypriot Orthodox Church.

Damascus

The Chapel of Saint Paul, said to be Bab Kisan where St. Paul escaped from Old Damascus. *Syriac Orthodox Church and Christianity in Syria* Damascus is the capital of Syria and claims to be the oldest continuously inhabited city in the world. According to the New Testament, the Apostle Paul was converted on the Road to Damascus. In the three accounts (Acts 9:1–20,), he is described as being led by those he was traveling with, blinded by the light, to Damascus where his sight was restored by a disciple called <u>Ananias</u> (who is thought to have been the first bishop of Damascus) then he was <u>baptised</u>.

Greece

Church of Greece

Thessalonica, the major northern Greek city where it is believed Christianity was founded by Paul, thus an Apostolic See, and the surrounding regions of Macedonia, Thrace, and Epirus, which also extend into the neighboring Balkan states of Albania and Bulgaria, were early centers of Christianity. Of note are Paul's Epistles to the *Thessalonians* and to Philippi, which is often considered the first contact of Christianity with Europe. The *Apostolic Father* Polycarp wrote a letter to the Philippians, c. 125.

Nicopolis was a city in the Roman province of Epirus Vetus, today a ruin on the northern part of the western Greek coast. In the Epistle to Titus, Paul said he intended to go there. It is possible that there were some Christians in its population. According to Eusebius, Origen (c. 185–254) stayed there for some time.

Ancient Corinth, today a ruin near modern Corinth in southern Greece, was an early centre of Christianity. According to the Acts of Apostles, Paul stayed eighteen months in Corinth to preach. He initially stayed with Aquila and Priscilla, and was later joined by Silas and Timothy. After he left Corinth, Apollo was sent from Ephesus by Priscilla to replace him. Paul returned to Corinth at least once. He wrote the First Epistle to the Corinthians from Ephesus in 57 and then the Second Epistle to the Corinthians from Macedonia in the same year or in 58. The earliest evidence of the primacy of the Roman Church can be seen in the First Epistle of Clement written to the Corinthian church, dated around 96. The bishops in Corinth include Apollo, Sosthenes, and Dionysius.

Athens, the capital and largest city in Greece, was visited by Paul. He probably traveled by sea, arriving at Piraeus, the harbor of Athens, coming from Berœa of Macedonia around the year 53. According to Acts 17, when he arrived at Athens, he immediately sent for Silas and Timotheos who had stayed behind in Berœa. While waiting for them, Paul explored Athens and visited the synagogue, as there was a local Jewish community. A Christian community was quickly established in Athens, although it may not have been large initially. A common tradition identifies the Areopagite as the first bishop of the Christian community in Athens, while another tradition mentions Hierotheos the Thesmothete. The succeeding bishops were not all of Athenian descent: Narkissos was believed to have come from Palestine, and Publius from Malta. Quadratus is known for an apology addressed to Emperor Hadrian during his visit to Athens, contributing to early Christian literature. Aristeides and Athenagoras also wrote apologies during this time. By the second century, Athens likely had a significant Christian community, as Hygeinos, bishop of

Rome, write a letter to the community in Athens in the year 139.

Gortyn on Crete was allied with Rome and was thus made capital of Roman Creta et Cyrenaica. St. Titus is believed to have been the first bishop. The city was sacked by the pirate Abu Hafs in 828.

Paul the Apostle preached in Macedonia, and also in Philippi, located in Thrace on the Thracian Sea coast. According to Hippolytus of Rome, Andrew the Apostle preached in Thrace, on the Black Sea coast and along the lower course of the Danube River. The spread of Christianity among the Thracians and the emergence of centers of Christianity like Serdica (present day Sofia), Philippopolis (present day Plovdiv) and Durostorum (present day Silistra) was likely to have begun with these early Apostolic missions.[107] The first Christian monastery in Europe was founded in Thrace in 344 by Saint Athanasius near modern-day Chirpan, Bulgaria, following the Council of Serdica.

Libya

Christianity in Libya

Cyrene and the surrounding region of Cyrenaica or the North African "Pentapolis", south of the Mediterranean from Greece, the northern Eastern part of modern Libya, was a Greek colony in North Africa later converted to a Roman province. In addition to Greeks and Romans, there was also a significant Jewish population, at least up to the Kitos War (115–117). According to Mark 15:21, Simon of Cyrene carried Jesus' cross. *Cyrenians* are also mentioned in Acts 2:10, 6:9, 11:20, 13:1. According to Byzantine legend, the first bishop was Lucius, mentioned in

Exactly when Christians first appeared in Rome is difficult to deterine. The Acts of the Apostles claims that the Jewish Christian couple Priscilla and Aquila had recently come from Rome to Corinth when, in about the year 50, Paul reached the latter city,[109] indicating that belief in Jesus in Rome had preceded Paul.

Historians consistently consider Peter and Paul to have been martyred in Rome under the reign of Nero in 64, after the Great Fire of Rome which, according to Tacitus, the Emperor blamed on the Christians. In the second century Irenaeus of Lyons, reflecting the ancient view that the church could not be fully present anywhere without a bishop, recorded that Peter and Paul had been the founders of the Church in Rome and had appointed Linus as bishop.

However, Irenaeus does not say that either Peter or Paul was "bishop" of the Church in Rome and several historians have questioned whether Peter spent much time in Rome before his martyrdom. While the church in Rome was already flourishing *when Paul wrote his Epistle to the Romans to them from Corinth (c. 58) he attests to a large Christian community already there and greets some fifty people in Rome by name, but not Peter, whom he knew*. There is also no mention of Peter in Rome later <u>during Paul's two-year stay there in Acts 28,</u> about 60–62. Most likely he did not spend any major time at Rome before 58 when Paul wrote to the Romans, and so it may have been only in the 60s and relatively shortly before his martyrdom that Peter came to the capital.

<u>Oscar Cullmann</u> sharply rejected the claim that **Peter began the papal succession, and concludes that while Peter** *was* **the original head of the apostles,** Peter was not the founder of any visible church succession. A scene

showing Christ Pantocrator from a Roman mosaic in the church of Santa Pudenziana in Rome, c. 410 AD

The original seat of Roman imperial power soon became a centre of church authority, grew in power decade by decade, and was recognised during the period of the Seven Ecumenical Councils, when the seat of government had been transferred to Constantinople, as the "head" of the church.

Rome and Alexandria, which by tradition held authority over sees outside their own province, were not yet referred to as patriarchates.

The earliest Bishops of Rome were all Greek-speaking, the most notable of them being: Pope Clement I (c. 88–97), author of an Epistle to the Church in Corinth; Pope Telesphorus (c. 126–136), probably the only martyr among them; Pope Pius I (c. 141–154), said by the Muratorian fragment to have been the brother of the author of the Shepherd of Hermas; and Pope Anicetus (c. 155–160), who received Saint Polycarp and discussed with him the dating of Easter.

Pope Victor I (189–198) was the first ecclesiastical writer known to have written in Latin; however, his only extant works are his encyclicals, which would naturally have been issued in Latin and Greek.

Greek New Testament texts were translated into Latin early on, well before Jerome, and are classified as the Vetus Latina and Western text-type.

During the 2nd century, Christians and semi-Christians of diverse views congregated in Rome, notably Marcion and Valentinius, and in the following century there were schisms connected with Hippolytus of Rome and Novatian.

The Roman church survived various persecutions. Among the prominent Christians executed as a result of their refusal to perform acts of worship to the Roman gods as ordered by emperor Valerian in 258 were Cyprian, bishop of Carthage. The last and most severe of the imperial persecutions was that under Diocletian in 303; they ended in Rome, and the West in general, with the accession of Maxentius in 306.

Early Christian quarter in ancient Carthage.

Carthage, in the Roman province of Africa, south of the Mediterranean from Rome, gave the early church the Latin fathers Tertullian (c. 120 – c. 220) and Cyprian (d. 258). Carthage fell to Islam in 698.

The Church of Carthage thus was to the Early African church what the Church of Rome was to the Catholic Church in Italy. The archdiocese used the African Rite, a variant of the Western liturgical rites in Latin language, possibly a local use of the primitive Roman Rite. Famous figures include Saint Perpetua, Saint Felicitas, and their Companions (died c. 203), Tertullian (c. 155–240), Cyprian (c. 200–258), Caecilianus (floruit 311), Saint Aurelius (died 429), and Eugenius of Carthage (died 505). Tertullian and Cyprian are considered Latin Church Fathers of the Latin Church. Tertullian, a theologian of part Berber descent, was instrumental in the development of trinitarian theology, and was the first to apply Latin language extensively in his theological writings. As such, Tertullian has been called "the father of Latin Christianity" and "the founder of Western theology." Carthage remained an important center of Christianity, hosting several councils of Carthage.

Southern Gaul

Amphithéâtre des Trois-Gaules, in Lyon. The pole in the arena is a memorial to the people killed during the persecution. *Christianity in Gaul*

The Mediterranean coast of France and the Rhone valley, then part of Roman Gallia Narborensis, were early centers of Christianity. Major Christian communities were found in Arles, Avignon, Vienne, Lyon, and Marseille (the oldest city in France). The Persecution in Lyon occurred in 177. The Apostolic Father Irenaeus from Smyrna of Anatolia was Bishop of Lyon near the end of the 2nd century and he claimed Saint Pothinus was his predecessor. The Council of Arles in 314 is considered a forerunner of the ecumenical councils. The Ephesine theory attributes the Gallican Rite to Lyon.

Aquileia

Bishop of Aquileia

The ancient Roman city of Aquileia at the head of the Adriatic Sea, today one of the main archaeological sites of Northern Italy, was an early center of Christianity said to be founded by Mark before his mission to Alexandria. Hermagoras of Aquileia is believed to be its first bishop. The Aquileian Rite is associated with Aquileia.

Milan

Bishop of Milan

It is believed that the Church of Milan in northwest Italy was founded by the apostle Barnabas in the 1st century. Gervasius and Protasius and others were martyred there. It has long maintained its own rite known as the Ambrosian Rite attributed to Ambrose (born c. 330) who was bishop in 374–397 and one of the most influential ecclesiastical figures of the 4th century. Duchesne argues that the Gallican Rite originated in Milan.

See also: Bishop of Syracuse and Bishop of Reggio Calabria

Syracuse was founded by Greek colonists in 734 or 733 BC, part of Magna Graecia. Syracuse is one of the first Christian communities established by Peter, preceded only by Antioch. Paul also preached in Syracuse. Historical evidence from the middle of the third century, during the time of Cyprian, suggests that Christianity was thriving in Syracuse, and the presence of catacombs provides clear indications of Christian activity in the second century as well. Across the Strait of Messina, Calabria on the mainland was also probably an early centre of Christianity, traditionally identified as the place where St Paul was shipwrecked. According to Acts, Paul was shipwrecked and ministered on an island which some scholars have identified as Malta (an island just south of Sicily) for three months during which time he is said to have been bitten by a poisonous viper and survived (Acts 27:39–42; Acts 28:1–11), an event usually dated c. AD 60. Paul had been allowed passage from Caesarea Maritima to Rome by Porcius Festus, procurator of Iudaea Province, to stand trial before the Emperor. Many traditions are associated with this episode, and catacombs in Rabat testify to an Early Christian community on the islands. According to tradition, Publius, the Roman Governor of Malta at the time of Saint Paul's shipwreck, became the first *Bishop of Malta* following his conversion to Christianity. After ruling the Maltese Church for thirty-one years, Publius was transferred to the See of Athens in 90 AD, where he was martyred in 125 AD. There is scant information about the continuity of Christianity in Malta in subsequent years, although tradition has it that there was a continuous line of bishops from the days of St. Paul to the time of Emperor Constantine.

Salona

Religion in Croatia Salona, the capital of the Roman province of Dalmatia on the eastern shore of the Adriatic Sea, was an early center of Christianity and today is a ruin in modern Croatia. Titus, a disciple of Paul, preached there. Some Christians suffered martyrdom. Seville was the capital of Hispania Baetica or the Roman province of southern Spain. The origin of the diocese of Seville can be traced back to Apostolic times, or at least to the first century AD. Gerontius, the bishop of Italica, near Hispalis (Seville), likely appointed a pastor for Seville. A bishop of Seville named Sabinus participated in the Council of Illiberis in 287. He was the bishop when Justa and Rufina were martyred in 303 for refusing to worship the idol Salambo. Prior to Sabinus, Marcellus is listed as a bishop of Seville in an ancient catalogue of prelates preserved in the "Codex Emilianensis"[1] After the Edict of Milan in 313, Evodius became the bishop of Seville and undertook the task of rebuilding the churches that had been damaged. It is believed that he may have constructed the church of San Vicente, which could have been the first cathedral of Seville. Early Christianity also spread from the Iberian peninsula south across the Strait of Gibraltar into Roman Mauretania Tingitana, of note is Marcellus of Tangier who was martyred in 298.

Roman Britain

History of the Church of England and Roman and Sub-Roman Christianity in the British Isles

Christianity reached Roman Britain by the third century of the Christian era, *the first recorded martyrs in Britain being. St. Alban of Verulamium and Julius and Aaron of Caerleon*, during the reign of Diocletian (284–305). Gildas dated the faith's arrival to the latter part of the reign of Tiberius, although stories connecting it with Joseph of Arimathea, Lucius, or Fagan are now generally considered pious forgeries. Restitutus, Bishop of London, is recorded as attending the 314 Council of Arles, along with the Bishop of Lincoln and Bishop of York.

Christianisation intensified and evolved into Celtic Christianity after the Romans left Britain c. 410.

Outside the Roman Empire

History of Eastern Christianity in Asia and Church of the East. Christianity also spread beyond the Roman Empire during the early Christian period.

Armenia

Etchmiadzin Cathedral, regarded the oldest cathedral in the world.

It is accepted that Armenia became the first country to adopt Christianity as its state religion. Although it has long been claimed that Armenia was the first Christian kingdom, according to some scholars this has relied on a source by Agathangelos titled "The History of the Armenians", which has recently been redated, casting some doubt. Christianity became the official religion of Armenia in 301, when it was still illegal in the Roman Empire. According to church tradition, the Armenian Apostolic Church was founded by Gregory the Illuminator of the late third – early fourth centuries while they trace their origins to the missions of Bartholomew the Apostle and Thaddeus (Jude the Apostle) in the 1st century

Georgia

According to Orthodox tradition, Christianity was first preached in Georgia by the Apostles Simon and Andrew in the 1st century. It became the state religion of Kartli (Iberia) in 319. The conversion of Kartli to Christianity is credited to a Greek lady called St. Nino of Cappadocia. The Georgian Orthodox Church, originally part of the Church of Antioch, gained its autocephaly and developed its doctrinal specificity progressively between the 5th and 10th centuries. The Bible was also translated into Georgian in the 5th century, as the Georgian alphabet was developed for that purpose.

India

Main articles: Christianity in India, Cristianity in Pakistan, and Saint Thomas Christians

According to tradition, the Indo-Parthian king Gondophares was proselytised by St Thomas, who continued on to southern India, and possibly as far as Malaysia or China. According to Eusebius' record, the apostles Thomas and Bartholomew were assigned to Parthia (modern Iran) and India. By the time of the establishment of the Second Persian Empire (AD 226), there were bishops of the Church of the East in northwest India, Afghanistan and Baluchistan (including parts of Iran, Afghanistan, and Pakistan), with laymen and clergy alike engaging in missionary activity.

An early third-century Syriac work known as the *Acts of Thomas* connects the apostle's Indian ministry with two kings, one in the north and the other in the south. According to the *Acts*, Thomas was at first reluctant to accept this mission, but the Lord appeared to him in a night vision and compelled him to accompany an Indian merchant, Abbanes (or Habban), to his native place in northwest India. There, Thomas found himself in the service of the Indo-Parthian King, Gondophares. The Apostle's ministry resulted in many conversions throughout the kingdom, including the king and his brother.

Thomas thereafter went south to Kerala and baptised the natives, whose descendants form the Saint Thomas Christians or the Syrian Malabar Nasranis.

Piecing together the various traditions, the story suggests that Thomas left northwest India when invasion threatened, and travelled by vessel to the Malabar Coast along the south western coast of the Indian continent, possibly visiting southeast Arabia and Socotra en route, and landing at the former flourishing port of Muziris on an island near Cochin in 52. From there he preached the gospel throughout the Malabar Coast. The various churches he founded were located mainly on the Periyar River and its tributaries and along the coast. He preached to all classes of people and had about 170 converts, including members of the four principal castes. Later, stone crosses were erected at the places where churches were founded, and they became pilgrimage centres. In accordance with apostolic custom, **Thomas ordained teachers and leaders or elders, who were reported to be the earliest ministry of the Malabar church.**

Thomas next proceeded overland to the Coromandel Coast in South Eastern India, and ministered in what is now Chennai (earlier Madras), where a local king and **many people were converted.** One tradition related that he went from there to China via Malacca in Malaysia, and after spending some time there, returned to the Chennai area. *Apparently Thomas' renewed ministry outraged the Brahmins, who were fearful lest Christianity undermine their social caste system. So according to the Syriac version of the Acts of Thomas, Mazdai, the local king at Mylapore, after questioning the Apostle condemned him to death about the year AD 72.* Anxious to avoid popular excitement, the King ordered Thomas conducted to a nearby mountain, where, **after being allowed to pray, he was then stoned and stabbed to death with a lance wielded by an angry Brahmin.**

Mesopotamia and the Parthian Empire

Edessa, which was held by Rome from 116 to 118 and 212 to 214, but was mostly a client kingdom associated either with Rome or Persia, was an important Christian city. Shortly after 201 or even earlier, its royal house became Christian.

Edessa (now Şanlıurfa) in northwestern Mesopotamia was from apostolic times the principal center of Syriac-speaking Christianity. it was the capital of an independent kingdom from 132 BC to AD 216, when it became tributary to Rome. Celebrated as an important centre of Greco-Syrian culture, Edessa was also noted for its Jewish community, with proselytes in the royal family. Strategically located on the main trade routes of the Fertile Crescent, it was easily accessible from Antioch, where the mission to the Gentiles was inaugurated. When early Christians were scattered abroad because of persecution, some found refuge at Edessa. Thus the Edessan church traced its origin to the Apostolic Age (which may account for its rapid growth), and Christianity even became the state religion for a time.

The Church of the East had its inception at a very early date in the buffer zone between the Parthian and Roman Empires in Upper Mesopotamia, known as the Assyrian Church of the East. The vicissitudes of its later growth were rooted in its minority status in a situation of international tension. The rulers of the Parthian Empire (250 BC – AD 226) were on the whole tolerant in spirit, and with the older faiths of Babylonia and Assyria in a state of decay, the time was ripe for a new and vital faith. The rulers of the Second Persian empire (226–640) also followed a policy of religious toleration to begin with, though later they gave Christians the same status as a subject race. However, these rulers also encouraged the revival of the ancient Persian dualistic faith of Zoroastrianism and established it as the state religion, with the result that the Christians were increasingly subjected to repressive measures. Nevertheless, it was not until Christianity became the state religion in the West (380) that enmity toward Rome was focused on the Eastern Christians. After the Muslim conquest in the 7th century, the caliphate tolerated other faiths but forbade proselytism and subjected Christians to heavy taxation.

The missionary Addai evangelized Mesopotamia (modern Iraq) about the middle of the 2nd century. An ancient legend recorded by Eusebius (AD 260–340) and also found in the *Doctrine of Addai* (c. AD 400) (from information in the royal archives of Edessa) describes how King Abgar V of Edessa communicated to Jesus, requesting he come and heal him, to which appeal he received a reply. It is said that after the resurrection, Thomas sent Addai (or Thaddaeus), to the king, with the result that the city was won to the

Christian faith. In this mission he was accompanied by a disciple, Mari, and the two are regarded as co-founders of the church, according to the *Liturgy of Addai and Mari* (c. AD 200), which is still the normal liturgy of the Assyrian church. The *Doctrine of Addai* further states that Thomas was regarded as an apostle of the church in Edessa.

Addai, who became the first bishop of Edessa, was succeeded by Aggai, then by Palut, who was ordained about 200 by Serapion of Antioch. Thence came to us in the 2nd century the famous *Peshitta*, or Syriac translation of the Old Testament; also Tatian's *Diatessaron*, which was compiled about 172 and in common use until St. Rabbula, Bishop of Edessa (412–435), forbade its use. This arrangement of the four canonical gospels as a continuous narrative, whose original language may have been Syriac, Greek, or even Latin, circulated widely in Syriac-speaking Churches.

A Christian council was held at Edessa as early as 197. In 201 the city was devastated by a great flood, and the Christian church was destroyed. In 232, the Syriac Acts were written supposedly on the event of the relics of the Apostle Thomas being handed to the church in Edessa. Under Roman domination many martyrs suffered at Edessa: Sts. Scharbîl and Barsamya, under Decius; Sts. Gûrja, Schâmôna, Habib, and others under Diocletian. In the meanwhile Christian priests from Edessa had evangelized Eastern Mesopotamia and Persia, and established the first churches in the kingdom of the Sasanians. Atillâtiâ, Bishop of Edessa, assisted at the First Council of Nicaea (325).

Persia and Central Asia

By the latter half of the 2nd century, Christianity had spread east throughout Media, Persia, Parthia, and Bactria.

The twenty bishops and many presbyters were more of the order of itinerant missionaries, passing from place to place as Paul did and supplying their needs with such occupations as merchant or craftsman. By AD 280 the metropolis of Seleucia assumed the title of "Catholicos" and in AD 424 a council of the church at Seleucia elected the first patriarch to have jurisdiction over the whole church of the East. The seat of the Patriarchate was fixed at Seleucia-Ctesiphon, since this was an important point on the east–west trade routes which extended to India and China, Java and Japan. Thus the shift of ecclesiastical authority was away from Edessa, which in AD 216 had become tributary to Rome, the establishment of an independent patriarchate with nine subordinate metropoli contributed to a more favourable attitude by the Persian government, which no longer had to fear an ecclesiastical alliance with the common enemy, Rome.

By the time that Edessa was incorporated into the Persian Empire in 258, the city of Arbela, situated on the Tigris in what is now Iraq, had taken on more and more the role that Edessa had played in the early years, as a centre from which Christianity spread to the rest of the Persian Empire.

Bardaisan, writing about 196, speaks of Christians throughout Media, Parthia and Bactria (modern-day Afghanistan) and, according to Tertullian (c. 160–230), there were already a number of bishoprics within the Persian Empire by 220. By 315, the bishop of Seleucia–Ctesiphon had assumed the title "Catholicos". By this time, neither Edessa nor Arbela was the centre of the Church of the East anymore; ecclesiastical authority had moved east to the heart of the Persian Empire. The twin cities of Seleucia-Ctesiphon, well-situated on the main trade routes between East and West, became, in the words of John Stewart, "a magnificent centre for the missionary church that was entering on its great task of carrying the gospel to the far east".

During the reign of Shapur II of the Sasanian Empire, he was not initially hostile to his Christian subjects, who were led by Shemon Bar Sabbae, the Patriarch of the Church of the East, however, the conversion of Constantine the Great to Christianity caused Shapur to start distrusting his Christian subjects. He started seeing them as agents of a foreign enemy. The wars between the Sasanian and Roman empires turned Shapur's mistrust into hostility. After the death of Constantine, Shapur II, who had been preparing for a war against the Romans for several years, imposed a double tax on his Christian subjects to finance the conflict. Shemon, however, refused to pay the double tax. Shapur started pressuring Shemon and his clergy to convert to Zoroastrianism, which they refused to do. It was during this period the 'cycle of the martyrs' began during which 'many thousands of Christians' were put to death. During the following years, Shemon's successors, Shahdost and Barba'shmin, were also martyred.

A near-contemporary 5th-century Christian work, the *Ecclesiastical History* of Sozomen, contains considerable detail on the Persian Christians martyred under Shapur II. Sozomen estimates the total number of Christians killed as follows:

The number of men and women whose names have been ascertained, and who were martyred at this period, has been computed to be upwards of sixteen thousand, while the multitude of martyrs whose names are unknown was so great that the Persians, the Syrians, and the inhabitants of Edessa, have failed in all their efforts to compute the number.

To understand the penetration of the Arabian peninsula by the Christian gospel, it is helpful to distinguish between the Bedouin nomads of the interior, who were chiefly herdsmen and unreceptive to foreign control, and the inhabitants of the settled communities of the coastal areas and oases, who were either middlemen traders or farmers and were receptive to influences from abroad. Christianity apparently gained its strongest foothold in the ancient center of Semitic civilization in South-west Arabia or Yemen (sometimes known as Seba or Sheba, whose queen visited Solomon). Because of geographic proximity, acculturation with Ethiopia was always strong, and the royal family traces its ancestry to this queen.

The presence of Arabians at Pentecost and Paul's three-year sojourn in Arabia suggest a very early gospel witness. A 4th-century church history, states that the apostle Bartholomew preached in Arabia and that Himyarites were among his converts. The Al-Jubail Church in what is now Saudi Arabia was built in the 4th century. Arabia's close relations with Ethiopia give significance to the conversion of the treasurer to the queen of Ethiopia, not to mention the tradition that the Apostle Matthew was assigned to this land. Eusebius says that "one Pantaneous (c. A.D. 190) was sent from Alexandria as a missionary to the nations of the East", including southwest Arabia, on his way to India.

Nubia

Christianity arrived early in Nubia. In the New Testament of the Christian Bible, *a treasury official of "Candace*, **queen of the Ethiopians" returning from a trip to Jerusalem was baptised by Philip the Evangelist:**

Then the Angel of the Lord said to Philip, Start out and go south to the road that leads down from Jerusalem to Gaza, which is desert. And he arose and went: And behold, a man of Ethiopia, an Eunuch of great authority under Candace, Queen of E-thi-o'pi-ans, who had the charge of all her treasure, and had come to Jerusalem to worship.

Ethiopia at that time meant any upper Nile region. Candace was the name and perhaps, title for the Meroë or Kushite queens.

In the fourth century, bishop Athanasius of Alexandria consecrated Marcus as bishop of Philae before his death in 373, showing that Christianity had permanently penetrated the region. John of Ephesus records that a Monophysite priest named Julian converted the king and his nobles of Nobatia around 545 and another kingdom of Alodia converted around 569. By the 7th century Makuria expanded becoming the dominant power in the region so strong enough to halt the southern expansion of Islam after the Arabs had taken Egypt. After several failed invasions the new rulers agreed to a treaty with Dongola allowing for peaceful coexistence and trade. This treaty held for six hundred years allowing Arab traders introducing Islam to Egypt.

PART FIVE

THE UNDILUTED TEACHINGS OF OUR LORD JESUS CHRIST

CHAPTER 5

In Christianity, Jesus is believed to be the Son of the Father in human form as written in the Bible's New Testament, and in most Christian denominations he is held to be the Son of the Father, a person of the Trinity.

Christians believe him to be the messiah, or a saviour, (giving him the title *Christ*) prophesied in the Bible's Old Testament. Through Jesus' crucifixion and resurrection, Christians believe that the Father offers humans salvation and eternal life, with Jesus' death atoning for all sin, thus making humanity right with Father. The commonly held belief among Christians is the phrase, "**Jesus died for your sins**," and thus they accept that **salvation is only possible through him**.

These teachings emphasise that as the Lamb, Jesus chose to suffer nailed to the cross at Calvary as a sign of his obedience to the will of the

Father, as an "agent and servant of the Father". Jesus' choice positions him as a man of obedience, in contrast to Adam's disobedience. According to the New Testament, after the Father raised him from the dead, Jesus ascended to heaven to sit at the right hand of the Father with his followers awaiting his return to Earth and subsequent Last Judgment.

According to the canonical gospel accounts, Jesus was born of a virgin, instructed other Jews how to follow the (sometimes using parables), performed miracles and gathered disciples. Christians generally believe that this narrative is historically true.

While there has been theological debate over the nature of Jesus, Trinitarian Christians believe that Jesus is the Logos, the Son, and "true man"—both fully divine and fully human. Jesus, having become fully human in all respects, suffered the pains and temptations of a mortal man, yet he did not sin.

Although Christian views of Jesus vary, it is possible to summarise the key elements of the beliefs shared by major Christian denominations by analysing their catechetical or confessional texts. Christian views of Jesus are derived from various biblical sources, particularly from the canonical gospels and New Testament letters such as the Pauline epistles. Christians predominantly hold that these works are historically true. Those Christian groups or denominations which are committed to what are considered biblically orthodox Christianity nearly all agree that Jesus:

- was born of a virgin
- is a human being who is also fully divine
- had never sinned during his existence
- was crucified and buried in a tomb
- rose from the dead on the third day
- eventually ascended back to the Father
- will return to earth

Some groups which are considered to be Christian hold beliefs which are considered to be heterodox. For example, believers in monophysitism reject the idea that Christ has two natures, one human and one divine.

The five major milestones in the gospel narrative of the life of Jesus are his baptism, transfiguration, Crucifixion, Resurrection and Ascension. These are usually bracketed by two other episodes: his nativity at the beginning and the sending of the Paraclete (Holy Spirit) at the end. The gospel accounts of the teachings of Jesus are often presented in terms of specific categories involving his "works and words", e.g., his ministry, parables and miracles.

Christians not only attach theological significance to the *works* of Jesus, but also to his *name*. Devotions to the name of Jesus go back to the earliest days of Christianity. These exist today both in Eastern and Western Christianity—both Catholic and Protestant.

Christians predominantly profess that through Jesus' life, death, and Resurrection, he restored humanity's communion with the Father with the blood of the New Covenant. **His death on a cross is understood as a redemptive sacrifice: the source of humanity's salvation and the atonement for sin which had entered human history through the sin of Adam.**

Christ, *Logos* and Son of the Father.

First page of Mark, by Sargis Pitsak (14th century): "The beginning of the gospel of Jesus Christ, the Son of the Father".

But who do you say that I am? Only Simon Peter answered him: *You are the Christ, the Son of Father* and humanity. As true Divine he brings the Father to mankind. As true man he brings mankind to the Father.

Most Christians generally consider Jesus to be the Christ, the long-awaited Messiah, as well as the one and only Son of the Father. The opening words in the Gospel of Mark (1:1), "The beginning of the gospel of Jesus Christ, the Son of the father", provide Jesus with the two distinct attributions as Christ and as the Son of the Father. His divinity is again re-affirmed in Mark 1:11. Matthew 1:1 which begins by calling Jesus the Christ and in verse 16 explains it again with the affirmation: "Jesus, who is called Christ".

In the Pauline epistles, the word *Christ* is so closely associated with Jesus that apparently for the early Christians there was no need to claim that Jesus was Christ, for that was considered widely accepted among them. Hence Paul could use the term *Christos* with no confusion about who it referred to, and as in 1 Corinthians 4:15 and Romans 12:5 he could use expressions such as "in Christ" to refer to the followers of Jesus.

In the New Testament, the title "Son of the Father" is applied to Jesus on many occasions, from the Annunciation up to the Crucifixion. The declaration that Jesus is the Son of the Father is made by many individuals in the New Testament, and on two occasions by the Father as a voice from Heaven, and is asserted by Jesus himself.

In Christology, the concept that Christ is the *Logos* (i.e., "The Word") has been important in establishing the doctrine of the divinity of Christ and his position as the Father the Son in the Trinity as set forth in the Chalcedonian Creed. This derives from the opening of the Gospel of John, commonly translated into English as: **"In the beginning was the Word, and the Word was with the Father, and the Word was Father."** In the original Koine Greek is translated as *Word* and in theological discourse, this is often left in its English transliterated form, *Logos*. The easiest way to understand this is the teaching that Jesus (The Word of the Father) came from the bosom of the Father and became a living being who then translated into a foetus in the womb of (Virgin Mary) through a supernatural means, as professed by believers in Christ.

The pre-existence of Christ refers to the existence of Christ before his incarnation as Jesus. One of the relevant New Testament passages is John 1:1-18 where, in the Trinitarian view, Christ is identified with a pre-existent divine hypostasis called the Logos or Word. This doctrine is reiterated in John 17:5 when Jesus refers to the glory which he had with the Father "before the world was" during the Farewell Discourse. John 17:24 also refers to the Father loving Jesus "before the foundation of the world". Nontrinitarian views about the pre-existence of Christ vary, with some rejecting it and others accepting it.

Following the Apostolic Age, from the 2nd century forward, several controversies developed about how the human and divine are related within the person of Jesus. Eventually in 451, the concept of a hypostatic union was stated **at the Council of Chalcedon, namely that Jesus is both fully divine and fully human**. However, differences among Christian denominations continued thereafter, with some rejecting the hypostatic union in favour of monophysitism.

Incarnation, Nativity and Second Adam.

He is the image of the invisible Word, the firstborn of all creation. For **by him all things were created, in heaven and on earth, visible and invisible.** — Colossians 1:15-16. The above verse Colossians regards the birth of Jesus as the model for all creation.

Paul the Apostle viewed the birth of Jesus as an event of cosmic significance which brought forth a "new man" who undid the damage caused by the fall of the first man, Adam.

Just as the Johannine view of Jesus as the incarnate Logos proclaims the universal relevance of his birth, the Pauline perspective emphasises the birth of a new man and a new world in the birth of Jesus. Paul's eschatological view of Jesus counter-positions him as a new man of morality and obedience, in contrast to Adam. Unlike Adam, the new man born in Jesus obeys the Father and ushers in a world of morality and salvation.

In the Pauline view, Adam is positioned as the first man and Jesus as the second: Adam, having corrupted himself by his disobedience, also infected humanity and left it with a curse as its inheritance. The birth of Jesus counterbalanced the fall of Adam, bringing forth redemption and repairing the damage done by Adam.

In the 2nd century Church Father Irenaeus writes:

"When He became incarnate and was made man, He commenced afresh the long line of human beings, and furnished us, in a brief, comprehensive manner, with salvation; so that what we had lost in Adam—namely to be according to the image and likeness of the Father- that we might recover in Christ Jesus."

In patristic theology, Paul's contrasting of Jesus as the new man versus Adam provided a framework for discussing the uniqueness of the birth of Jesus and the ensuing events of his life. The nativity of Jesus thus began to serve as the starting point for "cosmic Christology" in which the birth, life and Resurrection of Jesus have universal implications. The concept of Jesus as the "new man" repeats in the cycle of birth and rebirth of Jesus from his nativity to his Resurrection: following his birth, through his morality and obedience to the Father, Jesus began a "new harmony" in the relationship between the Father and man. The nativity and Resurrection of Jesus thus created the author and exemplar of a new humanity. In this view, the birth, death and Resurrection of Jesus brought about salvation, undoing the damage of Adam.

As the biological son of David, Jesus would be of the Jewish race, ethnicity, nation, and culture. One argument against this would be a contradiction in Jesus' genealogies: Matthew saying he is the son of Solomon and Luke saying he is the son of Nathan—Solomon and Nathan being brothers. John of Damascus taught that there is no contradiction, for Nathan wed Solomon's wife after Solomon died in accordance with scripture, namely, yibbum (the mitzvah that a man must marry his brother's childless widow).

Jesus grew up in Galilee and much of his ministry took place there. The languages spoken in Galilee and Judea during the 1st century AD include Jewish Palestinian Aramaic, Hebrew, and Greek, with Aramaic being predominant. There is substantial consensus that Jesus gave most of his teachings in Aramaic in the Galilean dialect.

The canonical gospels describe Jesus wearing tzitzit – the tassels on a tallit – in Matthew 14:36 and Luke 8:43–44. Besides this, the New Testament includes no descriptions of Jesus' appearance before his death and the gospel narratives are generally indifferent to people's racial appearance or features.

Ministry.

Ministry of Jesus: New Testament places associated with Jesus The *Comunion of the Aposties, Jesus says the thief comes only in order to steal and kill and destroy. I came that they may have and enjoy life, and have it in abundance (to the full, till it overflows).*—John 10:10 (Ampl)

173

Jesus seemed to have two basic concerns with reference to people and the material: (1) that they be freed from the tyranny of things and (2) that they be actively concerned for the needs of others.

In the canonical gospels, the Ministry of Jesus begins with his baptism in the countryside of Judea, near the River Jordan and ends in Jerusalem, following the Last Supper. The Gospel of Luke (3:23) states that Jesus was "about 30 years of age" at the start of his ministry. The date of the start of his ministry has been estimated at around AD 27 to 29 and the end in the range AD 30 to 36.

Jesus' early Galilean ministry begins when after his baptism, he goes back to Galilee from his time in the Judean desert. In this early period he preaches around Galilee and recruits his first disciples who begin to travel with him and eventually form the core of the early Church. The major Galilean ministry which begins in Matthew 8 includes the commissioning of the Twelve Apostles, and covers most of the ministry of Jesus in Galilee. The final Galilean ministry begins after the death of John the Baptist as Jesus prepares to go to Jerusalem.

In the later Judean ministry Jesus starts his final journey to Jerusalem through Judea. As Jesus travels towards Jerusalem, in the later Perean ministry, about one third the way down from the Sea of Galilee along the River Jordan, he returns to the area where he was baptised.

The final ministry in Jerusalem is sometimes called the *Passion Week* and begins with the Jesus' triumphal entry into Jerusalem. The gospels provide more details about the final ministry than the other periods, devoting about one third of their text to the last week of the life of Jesus in Jerusalem.

The words that I say unto you I speak not from myself: **but the Father** *who dwells in me does his works....* John 14:10

In the New Testament the teachings of Jesus are presented in terms of his "words and works". The words of Jesus include several sermons, in addition to parables that appear throughout the narrative of the Synoptic Gospels (the gospel of John includes no parables). The works include the miracles and other acts performed during his ministry.

Although the Canonical Gospels are the major source of the teachings of Jesus, the Pauline epistles, which were likely written decades before the gospels, provide some of the earliest written accounts of the teachings of Jesus.

The New Testament does not present the teachings of Jesus as merely his own teachings, but equates the words of Jesus with divine revelation, with John the Baptist stating in John 3:34: "For the one whom the Father has sent speaks the words of the Father, for the Father gives the Spirit without limit." and Jesus stating in John 7:16: **"My teaching is not my own. It comes from the one who sent me"**. In Matthew 11:27 Jesus claims divine knowledge, stating: "**No one knows the Son except the Father and no one knows the Father except the Son"**, asserting the mutual knowledge he has with the Father.

One of the most important of Jesus' teachings is his second coming in Matthew 24 and Luke 21. There Jesus explained the signs of the last days, popularly known as the end-time. These are the days that precedes the second coming of Jesus Christ, there he spoke of the signs of the end of days and what will happen to the believers in Christ, the persecution and the troubles that will come upon the world. The second coming of Jesus is mainly divided into two, namely; the Rapture and the Second Coming. The rapture being the time

Jesus comes in the air to take up his saints to Heaven for a period of seven years and the second coming, being a time he comes with the saints to rule the earth for a thousand years. It is also referred to as the millennial reign.

Discourses

The *Five Jesus' Discourses of Matthew, Sermon on the Mount, and Beatitudes, Farewell Discourse* to His eleven remaining disciples after the Last Supper, from the *Maestà* by Duccio

The gospels include several discourses by Jesus on specific occasions, such as the Farewell discourse delivered after the Last Supper, the night before his Crucifixion. Although some of the teachings of Jesus are reported as taking place within the formal atmosphere of a synagogue (e.g., in Matthew 4:23) many of the discourses are more like conversations than formal lectures.

The Gospel of Matthew has a structured set of sermons, often grouped as the Five Discourses of Matthew which present many of the key teachings of Jesus. Each of the five discourses has some parallel passages in the Gospel of Mark or the Gospel of Luke. The five discourses in Matthew begin with the Sermon on the Mount, which encapsulates many of the moral teaching of Jesus and which is one of the best known and most quoted elements of the New Testament. The Sermon on the Mount includes the *Beatitudes* which describe the character of the people of the Kingdom of the Father, expressed as "blessings". The Beatitudes focus on love and humility rather than force and exaction and echo the key ideals of Jesus' teachings on spirituality and compassion. The other discourses in Matthew include the *Missionary Discourse* in Matthew 10 and the *Discourse on the Church* in Matthew 18, providing instructions to the disciples and laying the foundation of the codes of conduct for the anticipated community of followers.

Parables

The Parable of the Good Samaritan is one of the parables of Jesus.

The parables of Jesus represent a major component of his teachings in the gospels, the approximately thirty parables forming about one third of his recorded teachings. The parables may appear within longer sermons, as well as other places within the narrative. Jesus' parables are seemingly simple and memorable stories, often with imagery, and each conveys a teaching which usually relates the physical world to the spiritual world.

In the 19th century, Lisco and Fairbairn stated that in the parables of Jesus, "the image borrowed from the visible world is accompanied by a truth from the invisible (spiritual) world" and that the parables of Jesus are not "mere similitudes which serve the purpose of illustration, but are internal analogies where nature becomes a witness for the spiritual world". Similarly, in the 20th century, calling a parable "an earthly story with a heavenly meaning", William Barclay states that the parables of Jesus use familiar examples to lead others' minds towards heavenly concepts. He suggests that Jesus did not form his parables merely as analogies but based on an "inward affinity between the natural and the spiritual order."

One of the major reasons why Jesus spoke in parables to the Jews was explained to the disciples of Jesus by Jesus himself. It is found in Matthew 13:13-14; there Jesus explains why he used much of parables to the people of Israel. Jesus explained that it was so for the fulfilment of the prophecy of Isaiah the prophet, and this is found in Isaiah 6:9-10. This was for the people of Israel not to understand and realise who Jesus is and accept him, he purposely did this to make provision for Gentiles to be part of the children of the Father in heaven.

Miracles of Jesus

*Believe the miracles, that you may know and understand that the Father is in me, and I in the Father...*John 10:38

In Christian teachings, the miracles of Jesus were as much a vehicle for his message as were his words. Many of the miracles emphasise the importance of faith, for instance in cleansing ten lepers, Jesus did not say: "My power has saved you" but says "Rise and go; your faith has saved you." Similarly, in the Walking on Water miracle, Apostle Peter learns an important lesson about faith in that as his faith wavers, he begins to sink.

Jesus healing the paralytic in *the Pool.*

One characteristic shared among all miracles of Jesus in the Gospel accounts is that he delivered benefits freely and never requested or accepted any form of payment for his healing miracles, unlike some high priests of his time who charged those who were healed. In Matthew 10:8 he advised his disciples to heal the sick, raise the dead, cleanse those who have leprosy, and drive out demons without payment and stated: **"Freely you have received; freely give"**.

Christians in general believe that Jesus' miracles were actual historical events and that his miraculous works were an important part of his life, attesting to his divinity and the

Hypostatic union, i.e., the dual natures of Christ's humanity and divinity in one hypostasis. Christians believe that while Jesus' experiences of hunger, weariness, and death were evidences of his humanity, the miracles were evidences of his deity.

Christian authors also view the miracles of Jesus not merely as acts of power and omnipotence, but as works of love and mercy: they were performed to show compassion for sinful and suffering humanity. Authors Ken and Jim Stocker state that "every single miracle Jesus performed was an act of love". And each miracle involves specific teachings.

Since according to the Gospel of John it was impossible to narrate all the miracles performed by Jesus, the Catholic Encyclopedia states that the miracles presented in the Gospels were selected for a twofold reason: first for the manifestation of God's glory, and then for their evidential value. Jesus referred to his "works" as evidences of his mission and his divinity, and in John 5:36 he declared that his miracles have greater evidential value than the testimony of John the Baptist.

Crucifixion and atonement

The accounts of the Crucifixion and subsequent Resurrection of Jesus provide a rich background for Christological analysis, from the canonical gospels to the Pauline epistles.

Johannine "agency christology" combines the concept that Jesus is the Son of his Father with the idea that he has come into the world as his Father's agent, commissioned and sent by the Father to represent the Father and to accomplish his Father's work. Implied in each Synoptic portrayal of Jesus is the doctrine that the salvation Jesus gives is inseparable from Jesus himself and his divine identity. Sonship and agency come together in the Synoptic gospels only in the Parable of the Vineyard (Matthew 21:37; Mark 12:6; Luke 20:13). The submission of Jesus to crucifixion is a sacrifice made as an *agent of the Father* or *servant of the Father*, for the sake of eventual victory. This builds upon the salvific theme of the Gospel of John which begins in John 1:36 with John the Baptist's proclamation: "The Lamb of the Father who takes away the sins of the world". Further reinforcement of the concept is provided in Revelation 21:14 where the "lamb slain but standing" is the only one worthy of handling the scroll (i.e., the book) containing the names of those who are to be saved.

A central element in the Christology presented in the Acts of the Apostles is the affirmation of the belief that the death of Jesus by crucifixion happened "with the foreknowledge of the Father, according to a definite plan". In this view, as in Acts 2:23, the cross is not viewed as a scandal, for the Crucifixion of Jesus "at the hands of the lawless" is viewed as the fulfilment of the plan of the Father.

Paul's Christology has a specific focus on the death and Resurrection of Jesus. For Paul, the Crucifixion of Jesus is directly related to his Resurrection and the term "the cross of Christ" used in Galatians 6:12 may be viewed as his abbreviation of the message of the gospels. For Paul, the Crucifixion of Jesus was not an isolated event in history, but a cosmic event with significant eschatological consequences, as in 1 Corinthians 2:8. In the Pauline view, Jesus, obedient to the point of death (Philippians 2:8) died "at the right time" (Romans 4:25) based on the plan of God.[131] For Paul the "power of the cross" is not separable from the Resurrection of Jesus. John Calvin supported the "agent of God" Christology and argued that in his trial in Pilate's Court Jesus could have successfully argued for his innocence, but instead submitted to crucifixion in **obedience to the Father**. This Christological theme continued into the 20th century, both in the Eastern and Western Churches. In the Eastern Church Sergei Bulgakov argued that the Crucifixion of Jesus was "pre-eternally" determined by the Father before the creation of the world, to redeem humanity from the disgrace caused by the fall of Adam. In the Western Church, Karl Rahner elaborated on the analogy that the blood of the Lamb of God (and the water from the side of Jesus) shed at the Crucifixion had a cleansing nature, similar to baptismal water.

Mormons believe that the Crucifixion was the culmination of Christ's atonement, which began in the Garden of Gethsemane.

The New Testament teaches that the Resurrection of Jesus is a foundation of the Christian faith. Christians, through faith in the working of the Father are spiritually resurrected with Jesus, and are redeemed so that they may walk in a new way of life.

In the teachings of the apostolic Church, the Resurrection was seen as heralding a new era. Forming a theology of the Resurrection fell to Apostle Paul. It was not enough for Paul to simply repeat elementary teachings, but as Hebrews 6:1 states, "go beyond the initial teachings about Christ and advance to maturity". Fundamental to Pauline theology is the connection between Christ's Resurrection and redemption. Paul explained the importance of the Resurrection of Jesus as the cause and basis of the hope of Christians to share a similar experience in 1 Cor 15:20–22: But Christ has indeed been raised from the dead, the firstfruits of those who have fallen asleep. For, since death came through a man, the resurrection of the dead comes also through a man. For as in Adam all die, so in Christ all will be made alive.

If the cross stands at the centre of Paul's theology, so does the Resurrection: unless the one died the death of *all*, the *all* would have little to celebrate in the Resurrection of the one. Paul taught that, just as Christians share in Jesus' death in baptism, so they will share in his Resurrection for Jesus was designated the Son of the Father by his Resurrection. Paul's views went against the thoughts of **the Greek philosophers** to whom a bodily resurrection meant a new imprisonment in a corporeal body, which was what they wanted to avoid, given that for them the corporeal and the material fettered the spirit. At the same time, Paul believed that the newly resurrected body would be a spiritual body—immortal, glorified and powerful, in contrast to an earthly body which is mortal, dishonoured and weak.

The Apostolic Fathers, discussed the death and Resurrection of Jesus, including Ignatius (50–115), Polycarp (69–155), and Justin Martyr (100–165). Following the conversion of Constantine and the liberating Edict of Milan in 313, the ecumenical councils of the 4th, 5th and 6th centuries, that focused on Christology helped shape the Christian understanding of the redemptive nature of Resurrection, and influenced both the development of its iconography, and its use.

What Are the Basics of Jesus' Teaching?

Jesus taught that He was the fulfilment of messianic prophecy, that the Father requires more than external obedience to rules, that salvation comes to those who believe in Christ. **That judgment is coming to the unbelieving and unrepentant.**

TAMMY KENNINGTON

This is Tammy's true story to learn from and goes like this, from the time they could hold chubby cardboard books in their dimpled hands, I began reading simple Bible stories and books about Christ's teachings to my children. I wanted each story to convey truth and share the basics of Jesus' teaching in a format even little ones could understand.

Unlike my children, not all of us were raised in Christian homes and many have not had the opportunity to learn about the teachings and parables of Jesus. This article will explore a few of Jesus' teachings while you can read more about His parables. Perhaps the most fundamental of Christ's teachings come from Mark 12:30-31(NKJV),

"Love the Lord your Father with all your heart and with all your soul and with all your mind and with all your strength.' The second is this: 'Love your neighbour as yourself. There is no commandment greater than these." Christ, as Divine incarnate, told the disciples that He wanted their love. **Not good deeds. Not a series of sacrifices, but Love.**

The English word translated love in these verses comes from the **Greek,** agape, which means "to regard the welfare of and to long for." God wants His people to long for Him emotionally, intellectually, and spiritually. Not only that, but the Father intends for us to **love one another.** It may seem remarkable, but the word agape? It's the same type of love Jesus spoke of when He told the crowds to **"love your enemies"** (Matthew 5:44). When Jesus taught about love, He meant for it to move beyond a transitory feeling. **Love involves dedicating our lives to the Father and to others through His power.**

What Are the Essentials of Jesus' Teachings?

If you asked me to share the most essential teachings of Christ, I would narrow them down to the following—**the identity of Jesus as Divine, salvation, forgiveness, and following Him**.

Everything we know about Christ hinges on His identity. If He is not the Messiah—the one of whom Israel's prophets spoke, then our faith is useless. But Jesus said, "Most assuredly, I say to you, before Abraham was, I AM" (John 8: 58 NKJV). He was referencing Exodus 14 in which the Father gave Himself the name **I AM,** which means "self-existent or eternally existent." Furious that Jesus would claim **to be Divine, the religious leaders threatened to stone Him.**

Because we know Christ is Divine incarnate, which you read more about here, we can trust Him for salvation—one of the topics about which He spoke most frequently. **The Father who formed the Earth from emptiness and crafted people out of love, is also the Lord who stepped out of heaven to rescue the hopeless and hurting. John 14:6 is as significant today as it was two thousand years ago when Jesus said, "I am the way, the truth, and the life. No one comes to the Father except through Me."**

There are other religions, teachers, and prophets—but only Christians have a Christ who gave up glory to save His people, was crucified, and then rose from the dead three days later.

Forgiveness, another of Christ's key teachings, was a concept that He emphasised throughout His three years of ministry. Not only did Jesus forgive others for various sins including adultery and murder, but He expects us to offer others the same grace and forgiveness we have received. As Matthew 6:14-15 (NIV) explains, "For if you forgive other people when they sin against you, your heavenly Father will also forgive you. But if you do not forgive others their sins, your Father will not forgive your sins."

While this may be one of Christ's most difficult teachings, few of us will need to forgive people for the sort of heinous treatment Jesus experienced. He spoke words of forgiveness from the cross.

Because Jesus is Lord and the way to salvation through forgiveness, He is worthy to receive the pouring out of our lives as an act of worship. Like the disciples of old, we are called to "take up the cross" (Matthew 16:24) and follow Him.

For some, this may look like choosing a different lifestyle than what you have been living. Others may need to leave religiosity behind and discover the freedom of relationship with Jesus. Still, others may realise this means pressing forward in faith knowing your cross for the season is loving that dear one with mental illness struggles, managing that ongoing health issue, or caring for the live-in relative.

What Did Jesus Teach about the Father's Kingdom?

While Jesus taught about several topics including those we discussed above, the one He addressed most often was the Kingdom.

When speaking about the kingdom of the Father, Jesus established that, **the kingdom of the Father is not an earthly kingdom**. Jesus said, "My kingdom is not of this world. If it were, my servants would fight to prevent my arrest by the Jewish leaders. But now my kingdom is from another place" **(John 13:36 NIV)**.

Believers participate in bringing the kingdom to earth. "This, then, is how you should pray: "'Our Father in heaven, hallowed be your name, your kingdom come, your will be done, on earth as it is in heaven" **(Matthew 6:9-10 NIV)**.

The kingdom of the Father, which is eternal, is more important than that which is temporal. "But seek ye first the kingdom of the Father, and his righteousness; and all these things shall be added unto you" **(Matthew 6:33 KJV)**.

The kingdom of the Father is constructed in a person's heart and mind. "the Father's kingdom does not come simply by obeying principles or waiting for signs. The kingdom is not discovered in one place or another, for the Father's kingdom realm is already expanding within some of you" (Luke 17:20-21).

While Christ has come, we wait for His return and the promise of the Father's kingdom to be fully realised. This is the tenuous relationship of the "already but not yet" which is examined in the following article.

Why Did Jesus Come to Earth and Teach?

If we consider the bulk of Christ's teachings and the years of His ministry, a picture of a man who lived what He taught begins to emerge. Jesus wasn't an esoteric intellectual trying to impress the elite in society.

He was, instead, the **Father's only Son** who taught those with tender hearts in word pictures they would understand. Jesus spoke about soil to explain responsive and unresponsive spirits and water to convey eternal life.

Christ spoke about what made sense in order to demystify that which could free people from the consequences of sin specifically salvation as a result of the forgiveness of sins and freedom as followers of the Messiah.

How Did Prayer Play a Role in Jesus' Ministry?

In addition to teaching, Jesus devoted a significant amount of time to prayer both personally, for His disciples, and for others. Depending upon how they are counted, at least 25 Bible verses record at least twenty-five of these instances.

His regular practice of prayer, along with the direct teaching of how and what to pray about, forged a mold the disciples and Christians for years to come, continue to follow.

Jesus prayed:

The Fatherwalking on water (Mark 6:46) before choosing His disciples (Luke 6:12-13), while healing people (Mark 7:34-35), before eating (John 6:11) when He blessed the children (Matthew 19:13-15), at His baptism (Luke 3:21-22), in the Garden of Gethsemane (Matthew 26:36-46), as He took His last breath (Luke 23:46)

Through Christ's demonstration of prayer and teaching, His followers gained an understanding of how they were to love the Father, love others, and discover hope and eternal security. **"Your kingdom come…"**

DEFINITION

Jesus' teachings were striking and memorable, not only because he used a variety of teachings methods but more so because of what he taught, that he was the incarnate, divine Lord who had brought his heavenly kingdom to earth and that the rules of this kingdom were much different from the rules of the kingdoms of earth. Jesus was known for his teachings because of the methods that he used and the message that he preached. *Throughout his teaching ministry, Jesus used a variety of methods that made his teachings both striking and memorable, understandable and provoking. These methods included many well-known methods of his day, as well as qualities that we are still familiar with—poetry, proverbs, exaggeration, parables, similes, riddles, and paradoxes. However, what set his teachings apart from others was the message that they contained. Jesus taught that the kingdom of the Father had come, and that he, as the incarnate and divine Lord, was its ruler. This kingdom challenged the standards of the kingdoms of men and called its citizens to live in radically different ways.*

Jesus was known for his ability to teach. **He is called "teacher" forty-five times in the New Testament. The Aramaic title "Rabbi" is used fourteen times of Jesus, even though he was not formally trained as a Rabbi.** The people, however, recognized that Jesus was indeed a teacher sent from the Father. Like other teachers, Jesus had disciples, announced divine commands, buttressed his teaching with Scripture, debated with others, was questioned about legal disputes, and employed various techniques to make his teaching more memorable. He taught both in the countryside and in the cities. **He taught in the synagogues and, on at least one occasion,** from a boat. He often was able to gather large crowds who could be so enthralled by his teaching that they simply forgot about their need for food. What made Jesus' teaching unique was not only *what* he taught but also *how* he taught it.

The Method of Jesus' Teaching

Jesus used a variety of teaching techniques to impress his teaching on his hearers. Such techniques were used to clarify his meaning, motivate (or sometimes shock) the listeners, or reveal the true intent of the Father's Word all the while making his teaching memorable. **Some forms of Jesus' teaching include poetry, proverbs, exaggeration, and parables, and many others (such as puns [Matt. 23:24], similes [Luke 17:6], metaphors [Matt. 5:13–14], riddles [Mark 14:58], paradoxes [Mark 12:41–44], irony [Matt. 16:2–3], and questions [Mark 3:1–4]).**

Poetry

Most of the poetry Jesus used (expressed by the Gospel writers) involve parallelism, with about two hundred examples in the Gospels. There are four main types of parallelism: synonymous, antithetical, step (or climactic), and chiastic.

In *synonymous parallelism*, a subsequent line (or lines) expresses a similar (synonymous) thought to the previous line. The second line, while it may be virtually synonymous, can also clarify or intensify the first line. About fifty examples Jesus' use of synonymous parallelism appear in the Gospels. For example, Jesus says, "For nothing is hidden except to be made manifest; nor is anything secret except to come to light" (Mark

4:22). Here, "hidden" parallels "secret" and "manifest" parallels "come to light."

In *antithetical parallelism*, the second line contrasts with the first line. This is the most common form of parallelism in Jesus' teaching, with nearly 140 instances. For example, "every healthy tree bears good fruit, but the diseased tree bears bad fruit" (Matt. 7:17). The terms "healthy" contrasts with "diseased" and "good fruit" contrasts with "bad fruit."

In *step* (or climactic) *parallelism*, the second line continues *and advances* the thought of the first line. There are about twenty examples of this type of parallelism in Jesus's teaching. One is, "Whoever receives you receives me, and whoever receives me receives him who sent me" (Matt. 10:40). Notice that the first line is repeated ("whoever receives me") and then an additional element is added which advances the teaching ("receives him who sent me").

Finally, *chiastic parallelism* involves the inversion of parallel statements (A, B, B¹, A¹). There are 16 cases of this type of parallelism in the Gospels. For example, "The Sabbath [A] was made for man [B], not man [B¹] for the Sabbath [A¹]" (Mark 2:27).

Proverbs

Proverbial statements are also employed by Jesus. Such statements are not to be taken as absolutes but are general principles. For example, Jesus states, "For all who take the sword will perish by the sword" (Matt. 26:52). As is the case with a proverb, exceptions are not provided. Jesus' statement does not mean that *all* who fight with swords will die by a sword. Rather, the meaning is that, generally speaking, those who are accustomed to fighting with swords are likely to be killed by a sword. Thus, a person knowing the truthfulness of the proverb will be wise to heed its teaching.

Exaggeration

Exaggeration can be wrong if it is used deceitfully especially when the listener is not anticipating exaggerated language. However, in ethical teachings, exaggerated language is a powerful tool that can leave an indelible impression on the hearer (or reader). There are two types of exaggerated language: overstatement and hyperbole. Overstatement is an exaggerated statement that is possible (though not intended) to complete. For example, when Jesus taught, "If your right eye causes you to sin, tear it out and throw it away" (Matt. 5:29), although such an action could be done, that is not the desired intent of Jesus' statement. Hyperbole, however, is an exaggerated statement that is impossible to complete. For example, Jesus says to the scribes and Pharisees, "You blind guides, straining out a gnat and swallowing a camel!" (Matt. 23:24). Although it is impossible for someone to swallow a camel, the ethical point is clear: don't be so careful about the little things so as to ignore to do the big things. Exaggeration is a powerful form of communication as it arrests the attention of the hearers. It also demonstrates the seriousness of a situation. For example, if removing an eye would help you avoid hell, it's worth removing.

Parables

Perhaps Jesus' most well-known method of teaching is the parable, which accounts for about one-third of all his teaching. In the Gospels, Jesus tells at least fifty different parables. Unfortunately, the parables are not only some of Jesus' most cherished teachings, they also constitute some of his most misunderstood teachings.

At its basic definition, a parable involves a comparison. For example, "The kingdom of heaven is like treasure hidden in a field" (Matt. 13:44). Thus, the "kingdom of heaven" is compared (has some resemblance) to a "treasure." Such parables are fairly easy to comprehend since the point of the comparison is usually highlighted in the parable itself (e.g., sacrifice whatever you need to enter the kingdom since it is worth it). In other parables (e.g., the parable of the sower/soils and the parable of the wheat and tares), Jesus explains the various comparisons since it may not be obvious to his hearers. Although parables have often been allegorized, it is best to seek the main idea of the parable based on the parable's context (why did Jesus give the parable?). Additionally, it is helpful to seek to understand the parable from the perspective of the original audience before applying it to a modern context.

The Message of Jesus' Teaching

Jesus was the consummate teacher, not only because of how he taught but because of what he taught. The following section will explain three prominent topics in Jesus' teachings: (1) the reality of the kingdom of the Father, (2) living in the kingdom of the Father, and (3) the Lord of the kingdom of the Father.

The Reality of the Kingdom of the Father

The kingdom of the Father is the central theme in Jesus' teaching. According to Mark, Jesus' message can be summarised as: "The time is fulfilled, and the kingdom of the Father is at hand; repent and believe in the gospel" (Mark 1:15; see also Matt. 4:17, 23; Luke 4:43). The Gospels contain seventy-six different kingdom sayings of Jesus (and just over one hundred including parallels). The kingdom refers not to a physical realm but to the reign of the Father. Jesus himself said, "My kingdom is not of this world" (John 18:36). The kingdom can, therefore, be defined as the Father's final, decisive exercising of his sovereign reign, which was inaugurated during Jesus' ministry and will be consummated at his return.

Although the phrase "kingdom of the Father" is not used in the Old Testament, the concept of Father as king and one who rules over his kingdom abounds (Dan. 2:44; Pss. 22:27–28; 103:19). The Father is frequently spoken of as the King of both Israel and all the world. And yet, there is also the expectation that the Father will one day rule over all his people in an unparalleled fashion. Therefore, when Jesus came preaching that the kingdom of Father had come, his Jewish audience knew that he was referring to the complete rule of the over Israel and all the nations.

Jesus taught that the kingdom of the Father is both present (already) and future (not yet). That is, the kingdom of the Father is both a present reality (Matt. 11:11; 12:28; Mark 1:15; 9:1; Luke 11:2; 17:20–21) and a future hope (Matt. 6:9–10; 7:21; 8:11–12; Mark 14:25). When Jesus (the King) came to earth he ushered in the kingdom. This kingdom, however, is still contested in the world and will not be fully experienced until every knee bows and every tongue confesses Jesus as the King. That would have to wait until the King returns (Jesus' second coming).

The phrases "kingdom of the Father" and "kingdom of heaven" are synonymous, representing the same reality. This can be demonstrated by comparing parallel passages where one text reads "kingdom of *heaven*" (Matt. 5:3) but the other has "kingdom of the Father" (Luke 6:20). "Heaven" is a substitute for the divine name "Father." Furthermore, Matthew uses the terms interchangeably in the same context: "Only with difficulty will a rich person enter the kingdom of *heaven*. Again I tell you, it is easier for a camel to go through the eye of a needle than for a rich person to enter the kingdom of *the Father*" (Matt. 19:23-24). Also, the kingdom of the Father (the Father's rule) is not identical to the church (Father's people).

Living in the Kingdom of the Father

Jesus came not only in fulfilment of promises of the Davidic king who would rule over Israel and the nations, he also came as a prophet who is greater than Moses (Deut. 18:18). In that role, he taught how kingdom citizens should conduct themselves. And yet, Jesus never offers a systematic ethical system. Moreover, some of Jesus' teachings appear to be contradictory. For example, the law is eternally valid (Matt. 5:17–20; Mark 12:28–34), but certain commands are abolished (Matt. 5:31–42; Mark 7:14–23). In other places, it appears that Jesus' expectation of obedience is impossible. For example, he states, "You therefore must be perfect, as your heavenly Father is perfect" (Matt. 5:48). And it's not just outward obedience that is required: even inward obedience including one's motives is demanded (Matt. 5:3–8; 12:33–37; 23:35–36; Luke 11:33–36). Finally, it is possible that some of Jesus' teachings are binding only on certain individuals. For example, Jesus tells the rich young ruler to "go, sell all that you have and give to the poor" (Mark 10:21) but he doesn't specifically require that of everyone.

You cannot serve both the Father and money – Luke 16:13We have probably all heard this one before and yet most of us have probably spend a good part of our lives living like it isn't true. Jesus makes it *very* clear that it is not possible for us to fully love and serve the Father and money at the same time. We must choose. If we choose to love our money, our stuff, and our jobs that provide us with money more than we love serving the Father and doing gospel ministry – we might as well declare to the Lord that we don't *really* worship and serve him because we'd rather serve our money.

Love and pray for your enemies Luke 6:27-28,35. An enemy is a person who is actively opposed or hostile to something. As Christians, our "enemies" are therefore many. Jesus not only encourages, but commands that his followers both love *and* pray for those who are hostile and actively opposed to everything that they stand for. Are you regularly praying for and seeking to do good to those who are actively fighting against religious freedom in America? Those who seek to kill Christians worldwide? Those who post on **Facebook** about the Father's "non-existence" and ridicule and condemn all who believe in such "nonsense"? In recent months it has become more clear to me than ever how many Christians in our country seem to think that evangelism means condemning the unbelieving world.

Jesus doesn't command us to sit on our computers and condemn those who disagree with our beliefs or are even hostile and actively opposed-instead he commands us to pray for them and do good to them.

Turn the other cheek – Luke 6:29. When was the last time someone hurt you or insulted you? I don't mean called you a name, I mean *really* hurt you. How did you respond? For most people, our natural response is either to lash out and strike back or run away. But Jesus commands his disciples to fight the natural response and instead to simply take the beating, absorb the insult, and respond with kindness and love. Paul hints at this when he writes about Christians suing one another he says, *"Why not rather suffer wrong? He further added, why not rather be defrauded."* instead of striking back and suing a brother in Christ. **Jesus also modelled is throughout his trial, torture, and crucifixion –** *"Father, forgive them, for they know not what they are doing."* **Christians are called to be hurt, wronged, defrauded, cheated, abused, and get hit on the cheek without retaliation.**

Deny self, take up Christlike suffering – Luke 9:23. In a nutshell, Jesus explains what would-be disciples must do in order to become followers. They must 1) deny themselves, 2) take up their cross (meaning suffering for Jesus), and 3) follow Him. But if we're being honest, many of us think we can jump straight to step 3 without denying ourselves or suffering. Paul writes extensively about Christian suffering in 2 Corinthians. He says, *"Through suffering, our bodies continue to share in the death of Jesus so that the life of Jesus may also be seen in our bodies. Yes, we live under constant danger of death because we serve Jesus, so that the life of Jesus will be evident in our dying bodies."* **Paul is arguing that if we do**

not receive daily suffering for Christ we will not be able to receive daily life with Christ. Suffering brings life. Denying self brings life. Losing our life means finding it. If we are truly, honestly, authentically, sacrificially living a Christ-centred life focused on gospel ministry – there *will* be suffering. Do you suffer on a daily basis for Christ's name and his mission in this world?

Following Jesus is more important even than family Luke 9:57-62, 14:26, 21:16-17. This may be a difficult one to swallow and it is not always easy to explain even for someone who believes it to be true. Following Jesus and preaching the gospel is more important than caring for elderly parents (Luke 9:60). Following Jesus and preaching the gospel is more important than our relationships with our parents, our siblings, or even our spouses and children. Don't believe me? In Luke 14:26 Jesus says, *"If you want to be my disciple, you must, by comparison, hate everyone else your father and mother, wife and children, brothers and sisters yes, even your own life. Otherwise, you cannot be my disciple."* Loving my wife more than I love Jesus prohibits me from being a disciple. Loving my children more than I love Jesus prohibits me from being a disciple. Jesus demands such a strong and resilient love from his disciples that our love for our families must by compassion look like hate. Think about how much you love your closest friends and family. Multiply that significantly and you are only beginning to scratch the surface of how deep your love for Jesus should be.

*It may sound harsh initially, but I believe that loving Jesus first and foremost is the only way to *truly* love our families.

Hell is real and most people are headed there Matthew 7:13, 13:50, 25:46. Many who identify as Christians either don't believe hell is real or don't believe that hell is eternal. Hell is both real and eternal and it will be far worse than even the most creatively sadistic mind could begin to imagine. Jesus spoke more bluntly about the realities of hell than most churches and pastors do today. Even those of us that do believe that hell is real, eternal, and terrible rarely live our lives like we care about the many who are headed there. Jesus said in Matthew 7:13, *"You can enter the Father's Kingdom only through the narrow gate. The highway to hell is broad, and its gate is wide for the many who choose that way."* Many/most of the people around us even the people that we love dearly and have strong relationships with are on the highway to hell. But do we do everything in our power to make sure that doesn't happen? Do we pray every day for the unbelievers in our lives? Do we talk about the Father with them often and purposefully? Do we actually share the good news with them? You may believe that hell is real, eternal, and terrible but do you share the gospel with your friends who are headed there?

We cannot be loved and accepted by both Jesus AND the world Luke 21:17. Jesus told his disciples just days before his death. *"And everyone will hate you because you are my followers."* Paul understood this when he wrote, *"Obviously, I'm not trying to win the approval of people, but of the Father. If pleasing people were my goal, I would not be Christ's servant."* Most of us spend our whole lives trying to find love and acceptance from other people. The way we dress, the hobbies we take up, and the things we spend our money can usually be traced back to us trying to find love and acceptance from the people in our lives. But Jesus warned his disciples against this. If we are living lives that are truly obedient to Christ the world *will* hate us. Being Christ's servant rarely pleases the masses. So many Christians spend their lives trying to have both love and acceptance from both Jesus AND the world. And in the process, many have found acceptance in the world while sacrificing obedience to Christ.

Forgive others or the Father won't forgive you Matthew 6:14-15. Forgiveness isn't always easy, but for Christians, it is always required. We have been forgiven a greater debt than any debt anyone on earth could possibly owe to us. We wronged the Father more severely than anyone could possibly wrong us and yet he forgave us. Jesus said, *"If you forgive those who sin against you, your heavenly Father will forgive you. But if you refuse to forgive others, your Father will not forgive your sins."* If we do not forgive those who wrong us even in the worst possible ways, the Father will not forgive our sins.

Deny Jesus before men, get denied by him before the Father – Luke 12:8-9, Matthew 10:32. We must not be ashamed of Jesus. I always tell my youth group kids when no one will volunteer to pray, "Don't make Jesus that person that you're embarrassed to let everyone else know you're friends with." The point is that we cannot only identify with Christ quietly and internally. Part of following Christ is acknowledging him and identifying with him publicly to the world. Jesus says,*"I tell you the truth, everyone who acknowledges me publicly here on earth, the Son of Man will also acknowledge in the presence of the Father's angels. But anyone who denies me here on earth will be denied before the Father's angels."* Again, many of us might claim to know Jesus and be Christians, but do we tell the whole world that we are? Do we publicly identify with Jesus and associate ourselves with him in spite of the rejection from the

world that it will bring? We should because if we don't, Luke 12:9 will apply to us. These are just a few of the radical teachings of Jesus that so many Christians and churches have either chosen to ignore. What other major, crucial teachings of Christ would you say that many Christians fail to acknowledge regularly?

WAS THE EARLY CHURCH CATHOLIC OR CHRISTIAN?

CHAPTER 6

Protestants often claim that the Church that Jesus founded was the "Christian Church," not the Catholic Church. The biblical evidence cited for this claim is found in the Acts of the Apostles: "So Barnabas went to Tarsus to look for Saul; and when he had found him, he brought him to Antioch. For a whole year they met with the church, and taught a large company of people; and in Antioch the disciples were for the first time called Christians" (Acts 11:25-26).

Many modern Christians then suppose that **the Catholic Church was founded by mere men much later in Christian history**.

No doubt, disciples in the early Church became known as *Christians*. But does this mean that their Church was not the Catholic Church? A little historical study into the church at Antioch reveals that these early Christians' church was, indeed, the Catholic Church.

One of the things Peter did before he went to Rome was to found the church in Antioch, the third largest city in the Roman Empire at the time. **He ordained a disciple there named Evodius to the episcopacy and appointed him the bishop of Antioch.** Evodius is believed by many to have been one of the seventy disciples Jesus appointed to go ahead of him to the towns and places where he taught during his second missionary journey (see Luke 10:1). It was during **Evodius's reign as bishop of Antioch that the disciples there were for the first time called Christians. But this isn't the end of the story!**

While Paul was teaching the Christians in Antioch during Evodius' reign, another young disciple was moving up through the ranks. His name was Ignatius, and he would later become known as Saint Ignatius of Antioch, an early Christian martyr. Ignatius was a disciple of John. Legend has it that, much earlier in his life, *Ignatius was the child whom Jesus took in his arms in a passage recorded by Mark:* Jesus sat down and called the twelve; and he said to them, "If any one would be first, he must be last of all and servant of all." And he took a child, and put him in the midst of them; and taking him in his arms, he said to them, "Whoever receives one such child in my name receives me; and whoever receives me, receives not me but him who sent me." (Mark 11:35-37)

This legend demonstrates the great esteem his memory has enjoyed since the early centuries of the Church.

At Antioch, Ignatius was ordained by Paul, and then, at the end of the reign of Evodius, he was appointed bishop of Antioch by Peter. He reigned there for many years before his martyrdom in Rome. On his way to Rome to be martyred, he wrote several letters to fellow Christians in various locations, expounding on Christian theology. He especially emphasised unity among Christians (see John 17) and **became known as an Apostolic Father of the Church**.

In one of his letters (to Christians in Smyrna), **he wrote, "Where there is Christ Jesus, there is the Catholic**

Church." This is the earliest known written record of the term "Catholic Church" (written around A.D. 107), but Ignatius seemingly used it with the presumption that the Christians of his day were quite familiar with it. In other words, even though his is the earliest known written record of the term, the term likely had been in use for quite some time by then, dating back to the time of the apostles.

The term "Catholic Church" (Gk. *katholike ekklesia*) broadly means "universal assembly," and Ignatius used it when writing to the Christians of Smyrna as a term of unity. He exhorted these Christians to follow their bishop just as the broader universal assembly of Christians follows Christ. He clearly uses the terms "Christian" and "Catholic Church" distinctly: disciples of Christ are Christians; the universal assembly of Christians is the Catholic Church.

Some might claim that Ignatius intended to use the term "Catholic Church" not as a proper name for the Church, but only as a general reference to the larger assembly of Christians. If so, then the universal assembly had no proper name yet, but "Catholic Church" continued in use until it became the proper name of the one church that Christ built on Peter and his successors.

Thus, we see that the Christians of Antioch were part of the Catholic Church. They were indeed *Christian* disciples, but they were also *Catholic*. Given the unbroken chain of succession at Antioch from Peter (sent by Christ) to Evodius to Ignatius if any Christian today wishes to identify with the biblical Christians of the first century mentioned in Acts 11, it follows quite logically that he must also identify Christians' universal assembly: the Catholic Church.

The Roman Empire was primarily polytheistic civilization

The Roman Empire was a primarily polytheistic civilization, which meant that people recognized and worshiped multiple gods and goddesses. Despite the presence of **monotheistic** religions within the empire, such as **Judaism** and early **Christianity**, Romans honoured multiple deities. They believed that these deities served a role in founding the Roman civilization and that they helped shape the events of people's lives on a daily basis. **Romans paid allegiance to the gods both in public spaces and in private homes**. While the Roman state recognized main gods and goddesses by decorating public buildings and fountains with their images, families worshipping at home also put special emphasis on the deities of their choosing.

The gods and goddesses of Greek culture significantly influenced the development of Roman deities and mythology. Due to Rome's geographic position, its citizens experienced frequent contact with the Greek peoples, who had expanded their territories into the Italian peninsula and Sicily. As the Roman Republic was rising to prominence, it acquired these Greek territories, bringing them under the administration of the Roman state. Romans adopted many aspects of Greek culture, adapting them slightly to suit their own needs. For example, many of the gods and goddesses of Greek and Roman culture share similar characteristics. However, these deities were renamed and effectively rebranded for a Roman context, possessing names that are different from their Greek counterparts.

The main god and goddesses in Roman culture were Jupiter, Juno, and Minerva. Jupiter was a sky-god who Romans believed oversaw all aspects of life; he is thought to have originated from the Greek god Zeus. Jupiter also

concentrated on protecting the **Roman state. Military commanders would pay homage to Jupiter at his temple after winning in battle.**

Juno was Jupiter's wife and sister. She resembled the Greek goddess Hera in that she kept a particularly watchful eye over women and all aspects of their lives. Minerva was the goddess of wisdom and craft. **She watched over schoolchildren** and craftspeople such as carpenters and stonemasons. Minerva is thought to be the equivalent of the **goddess Athena, who was the Greek goddess of wisdom.**

Other Roman gods and goddesses who were adapted from Greek culture include **Venus,** who drew on **Aphrodite, goddess of love; Neptune, a sea god who was inspired by the Greek god Poseidon; Pluto,** who ruled the Roman underworld as the god Hades did in Greek culture; Diana, Roman goddess of the hunt who had her Greek equivalent in Artemis; and Mars, god of war, who was fashioned after the Greek god Ares. Just as the Greeks influenced Roman culture, the Romans inspired the cultural development of later societies. You may by now have noticed that **many of the planets in our solar system were named after Roman deities.**

Rome did have some of its own gods and goddesses who did not trace their origins back to Greek culture. For example, **Janus** was a god with two faces that represented the spirit of passages such as doorways and gates. Believed to preside over **beginnings,** it is fitting that the month of **January is named after Janus. Janus' son was Tiberinu**s, the god of the river Tiber, which runs through the city of Rome.

According to Roman mythology, the gods had a hand in the founding of the city of Rome itself. **Mars, god of wa**r, and a Vestal Virgin named Rhea Silvia were the parents of twin boys, **Romulus and Remus**. Vestal Virgins were not permitted to marry or bear children but were instead to devote their lives to serving Vesta, goddess of the hearth.

It is said that King Amulius ordered that the twins be thrown into the Tiber River as a punishment to Rhea Silvia for betraying her vow of celibacy. Luckily, the boys were rescued from the river by a mother wolf. She helped to raise them until a local couple adopted them.

As the boys grew up, they became important members of the community. They dethroned King Amulius and worked together to establish a new city. In a later argument about the city, however, Romulus killed his brother Remus. Romulus went on to name the city after himself, calling it Rome (or *Roma*).

The presence and influence of gods and goddesses were integral parts of life in the Roman state. The people of Rome built temples to their gods and observed rituals and festivals to honor and celebrate them. Any favourable or unfavourable circumstances in Roman life could be attributed to the mood of certain gods, so people would likewise make offerings to the gods in thanks, or in an attempt to appease their tempers. Unlike many monotheistic religious or spiritual traditions, the Romans gods were seen as caring little about the morality of the Roman people. Rather, their chief concern was being paid tribute through very specific rituals.

We can still recognise traces of the Roman gods and goddesses in the artifacts that remain from the ancient civilization and the art that pays homage to them. Carvings of Janus still survive and statues of Neptune spout water from city fountains. Today we appreciate the stories and mythology built around these deities as insights into **what life was like over 2,700 years ago for the ancient Romans.**

Some common meanings

Carpenter
A person who builds or repairs wooden structures.

Christianity
A religion based on the teachings of Jesus of Nazareth.

circumstance
Condition or situation.

civilization
Complex way of life that developed as humans began to develop urban settlements.

Culture
Learned behaviour of people: including their languages, belief systems, social structures, institutions, and material goods. Also: a group of people that share the same cultural traits and values.

Home Philosophy & Religion

Roman religion, beliefs and practices of the inhabitants of the Italian peninsula from ancient times until the ascendancy of Christianity in the 4th century CE, during a period known as Classical antiquity.

Nature and significance

The Romans, according to the orator and politician Cicero, excelled all other peoples in the unique wisdom that made them realise that everything is subordinate to the rule and direction of the gods. Yet Roman religion was based not on divine grace but instead on mutual trust (*fides*) between god and man. The object of Roman religion was to secure the cooperation, benevolence, and "peace" of the gods (*pax deorum*). The Romans believed that this divine help would make it possible for them to master the unknown forces around them that inspired awe and anxiety (*religio*), and thus they would be able to live successfully. Consequently, there arose a body of rules, the *jus divinum* ("divine law"), ordaining what had to be done or avoided.

These precepts for many centuries contained scarcely any moral element; they consisted of directions for the correct performance of ritual. Roman religion laid almost exclusive emphasis on cult acts, endowing them with all the sanctity of patriotic tradition. Roman ceremonial was so obsessively meticulous and conservative that, if the various partisan accretions that grew upon it throughout the years can be eliminated, remnants of very early thought can be detected near the surface.

This demonstrates one of the many differences between Roman religion and Greek religion, in which such remnants tend to be deeply concealed. The Greeks, when they first began to document themselves, had already gone quite a long way toward sophisticated, abstract, and sometimes daring conceptions of divinity and its relation to man. But the orderly, legalistic, and relatively inarticulate Romans never quite gave up their old practices. Moreover, until the vivid pictorial imagination of the Greeks began to influence them, they lacked the Greek taste for seeing their deities in personalised human form and endowing them with mythology. In a sense, there is no Roman mythology, or scarcely any. Although discoveries in the 20th century, notably in the ancient region of Etruria (between the

Tiber and Arno rivers, west and south of the Apennines), confirm that Italians were not entirely unmythological, their mythology is sparse. What is found at Rome is chiefly only a pseudomythology (which, in due course, clothed their own nationalistic or family legends in mythical dress borrowed from the Greeks). Nor did Roman religion have a creed; provided that a Roman performed the right religious actions, he was free to think what he liked about the gods. And, having no creed, he usually deprecated emotion as out of place in acts of worship.

In spite, however, of the antique features not far from the surface, it is difficult to reconstruct the history and evolution of Roman religion. The principal literary sources, antiquarians such as the 1st-century-BCE Roman scholars Varro and Verrius Flaccus, and the poets who were their contemporaries (under the late Republic and Augustus), wrote 700 and 800 years after the beginnings of Rome. They wrote at a time when the introduction of Greek methods and myths had made erroneous (and flattering) interpretations of the distant Roman past unavoidable. In order to supplement such conjectures or facts as they may provide, scholars rely on surviving copies of the religious calendar and on other inscriptions. There is also a rich, though frequently cryptic, treasure-house of material in coins and medallions and in works of art.

History: Early Roman religion

For the earliest times, there are the various finds and findings of archaeology. But they are not sufficient to enable scholars to reconstruct archaic Roman religion. They do, however, suggest that early in the 1st millennium BCE, though not necessarily at the time of the traditional date for the founding of Rome (753 BCE), Latin and Sabine shepherds and farmers with light plows came from the Alban Hills and the Sabine Hills, and that they proceeded to establish villages at Rome, the Latins on the Palatine Hill and the Sabines (though this is uncertain) on the Quirinal and Esquiline hills. About 620 the communities merged, and *c.* 575 the Forum Romanum between them became the town's meeting place and marke

Special offer for students! Check out our special academic rate and excel this spring semester!

Deification of functions

From such evidence it appears that the early Romans, like many other Italians, sometimes saw divine force, or divinity, operating in pure function and act, such as in human activities like opening doors or giving birth to children, and in nonhuman phenomena such as the movements of the sun and seasons of the soil. They directed this feeling of veneration both toward happenings that affected human beings regularly and, sometimes, toward single, unique manifestations, such as a mysterious voice that once spoke and saved them in a crisis (Aius Locutius). They multiplied functional deities of this kind to an extraordinary degree of "religious atomism," in which countless powers or forces were identified with one phase of life or another. Their functions were sharply defined; and in approaching them it was important to use their right names and titles. If one knew the name, one could secure a hearing. Failing that, it was often best to cover every contingency by admitting that the divinity was "unknown" or adding the precautionary phrase "or whatever name you want to be called" or "if it be a god or goddess."

Veneration of objects

The same sort of anxious awe was extended not only to functions and acts but also to certain objects that inspired a similar belief that they were in some way more than natural. This feeling was aroused, for example, by springs and woods, objects of gratitude in the torrid summer, or by stones that were often believed to be meteorites—*i.e.,* had apparently reached the earth in an uncanny fashion. To these were added products of human action, such as burial places and boundary stones, and inexplicable things, such as Neolithic implements (probably the mysterious meteorites were often these) or bronze shields (artifacts that had strayed in from more advanced cultures).

Jupiter

To describe the powers in these objects and functions that inspired the *horror,* or sacred thrill, the Romans eventually employed the word *numen,* suggestive of a god's nod, *nutus*; though so far there is no evidence that this usage was earlier than the 2nd century BCE. The application of the word spirit to *numen* is anachronistic in regard to early epochs because it presupposes a society capable of greater abstraction. Nor must the term mana, used by Melanesians to describe their own concept of superhuman forces, be introduced too readily. The two societies are not necessarily analogous and, besides, the deduction from such comparisons that the Romans experienced an impersonal, pre-deistic, primordial stage of religion that neatly preceded the personal stage cannot be regarded as correct. On the contrary, from the very earliest times, the supernatural forces that they envisaged included a number of deities in analogous human forms; among them were certain "high gods." Foremost among these was a divinity of the sky, Jupiter, akin to the sky gods of other early Indo-European-speaking peoples, the Sanskrit Dyaus and Greek Zeus. Not yet, probably, a Supreme Being, though superior in some sense to other divine powers, this god of the heavens was easily linked with the forces of function and object, with lightning and weather, or with the uncanny stone that came from on high and was called Jupiter Lapis.

Purpose of sacrifice and magic

These gods and sacred functions and objects seemed charged with power because they were mysterious and alarming. In order to secure their food supply, physical protection, and growth in numbers, the early Romans believed that such forces had to be propitiated and made allies. Sacrifice was necessary. The product sacrificed would revitalise the divinity, which was seen as a power of action and therefore likely to run down unless so revitalised. By this nourishment he or it would become able and ready to fulfil requests. And so the sacrifice was accompanied by the phrase *macte esto!* ("be you increased!").

Prayer was a normal accompaniment of sacrifice, and as a conception of the divine powers gradually developed, it contained varying ingredients of flattery, cajolery, and attempted justification; but it also was compounded by magic—the attempt not to persuade nature, but to coerce it. Though the authorities (*e.g., c.* 451–450 BCE, Law of the Twelve Tables) sought to limit its noxious aspects, magic continued to abound throughout the ancient world. Even official rites remained full of its survivals, notably the annual festival of the Lupercalia and the ritual dances of the Salii in honour of Mars. Romans in historical times regarded magic as an oriental intrusion, but Italian tribes, such as the Marsi and Paeligni, were famous for such practices. Among them curses figured prominently, and curse inscriptions from *c.* 500 BCE onward have been found in large numbers. There were also numerous survivals of taboo, a negative branch of magic: people were admonished to have no dealings with strangers, corpses, newborn children, spots struck by lightning, etc., lest harm would befall them.

Religion in the Etruscan period

The apparent amalgamation of the Latin and Sabine villages of Rome coincided with, or more probably was soon followed by, a period in which Rome was under the control of at least one dynasty (the Tarquins) from Etruria, north of the Tiber (*c.* 575–510 BCE, though some scholars would extend this domination to *c.* 450).

Importance of ritual

The Etruscans felt profound religious anxieties and were more devoted to ritual than any other people of the ancient Western world. Though sources are, again, late and unsatisfactory, it appears that they possessed a comprehensive collection of rules regulating these rites. Etruscan culture was heavily based on influences from Greece in its orientalising period, conveyed mainly through Greek centres (such as Cumae) in Campania, colonized by Euboeans, who were also prominent in Syrian markets. But the religion of Etruria proclaims a very un-Greek view of the abasement and nonentity of man before the gods and their will.

To the Etruscans the whole fanatical effort of life was directed toward forcing their deities, led by Tinia or Tin (Jupiter), to yield up their secrets by divination. They saw an intimate link existing between heaven and earth, which seemed to echo one another within a unitary system, and they were more ambitious than either Greeks or Romans in their claims to foretell the future. They also formed an exceptionally complex, rich, and imaginative picture of the afterlife. The living were perpetually obsessed by their care for the dead, expressed in elaborate, magnificently equipped and decorated tombs and lavish sacrifices. For, in spite of beliefs in an underworld, or Hades, there was also a conviction that the individuality of the dead somehow continued in their mortal remains; and it was therefore imperative that they take pleasure in their graves or tombs and not return to haunt the living. From the 4th century BCE onward, after the Etruscans had lost their political power to Rome, their art depicts horrors indicating an increasing fear of what death might bring.

Influence on Roman religion

The Roman religion continued to display certain obvious debts to the period when the city had been under Etruscan control. It is true that the Roman shades (Di Manes) were much less substantial than the fantastic Etruscan conceptions and, although Etruscan divination by the liver and entrails survived and later became increasingly fashionable in Rome, Roman diviners in general, products of a more realistic and prosaic society, never aspired to such precise information about the future as the Etruscans had hoped to gain. Yet, it was the Etruscans who first gave a vigorous definition to Italian religious forms. Indeed, many of the religious features that patriotic historians preferred to ascribe to the mythical King Numa Pompilius (who was supposed to have been Romulus' Sabine successor in the 8th century BCE the man of peace following the man of war) date, in fact, from the period of Etruscan domination two centuries later. Nevertheless, Romans acknowledged a debt to Etruria that included much ceremony and ritual and the plan, appearance, and decoration of a number of temples, notably the great shrine of the Capitoline Triad, Jupiter, Juno, and Minerva. The Romans also were indebted to the Etruscans for their first statues of gods, including the cult image of Jupiter commissioned from an Etruscan for the Capitoline temple. Such statuary, showing the gods in human shape, encouraged the Romans to think of their gods in this way, with the consequent possibility of investing them with myths, which thereafter gradually accumulated around them in the form of Hellenic stories ofteinfused with a native patriotic element.

Jupiter and Juno on Mount Ida, oil on canvas by Charles-Antoine Coypel.

Above all, Rome owed to its Etruscan kings its religious calendar. In addition to poetical works discussing the calendar in antiquarian fashion, such as the *Fasti* of Ovid, there are extant fragments of about 40 copies of the calendar itself, in a revised shape established by Julius Caesar. Besides the Julian revision, there is an incomplete pre-Caesarian, Republican calendar, the Fasti Antiates, discovered at Antium (Anzio); it dates from after 100 BCE. It is possible to detect in these calendars much that is very ancient, including a **pre-Etruscan 10-month solar year**. However, the basis of the calendars, in their surviving form, is later, since it consists of **an attempt to reconcile the solar and lunar year, in accordance with Babylonian calculations.** This endeavour belongs to the period of Etruscan domination of Rome for example, the names of the months April and June (in their Roman form) come from Etruria. Moreover, the presence or absence of certain festivals permits a dating approximating to the time of Etruscan domination in the later 6th century BCE.

Additional modifications were introduced in the following century and again when the calendar was subsequently published (30 BCE).

The festivals it records, of which the earliest are indicated in large letters, reflect a period of transition between country and town life. Though local cult continued to remain active, many forms of worship hitherto maintained by families and farms had now been taken over by the comparatively mature Roman state. The state management blocked any tendency toward spiritualization and removed the need for any vigorous individual participation; however, by ensuring that the gods were conciliated by a schedule corresponding to the regular process of nature, it made the individual citizens feel for centuries that relations with the supernatural were being maintained safely.

Religion in the early Republic

Even if, as tradition records, a coup d'état dislodged the Etruscan kings before 500 BCE, in the first half of the 5th century there was no weakening of trade relations with Etruria. Its southern cities, such as Caere (Cerveteri) and Veii close to Rome, had long used the Greek city of Cumae as a commercial outlet, converting it into an important grain supplier. And now Rome, faced with a shortage of grain, arranged for it to be imported from Cumae. The same city also influenced the foundation of Roman temples in the Greek style. Rome, which had already become accustomed to Greek religious customs in the Etruscan epoch, now showed a willingness to absorb them. This forms a strange contrast to its deeply ingrained religious conservatism. Moreover, at some quite early stage (though there is no positive evidence of the practice until the 3rd century), Romans borrowed from elsewhere in Italy a special ritual (*evocatio*) for inviting the patron deities of captured towns to abandon their homes and migrate to Rome.

In an emergency in 399 BCE, during a difficult siege of Veii, Rome carried Hellenization further by importing a Greek rite in which, as an appeal to emotional feeling, images of pairs of gods were exhibited on couches before tables spread with food and drink; this rite (*lectisternium*) was designed to make them Rome's welcome guests. From the same century onward, if not earlier, pestilences were averted by another ritual (*supplicatio*), in which the whole populace went around the temples and prostrated themselves in Greek fashion. Later the custom was extended to the celebration of victories.

Religion in the later Republic: crises and new trends

The *lectisternium* was repeated, with increased elaboration and pomp, in 217 BCE during a period in which emotional religion was running rampant because of Hannibal's invasion of Italy in the Second Punic War. Faced with a flood of fears and anxieties and reports of many alarming and extraordinary events, Rome took precautions to secure the favour of all manner of gods. Among them, as a desperate attempt at novelty when appeals to the usual deities seemed stale, was the introduction of the Great Mother of Asia Minor, Cybele (204 BCE). Eighteen years later, the equally orgiastic worship of Dionysus (Bacchus) was coming in so rapidly and violently, by way of southern Italy, that the Senate, scenting subversion, repressed its practitioners. But these and other mystery religions, promising initiation, afterlife, and an excitement that Roman national cults could not provide, had come to stay and, although there were long periods of official disapproval before acclimatisation was completed, they gradually played an immense part upon the religious scene. Eastern astrology, too, became extremely popular. It was based on the conviction that, since there is cosmic sympathy between the earth and other heavenly bodies, and since, therefore, the emanations of these bodies influence the earth, men must learn how to foresee their dictates and outwit them.

Astrological practices received encouragement from Stoic philosophy, which was introduced to Rome in the 2nd and early 1st centuries BCE, notably by Panaetius and Poseidonius. The Stoics saw this pseudoscience as proof of the Platonic unity of the universe. Stoicism affected Roman religious thinking in at least three other ways. First, it had a deterministic effect, encouraging a widespread belief in Fate and also, somewhat illogically, in Fortune, both of which were revered in other parts of the Mediterranean and Middle Eastern world. Second, Stoicism infused a new spirituality into religious thinking by its insistence that the human soul is part of the universal spirit and shares its divinity. Third, the moral implication of this, as the Stoics pointed out, was that all men are brothers and must treat each other accordingly. This demonstration struck a chord in the psychology of the Romans, who possessed strongly ethical inclinations and now, at last, saw this trend supported and justified by a philosophical sanction that their formalistic religion had not provided. In changing times of imperialism, materialism, and widespread heart-searching, the state religion had failed to fill the vacuum, and philosophy stepped in instead. At the same time the negative approach of Roman religion to the afterlife was counteracted by an influx of speculations that blended theology, mysticism, and magic and claimed the mythical Orpheus and the part historical, part legendary Pythagoras as prophets.

While their national poet Ennius helped to diffuse such beliefs, he and the comic dramatist Plautus ridiculed the traditional Roman gods on the stage. The upper-class attitude of the times was expressed by the historian Polybius, the priestly lawyer Scaevola, the scholarly Varro, and the orator and philosopher Cicero, who maintained that the importance of religion was political, residing in its power to keep the multitude under control, to prevent social chaos, and to promote patriotic feeling.

After the prolonged horrors of civil war had ended (30 BCE), the victorious Octavian, the adoptive son of the dictator Caesar and founder of the imperial regime or principate, decided, correctly, that the ancient religion was far from dead and that the restoration of all its forms would respond to a strong popular, instinctive belief that the disasters of the past generations had been due to the neglect of religious duties.

The imperial cult

Octavian himself took the name Augustus, a term indicating a claim to reverence. This did not make him a god in his lifetime, but, combined with the insertion of his *numen* and his *genius* (originally the procreative power that enables a family to be carried on) into certain cults, it prepared the way for his posthumous deification, just as Caesar had been deified before him. Both were deified by the state because they seemed to have given Rome gifts worthy of a god. From earliest times in Greece there had been an idea that, if someone saved you, you should pay him the honours you would offer to a god. Alexander the Great and his successors had demanded reverence as divine saviours, and Ptolemy II Philadelphus of Egypt introduced a cult of his own living person. The Stoic belief that the human soul was part of the world soul was a corollary of the view that great men possessed a larger share of this divine element. Moreover, the 3rd-century-BCE mythographer Euhemerus had elaborated a theory that the gods themselves had once been human; this idea was readily adapted to the supposed careers of Heracles (Hercules) and the Dioscuri (Castor and Polydeuces; and the Romans applied it to their own gods Saturn and Quirinus, the latter identified with the national founder, Romulus, risen to heaven. And so it became customary if emperors (and empresses) were approved of in their lives to raise them to divinity after their deaths. They were called *divi,* not *dei* like the Olympian gods; the latter were prayed to, but the former were regarded with veneration and gratitude.

As the empire proceeded and the old religion seemed more and more irrelevant to people's personal preoccupations and successive national emergencies, the cult of the *divi,* subsequently grouped together in a single Hall of Fame, remained foremost among the patriotic cults that were increasingly encouraged as unifying forces. Concentrating on the protectors of the emperor and the nation, they included the worship of Rome herself, and of the *genius* of the Roman people; for the army a number of special military celebrations are recorded on the Calendar of Doura-Europus in Mesopotamia (Feriale Duranum, *c.* 225–27 CE). As for the ruling emperors, they were more and more frequently treated as divine, with varying degrees of formality, and officially they often were compared with gods. As monotheistic tendencies grew, however, this custom led not so much to their identification with the gods as to the doctrine that they were the elect of the divine powers, who were defined as their companions (*comites*). In pursuance of this way of thinking, as official paganism approached its last days, the emperors Diocletian and Maximian took the names Jovius and Herculius, respectively, after their Companions and Patrons Jupiter and Hercules.

Introduction of Christianity and Mithraism

By now, however, the humanistic idea that men could become gods had ceased to have any plausibility. Plotinus and his Neoplatonism, the dominant philosophy of the pagan world from the mid-3rd century CE, had given powerful, mystical shape to the Platonic and Stoic conception that the universe is governed by a single force. On the other hand, the greatest religious figure of the century, the Iranian Mani, who had started to preach in Mesopotamia *c.* 240, dramatically preached the opposing dualistic idea that the world is the creation not only of a good power but of an evil one as well. Mani's church, which alarmed Diocletian and for a time attracted the great Christian theologian St. Augustine, absorbed many of the innumerable cults of Gnostics who claimed special knowledge (*gnōsis*) by illumination and revelation and taught how people can purge the nonspiritual from within themselves and escape their earthly prison. More impressively, the cult of the Persian Mithra blended the dualism of Mani with the emotional initiations of the mystery religions (corrected by a much sterner tone of moral endeavour) and became a strong link between **the cult of the Sun** (which appealed to contemporary monotheists) and the fashionable revulsion from the senses that was shortly to lead to Christian monasticism. Like Christianity, Mithraism had its sacraments; but the life of Mithra exercised a less far-reaching appeal than **the life of Christ, and Mithra's cult excluded women.**

Christianity, unique in its universal charity and unique also in its demand for a noble effort of faith in Jesus' blend of divinity and humanity, was the religion that prevailed in the Roman world. It satisfied the emperor Constantine's impulsive need for divine support, and from AD 312 CE onward, by a complex and gradual process, it became the official religion of the empire.

The survival of Roman religion

For a time, coins and other monuments continued **to link Christian doctrines with the worship of the Sun, to which Constantine had been addicted previously**. But even when this phase came to an end, **Roman paganism continued to exert other, permanent influences, great and small**. **The emperors passed on to the popes the title of chief priest,** *pontifex maximus*. The saints, with their distribution of functions, often seemed to perpetuate the many *numina* of ancient tradition. *The ecclesiastical calendar retains numerous remnants of pre-Christian festivals—notably Christmas, which blends elements including both the feast of the Saturnalia and the birthday of Mithra.* But, most of all, **the mainstream of Western Christianity owed ancient Rome the firm discipline** that gave it stability and shape, combining insistence on established forms with the possibility of recognising that novelties need not be excluded, since they were implicit from the start.

Beliefs, practices, and institutions.

The earliest divinities

The legend of Libra, explained: Libra is the seventh sign of the zodiac and is said to govern from about September 22 to about October 23.(more). The early Romans, like other Italians, worshiped not only purely functional and local forces but also certain high gods. Chief among them was the **sky god Jupiter**, whose cult, at first limited to the communities around the Alban Hills, later gained Rome as an adherent. The Romans gave Jupiter his own priest (*flamen*), and the fact that there were two other senior *flamines,* devoted to Mars and Quirinus, confirms other indications that the cults of these three deities, envisaged perhaps in some sort of association, belonged to a very early stratum (though the theory of their correspondence to the three-class social division of the early Indo-European-speaking peoples is generally unacceptable). Mars, whose name may or may not be Indo-European, was a high god of many Italian peoples, as liturgical bronze tablets found at Iguvium (Gubbio), the Tabulae Iguvinae (*c.* 200–*c.* 80 BCE), confirm, protecting them in war and defending their agriculture and animals against disease. Later, he was identified with **the Greek god of war, Ares,** and also was regarded as the father of Romulus. Mars Gradivus presided over the beginning of a war and MarQuirinus over its end, but earlier Quirinus had apparently, as a separate deity, been the patron of the Quirinal village before its amalgamation with the Palatine; subsequently he was believed to have been the god that Romulus became when he ascended into heaven.

Janus

Two-headed Janus, who sees forward and backward, a personification of the month of January; Romanesque high-relief stone sculpture, in the Museo del Duomo

Two other forces that belong to an early phase were Janus and Vesta, the powers of the door and hearth, respectively. Janus, who had no Greek equivalent, was worshiped beside the Forum in a small shrine with double doors at either end and originated either from a divine power that regulated the passage over running water or rather, perhaps, from sacred doorways like those found on the art of Bronze Age Mycenae. Janus originally stood for the magic of the door of a private house or hut and later became a part of the state religion. The gates of his temple were formally closed when the state was at peace, a custom going back to the primitive war magic that required armies to march out to battle by this properly sanctified route. Vesta, too, passed from the home to the state, always retaining a circular temple reminiscent of the primitive huts whose form can be reconstructed from traces left in the earth and from surviving funerary urns. Vesta's shrine contained the eternal fire, but the absence of a statue indicates that it preceded the anthropomorphic period; its correspondence with the Indian *garhapatya,* "house-father's fire," suggest an origin prior to the time of the differentiation of the Indo-European-speaking peoples. The cultic site just outside the area of the primitive Palatine settlement indicates that there had been a form of fire worship even earlier than Vesta's (dedicated to the deity Caca) on the Palatine itself. The cult of Vesta, tended by her Virgins, continued to flourish until the end of antiquity, endowed with an important role in the sacred protectorship of Rome.

Vesta and Vestal Virgins

Vesta (seated on the left) with Vestal Virgins, classical relief sculpture; in the Palermo Museum, Italy, The Di Manes, collective powers (later "spirits") of the dead, may mean "the good people," an anxious euphemism like the Greek name of "the kindly ones" for the Furies. As a member of the family or clan, however, the dead man or woman would, more specifically, be one of the Di Parentes; reverence for ancestors was the core of Roman religious and social life. Di Indigetes was a name given collectively to these forebears, as well as to other deified powers or spirits who likewise controlled the destiny of Rome. For example, the name Indiges is applied to Aeneas, whose mythical immigration from Troy led to the eventual foundation of the city. According to an inscription of the 4th century BCE (found at Tor Tignosa, 15 miles south of Rome), Aeneas is also called Lar, which indicates that the Lares, too, were originally regarded as divine ancestors and not as deities who presided over the farmland. The Lares were worshiped wherever properties adjoined, and inside every home their statuettes were placed in the domestic shrine (*lararium*). Under state control they moved from boundaries of properties to crossroads (where Augustus eventually associated his own *genius* with the cult) and were worshiped as the guardian spirits of the whole community (Lares Praestites). The cult of the Di Penates likewise moved from house to state. From very early times the Penates, the powers that ensured that there was enough to eat, were worshiped in every home. They also came to be regarded as national protectors, the Penates Publici. Originally they were synonymous with the Dioscuri. The legend that they had been brought to Italy by Aeneas with his followers from Troy was imported from Lavinium (Pratica di Mare) when the early Romans incorporated that town into their own state.

The divinities of the later Regal period

Diana the Huntress **Diana the Huntress, oil on canvas by an anonymous artist of the school of Fontainebleau, c. 1550; in the Louvre, Paris.(more). Two other deities whose Roman cults tradition attributed to the period of the kings were Diana and Fors Fortuna. Diana, an Italian wood goddess worshiped at Aricia (Ariccia) in Latium and prayed to by women who wanted children, was in due course identified with the Greek Artemis.**

Her temple on the Aventine Hill (*c.* 540 BCE) with its statue, an imitation of a Greek model from Massilia (Marseille), was based on the Temple of Artemis of Ephesus. By establishing such a sanctuary, the Roman monarch Servius Tullius hoped to emulate the Pan-Ionian League among the Latin peoples. Fors Fortuna, whose temple across the Tiber from the city was one of the few that slaves could attend, was similar to the oracular shrines of Fortuna at Antium (Anzio) and Praeneste (Palestrina). Originally a farming deity, she eventually represented luck. She came to be identified with Tyche, the patroness of cities and goddess of Fortune among the Hellenistic Greeks.

Juno

Juno, classical sculpture; in the National Archaeological Museum, Naples. In Roman tradition, Servius Tullius reigned between two Etruscan kings, Tarquinius Priscus and Tarquinius Superbus. The Etruscan kings began and perhaps finished the most important Roman temple, devoted to the cult of the Capitoline Triad, Jupiter, Juno, and Minerva (the dedication was believed to have taken place in 509 or 507 BCE after the expulsion of the Etruscans). Such triads, housed in temples with three chambers (*cellae*), were an Etruscan institution. But the grouping of these three Roman deities seems to be owed to Greek anthropomorphic ideas, since Hera and Athena, with whom Juno and Minerva were identified, were respectively the wife and daughter of Zeus (Jupiter). In Italy, Juno (Uni in Etruscan) was sometimes the warlike high goddess of a town (*e.g.,* Lanuvium [Lanuvio] in Latium), but her chief function was to supervise the life of women, and particularly their sexual life. The functions of Minerva concerned craftsmen and reflected the growing industrial life of Rome. Two gods with Etruscan names, both worshiped at open altars before they had temples in Rome, were Vulcan and Saturn, the former a fire god identified with the Greek blacksmiths' deity Hephaestus, and the latter an agricultural god identified with Cronus, the father of Zeus. Saturn was worshiped in Greek fashion, with head uncovered.

Commodus

The focal point of the cult of Hercules was the Great Altar (Ara Maxima) in the cattle market, just inside the boundaries of the primitive Palatine settlement. The altar may be traced to a shrine of Melkart established by traders from Phoenicia in the 7th century BCE. The name of the god, however, was derived from the Greek Heracles, whose worship spread northward from southern Italy, brought by traders who venerated his journeys, his labours, and his power to avert evil. In a market frequented by strangers, a widely recognized divinity of this type was needed to keep the peace. The Greek cult, at first private, perhaps dates from the 5th century BCE.

Ceres and Cupid

An important series of temples was founded early in the 5th century BCE. The completion of the temple of the Etruscan Saturn was attributed to this time (497). A shrine honouring the twin horsemen, the Dioscuri (Castor and Pollux), was also built in this period. An inscription from Lavinium describing them by the Greek term *kouroi* indicates a Greek origin (from southern Italy) without Etruscan mediation. In legend, the Dioscuri had helped Rome to victory in a battle against the Latins at Lake Regillus, and in historic times, on anniversaries of that engagement, they continued to preside over the annual parade of knights (*equites*). From southern

Italy, too, came the cult of Ceres, whose temple traditionally was vowed in 496 and dedicated in 493. Ceres was an old Italian deity who presided over the generative powers of nature and came to be identified with Demeter, the Greek goddess of grain. She owed her installation in Rome to the influence of the Greek colony of Cumae, from which the Romans imported grain during a threatened famine. The association of Ceres at this temple with two other deities, Liber (a fertility god identified with Dionysus) and Libera (his female counterpart), was based on the triad at Eleusis in Greece. The Roman temple, built in the Etruscan style but with Greek ornamentation, stood beside a Greek trading centre on the Aventine Hill and became a rallying ground for the plebeians, the humbler section of the community who were hard hit by the grain shortage at this time and who were pressing for their rights against the patricians.

Lorenzo Bernini: *Apollo and Daphne*

Cumae also played a part in the introduction of Apollo. The Sibylline oracles housed in Apollo's shrine at Cumae allegedly were brought to Rome by the last Etruscan kings. The importation of the cult (431 BCE) was prescribed by the Sibylline Books at a time when Rome, as on earlier occasions, had requested Cumae for help with grain. The Cumaean Apollo, however, was primarily prophetic, whereas the Roman cult, introduced at a time of epidemic, was concerned principally with his gifts as a healer. This role may possibly have been derived from the Etruscans, whose Apollo is known from a superb statue of *c.* 500 BCE from Veii, Etruria's nearest city to Rome. In 82 BCE the Sibylline Books were destroyed and replaced by a collection assembled from various sources. Later, Augustus elevated Apollo as the patron of himself and his regime, intending thereby to convert the brilliant Hellenic god of peace and civilization to the glory of Rome.

Tinted Venus

Unlike Apollo, Aphrodite did not keep her name when she became identified with an Italian deity. Instead, she took on the name Venus, derived, without complete certainty, from the idea of *venus,* "blooming nature" (the derivation from *venia,* "grace," seems less likely). She gained greatly in significance because of the legend that she was the mother of Aeneas, the ancestor of Rome, whom statuettes of the 5th century BCE from Veii show escaping from Troy with his father and son. From the time of the Punic Wars 200 years later the Trojan legend grew, for long before the 1st-century-BCE dictators Sulla and Caesar claimed Venus as their ancestor, the story was interpreted as the preface to the Carthaginian struggle.

A number of gods were spoken of as possessing accompaniments, often in the feminine gender; *e.g.,* Lua Saturni and Moles Martis. These attachments, sometimes spoken of as cult partners, were not the wives of the male divinities but rather expressed a special aspect of their power or will. A similar origin could be ascribed to the worship of divine powers representing "qualities." Fides ("Faith" or "Loyalty"), for example, may at first have been an attribute or aspect of a Latin-Sabine god of oaths, Semo Sanctus Dius Fidius; and in the same way Victoria may come from Jupiter Victor. Some of these concepts were worshiped very early, such as Ops ("Plenty," later associated with Saturn and equated with Hebe), and Juventas (who watched over the men of military age). The first of these qualities to receive a temple, as far as is known, is Concordia (367), in celebration of the end of civil strife. Salus (health or well-being) followed in *c.* 302, Victoria in *c.* 300, Pietas (dutifulness to family and gods, later exalted by Virgil as the whole basis of Roman religion) in 191. The Greeks, too, from the earliest days, had clothed such qualities in words; *e.g.,* Shame, Peace, Justice, and Fortune. In the Hellenic world they had a wide variety of signification, ranging from full-fledged divinity to nothing more than abstractions. But in early Rome and Italy they were in no sense abstractions or allegories and were likewise not thought of as possessing the anthropomorphic shape that the term personification might imply. They were things, objects of worship, like many other functions that were venerated. They were external divine forces working upon humans and affecting them with the qualities that their names described. Later on, under philosophical (particularly Stoic) influences that flooded into ethically minded Rome, they duly took their place as moral concepts, the Virtues and Blessings which abounded for centuries and were depicted in human form on Roman coinage as part of the imperial propaganda.

The Sun and stars

Little or no contribution to cosmology was made in the Roman world, and the demonstration of Aristarchus of Samos (*c.* 270 BCE) that the Earth revolves around the Sun received virtually no support. The complicated geocentric interpretation that held sway in Rome was summed up in Cicero's *Dream of Scipio*. It formed the basis for the concept of the solar system on which the popular pseudoscience of astrology was founded, the Sun being regarded as the centre of the concentric planetary spheres encircling the Earth— not the centre of the cosmos in the sense of Aristarchus but its heart. From the 5th century BCE onward this **solar god** was identified with Apollo in his role as the supreme dispenser of agricultural wealth. Possessor of a sacred grove at Lavinium, Sol Indiges was regarded as one of the divine ancestors of Rome. During the last centuries before the Christian era, worship of the **Sun spread throughout the Mediterranean world** and formed the principal rallying point of paganism's last years. Closely associated with the **sun cult was that of** Mithra, the Sun's ally and agent who was elevated to partake of communion and the love feast as the god's companion. Sun worship was popular in the army, and particularly on the Danube. Aurelian, one of the great military emperors produced by that area in the 3rd century, built a magnificent temple of Sol Invictus (the "**Unconquered Sun**") at Rome (274). Constantine the Great declared the Sun his Comrade on empire-wide coinages and devoted himself to the cult until he adopted Christianity in its stead.

Priests

Precedence among **Roman priests belonged to the** *rex sacrorum* ("king of the sacred rites"), who, after the expulsion of the kings, took over the residue of their religious powers and duties that had not been assumed by the Republican officers of state. Nevertheless, the hold exercised by the *rex sacrorum* and his colleagues was weakened by the Law of the Twelve Tables (*c.* 451–450 BCE), which displayed the secular arm exercising some control over sacral law. **As late as *c.* 275 BCE the religious calendar was still dated by the *rex sacrorum* but by this time he was already fading** into the background.

Very early origins can also be attributed to some of the *flamines,* the priests of certain specific cults, and particularly to the three major *flamines* of Jupiter, Mars, and Quirinus. Jupiter's priest, the *flamen dialis,* was encompassed by an extraordinary series of taboos, some dating to the Bronze

Age, which made it difficult to fill the office in historic times.

Except for the *rex sacrorum* and *flamen dialis,* whose duties were unusually professional and technical, almost all Roman priesthoods were held by men prominent in public life. The social distinction and political prestige carried by these part-time posts caused them to be keenly fought for.

There were four chief colleges, or boards, of priests: the *pontifices, augures, quindecimviri sacris faciundis and epulones.* Originally three, and finally 16 in number, the *pontifices* (whose name may recall antique tasks and magic rites in connection with bridges) had assumed control of the religious system by the 3rd century BCE. The chief priest, the *pontifex maximus* (the head of the state clergy), was an elected official and not chosen from the existing *pontifices.* The *augures,* whose name may have been **derived from the practice of magic in fertility rites** and perhaps meant "increasers," had the task of discovering **whether or not the gods approved of an action.** This they performed mainly **by interpreting divine signs** in the movements of birds (*auspicia*). Such divination was elevated, perhaps under Etruscan influence, into an indispensable preliminary to state acts, though the responsibility for the decision rested not with the priests but with the presiding state officials, who were said to "possess the auspices." In private life too, even as late as Cicero and Horace in the 1st century BCE, important courses of action were often preceded by consultation of the heavens. The Etruscan method of divining from the liver and entrails of animals (*haruspicina*) became popular in the Second Punic War, though its practitioners (who numbered 60 under the empire) never attained an official priesthood.

Of the other two major colleges, the *quindecimviri* ("Board of Fifteen," who earlier had been 10 in number) *sacris faciundis* looked after foreign rites, and the members of the other body, the *epulones,* supervised religious feasts. There were also *fetiales,* priestly officials who were concerned with various aspects of international relationships, such as treaties and declarations of war. Also six Vestal Virgins, chosen as young girls from the old patrician families, tended the shrine and fire of Vesta and lived in the House of Vestals nearby, amid a formidable array of prehistoric taboos.

Shrines and temples

The Roman calendar, as introduced or modified in the period of the Etruscan kings, contained 58 regular festivals. These included 45 Feriae Publicae, celebrated on the same fixed day every year, as well as the Ides of each month, which were sacred to Jupiter, and the Kalends of **March, which belonged to Mars**. Famous examples of Feriae Publicae were the Lupercalia **(February 15)** and **Saturnalia (December 17**, later extended). There were also the Feriae Conceptivae, the dates of which were fixed each year by the proper authority, and which included the Feriae Latinae ("Latin Festival") celebrated in the Alban Hills, usually at the end of **April**.

Templum is a term derived from Etruscan divination. First of all, it meant an area of the sky defined by the priest for his collection and interpretation of the omens. Later, by a projection of this area onto the earth, it came to signify a piece of ground set aside and consecrated to the gods. At first such areas did not contain sacred buildings, but there often were altars on such sites, and later shrines. In Rome, temples have been identified from *c.* 575 BCE onward, including not only **the round shrine of Vesta** but also a group in a sacred area (S. Omobono), close to the river Tiber beside the cattle market (Forum Boarium). The great Etruscan temples, made of wood with terra-cotta ornaments, were constructed later and culminated in the temple of the Capitoline Triad. Subsequently, more solid materials, such as tuff (tufa), travertine, marble, cement, and brick, gradually came into use. Temple <u>archives</u>, now vanished, play a large part in the historical tradition, and the anniversaries of the vows to build the temples and their dedication were scrupulously remembered and celebrated on numerous coins.

<u>Sacrifice</u> and burial rites

The characteristic offering of the Romans was a **sacrifice accompanied by a prayer or vow. (The Triumph, associated with Jupiter, was regarded as a thanksgiving in discharge of a vow.) Animal sacrifices were re**garded as more effective than anything else, **the pig being the commonest victim, with sheep and ox** added on important occasions. Considered best of all were the **basic elements of life: heart, liver, and kidneys**. <u>**Human sacrifice,**</u> on the whole, was extraneous to Roman custom, though its practice among the Etruscans may have contributed to the institution of gladiatorial funeral games in both Etruria and Rome, and it was resorted to in major crises, notably during the Second Punic War (216 BCE). Earlier in the century, perhaps once before, a member of the family of the Decii had given up his life by self-sacrifice (*devotio*) in a critical battle.

Although ancestors were meticulously revered, there was nothing resembling the <u>comprehensive</u> Etruscan attention to the <u>dead</u>. In spite of elaborate philosophising by Cicero and <u>Virgil</u> about the possibility of some sort of survival of the <u>soul</u> (especially for the deserving), most Romans' ideas of the <u>afterlife</u>, unless they believed in the promises of the mystery religions, were vague. Such ideas often amounted to a cautious hope or fear that the spirit in some sense lived on, and this was sometimes combined with an anxiety that the ghosts of the dead, especially the young dead who bore the living a grudge, might return and cause harm. Graves and tombs were inviolable, protected by supernatural powers and by taboos. In the earliest days of Rome both <u>cremation</u> and <u>inhumation</u> were practiced simultaneously, but by the 2nd century BCE the former had prevailed. Some 300 years later, however, there was a massive reversion to inhumation, probably because of an inarticulate revival of the feeling that the future welfare of the soul depended on comfortable repose of the body—a feeling that, as sarcophagi show, was fully shared by the adherents of the mystery cults, though, on the rational level, it contradicted their assurance of an afterlife in some spiritual sphere. The designs on these tombs reflect the soul's survival as a personal entity that has won its right to paradise.

Religious art

A vast gallery of architecture, sculpture, numismatics, painting, and mosaics illustrates Roman religion and helps to fill the gaps left by the fragmentary, though extensive, literary and epigraphic record. Starting with primitive statuettes and terra-cotta temple decorations, this array eventually included masterpieces such as the Apollo of Veii. Other works of art, more than 400 years later, include paintings illustrating Dionysiac mysteries at Boscoreale near Pompeii, and the reliefs of Augustus' Ara Pacis at Rome; and with the Christian emblems of Constantinian sarcophagi and coinage a thousand years of ancient Roman religious art comes to an end.

Conclusion

Though Roman religion never produced a comprehensive code of conduct, its early rituals of house and farm engendered a feeling of duty and unity. Its idea of reciprocal understanding **between man and god** not only imparted the sense of security that Romans needed in order **to achieve their successes** but stimulated, by analogy, the concept of mutual obligations and binding agreements between one person and another. Except for rare aberrations, such as human sacrifice, Roman religion was unspoiled by orgiastic rites and savage practices. Moreover—unlike ancient philosophy—it was neither sectarian nor exclusive. It was a tolerant religion, and it would be difficult to think of any other whose adherents committed fewer crimes and atrocities in its name

GOSPEL WRITERS QUOTED JESUS AS GOD FROM THE OLD TESTAMENT

CHAPTER 7

This conclusion chapter accesses the four Synoptic Gospel writers: Mark, John, Mathew and Luke. They referred to Jesus Christ the Saviour as Yahweh the Jewish pagan-God or the Son of Yahweh/God in reference to the Old Testament which refers to Jesus as Yaweh their pagan-God. Although Jesus Christ told His Disciples that He and the Father in Heaven are One, and that no one goes to the Father without through Him.

One possible inference from the use of the Old Testament in the Gospel of Mark is that the author created a new story with the aid of intertextual codes that helped him to communicate his own point of view. The Old Testament quotations and references formed part of the new story that Mark created in order to convince his readers of his point of view concerning Jesus and the implications of Jesus' life, works and words for the prevailing situation.

Mark and Old Testament Context

It is commonly maintained that the Gospel of Mark was originally written in Koine Greek, and that the final text represents a rather lengthy history of growth. For more than a century attempts have been made to explain the origin of the gospel material and to interpret the space between the related events and the final inscripturation of the contents of the Gospel.

C. H. Dodd asserted the earliest Christians shared oral accounts about Jesus but in order to make sense of what looked like failure on the part of Jesus' arrest, trial and crucifixion they were driven to interpret those memories in the light of Scripture. Dodd justified this model of how the stories evolved before becoming part of a written Gospel by pointing to passages in the Acts of the Apostles.

The Dodd camp's viewpoint has resulted in scholarship where the emphasis has been on the growth and not on the making of the Gospel to the extent that certain data beliefs and assumptions concerning the Gospel have become so dominant that very little progress has been made in the history of interpretation of the Gospel (see e.g. Peabody 1987:3ff). However some scholars, following the work of Alfred Suhl, have taken the intertextual production of the written Gospel seriously. The intertextuality of the Gospel of Mark has been recognized by scholars such as Thomas L. Brodie, Willem S. Vorster, Dennis R. MacDonald and Bartosz Adamczewski.

Traditional view

It is normally argued that the followers of Jesus transmitted his words and deeds by telling and retelling things he did and said, in view of the folkloric nature of many of the stories of and about Jesus, the aphoristic character of many of his sayings, the many parables he apparently told his followers, and the role of oral communication in that period.

Therefore, it is probable that Mark was informed about the story of Jesus by way of tradition. It is also probable that his audience would have known these traditions and others, such as the institution of the Lord's Supper, and controversy stories. Thus it is argued that Mark based his written story of Jesus on traditional material which he received and decided to put into written form.

This is also the way in which the origin of the material was explained in the early church. The earliest witness to the authorship of Mark is the quotation from Papias of Hierapolis (c 140 CE) in the history of Eusebius (*Hist Eccl* III 39:15), according to which the Gospel was based on "memory" of the things Peter had told Mark (see Breytenbach 1992).

Karl Ludwig Schmidt asserted that the accounts of the New Testament were to be regarded as fixed written versions of oral Gospel tradition. Using form criticism, Schmidt showed that an editor had assembled the narrative out of individual scenes that did not originally have a chronological order.

Precursor texts and intertextual relationships

In Mark we have a text, written in Greek with different allusions to and quotations from precursor texts. These include parables, miracle stories, controversy stories, bibliographies, stories of cult heroes, speeches about the future, stories of suffering and resurrection stories. In addition Mark apparently knew themes, words, phrases and stories from the Old Testament. He must have had acquaintance with the Elisha cycle and with other performers of miracles. He must also have known the economic, political and other cultural codes of his time. We still do not know exactly how Mark went about creating his story of Jesus — that is, how he made his Gospel, but some scholars such as Willem S. Vorster argue for an intertextual production of the Gospel. Vorster writes:

The relationship between the final text of the Gospel of Mark and precursor and other texts is an intertextual relationship. There is no causal relationship between this new text and the texts out of which Mark made his text. Mark quoted other texts, and his story alludes to other texts and absorbed other texts. This is how his story becomes meaningful and different from other stories with the same theme when the reader interprets Mark's texts in the light of other texts known to him/her.

There is no reason to doubt that the written Gospel of Mark echoes many different precursor texts and intertextual relationships. Other scholars that also argue for the making of the Gospel are:

Burton L. Mack maintains that Mark's Gospel was "not a pious transmission of revered tradition. It was composed at a desk in a scholar's study lined with texts and open to discourse with other intellectuals. In Mark's Study were chains of miracle stories, collections of pronouncement stories." Mack assumes that Mark had different Hellenistic Jewish texts, the Scriptures and other Christian texts in his study as a possible influence in the production of the Markan text in the first century (Mack 1988:322-323).

- Pieter J. J. Botha, on the other hand, maintains that the Mediterranean world of the first century was predominately oral. Mark came from an oral community and his Gospel should be seen as oral literature. Mark told his story of Jesus orally and at some stage dictated it to somebody who wrote down his words. It still bears the signs of oral literature. Per Botha, Mark is taken seriously as the producer of a text and not simply as a conduit through which a stream of tradition flowed, or a (passive) exponent of a community out of which his text arose (Botha 1989:76-77; see also Vorster 1980).

Whereas Matthew and Luke use the Old Testament within a promise-fulfilment scheme, Vorster, following Alfred Suhl, argues that Mark's use of the Old Testament is totally different.

Allusions to and quotations from the Old Testament are usually absorbed into Mark's story in such a manner that, except for a few cases where he specifically mentions the origin of the quotation, the allusions and quotations form part of the story stuff. They are so embedded into the story that, if it were not for the references in the margins and a knowledge of the Old Testament, the reader would not have noticed that Mark uses an allusion or a quotation (see Mk 15:24). This is best seen in Mark's story of the passion of Jesus.

It has often been noticed that psalms of lamentation such as Psalms 22, 38 and 69 concerning the suffering of "the just", are knitted into the passion narrative in such a manner that one can Say that the passion narrative of Mark is narrated in the language of the Old Testament. The point is, however, that the allusions and 'quotations' form such an integral part of the passion narrative that it is impossible for the naïve reader to realize that the text is enriched by its intertextual relationships concerning the suffering of the Just.

In addition to the many studies on the texts behind and in the Gospel of Mark, some scholars that argue for the Gospel as the rewriting of Old Testament stories are:

- Wolfgang Roth sees evidence that suggests Jewish midrashic influence was present in the production of the Gospel (see Roth 1988).

- Dale and Patricia Miller argue that New Testament writers created new "midrashim" on older texts. They argue that Mark did not simply interpret the Old Testament midrashically. Mark created a new midrash, i.e. "midrashim" as new Scripture in typical Jewish fashion. This is another way of seeing the importance of creativity in Mark's Gospel (see Miller & Miller 1990).

Robert M. Price, and Daniel Boyarin have noted the Jewish mode of scriptural interpretation termed midrash, embedded in the Gospel of Mark.

John Shelby Spong also sees a midrashic production of the Gospel, but clarifies his use of the term "midrashic" as "interpretation" or "literary borrowing" which is divergent from the traditional usage of the term "midrash", Spong writes:

I have used the word midrash only as the modifying adjective, midrashic, both to indicate the broadness of the way I am employing this concept and also to leave the word midrash to its special Jewish understanding.

Philip S Alexander holds that in modern usage the term "midrash becomes simply a fancy word for 'Bible interpretation'" and therefore its usage should be discontinued. Nathanael Vette also addresses the problem of definition and sides with those who believe that what is often being labelled as "midrash" is more like the Greco-Roman literary practice of "mimesis", that is, literary imitation, or simply "a creative use of Scriptural material".

A justification for the comparison of the Gospel of Mark with Jewish apocrypha and pseudepigrapha is given by Nathanael Vette, following Devorah Dimant's work "Use and Interpretation of Mikra": that these writings have in common the imitation of the styles and forms of the Old Testament biblical literature and can be read as if they are attempting to imitate that biblical world. Scripture is not primarily addressed directly in order to be explicitly interpreted in these writings but acts as an underlay that helps shape narrative episodes. Vette also borrows from Dimant the terms to describe these two types of Scripture reference: expositional and compositional. Most scholarship has attended to the expositional use of Scriptures in the Gospel of Mark, seeking to explain how the Gospel can be interpreted through its Scriptural references; but Vette seeks to redress that balance by examining the compositional function of biblical texts in the Gospel.

Mark and Old Testament context

A possible conclusion about the use of the Old Testament in the Gospel is that Mark had no respect for the original context of the quotations and allusions to Old Testament writings in his text. This can be seen in the story of John the Baptist at the beginning of the Gospel.

The first quotation (Mk 1:2-3) does not come entirely from Isaiah the prophet, as Mark asserts. It is a composite reference to Exodus 23:20, Malachi 3:1 and Isaiah 40:3 which he connects to Isaiah the prophet. The quotation is taken out of context and worked into his story of John and Jesus in order to show the relationship between the two. The beginning of the Gospel does not prove the fulfilment of the Old Testament, it characterizes John as the predecessor of Jesus. Only at a later stage does the reader realize the resemblance between the apocalyptic John and the apocalyptic Jesus.

John Dominic Crossan and Howard Clark Kee argue that Mark's citation of scripture is not representative of ignorance or editorial sloppiness, but rather represents combinations and alterations of scripture texts that cohere with Mark's intent to create a new story to communicate his own point of view.

Contra Mark as only compiling "Jesus tradition"

<u>Mark did not hesitate to use the Old Testament out of context, therefore it is probable that he did the same with the "Jesus tradition" he received.</u> This underscores the argument that he retold tradition for his own purposes. By doing this Mark created a new text from other texts, traces of which can be seen in his text.

Mark was not a conservative redactor; he not only reshaped his story of Jesus by retelling the story for the sake of a particular situation, he also told it from his own perspective. However, whether Mark transmitted tradition conservatively or creatively is of little significance, even eyewitnesses shape their messages for their own purposes. Jan Vansina (1985:5) observes:

Mediation of perception by memory and emotional state shapes an account. Memory typically selects certain features from the successive perceptions and interprets them according to expectation, previous knowledge or the logic of 'what must have happened', and fills the gaps in perception.

This is all the more true of the Jesus tradition which has been shaped by putative eyewitnesses as well as those who retold the tradition for their own purposes and in their own circumstances. That is already clear from the different versions of the same stories of and about Jesus in the canonical gospels. First of all we do not have any eyewitness reports; furthermore, the retelling of the Jesus tradition was done in different circumstances for different purposes. This is, for instance, confirmed by the 'same' version of the 'same' parable in different contexts in the different gospels. Retelling of the 'same' event or word of a specific person involves creativity. Bart Ehrman argues that an understanding of how memory—especially memory in oral cultures— works is crucial to understanding the production of the Gospel of Mark

John in the Old Testament

The Purpose of Signs in the Old Testament

The reason we need to start in the Old Testament is because that is the theological milieu of the mindset of the human author of John's Gospel. We can witness the apostle John's deep connection to the Old Testament in the very first verse of his Gospel, "In the beginning was the Word, and the Word was with God, and the Word was God." John begins his Gospel by echoing the opening verse of Genesis. A careful reader of his Gospel will note that John makes many other connections to the Old Testament, including references to the liturgical festivals and ceremonial laws of Israel. Thus, when John uses the motif of signs in his Gospel we can rightly assume his understanding is built upon what is revealed to us in the Old Testament.

There are two areas in the Old Testament where signs figure prominently: the book of Exodus and the prophets. While signs are operative in both of these areas, they function somewhat differently in each of them. When one studies the signs in Exodus, it becomes immediately apparent that they have a "shock and awe" nature to them. These signs, such as the plagues upon Egypt, represent miraculous displays of Yahweh's power and demonstrate that **Yahweh is more powerful than all the false gods of Egypt.** These signs have a threefold purpose: to authenticate Moses as Yahweh's appointed human leader (both to Israel and to Pharaoh), to scare the Egyptian adversaries, and to comfort the frightened Israelites. These signs are similar to a modern big-budget, special-effects laden blockbuster movie. The "wow" factor of the signs in Exodus is emphasised by the use of the phrase "signs and wonders" to describe them, Exod. 4:28–30;

When we turn to the prophets, however, we notice that they serve a more focused and narrow purpose. Instead of the big-budget special effects of the signs and wonders of Exodus, we encounter relatively low-budget and mundane signs. For example, the prophet Isaiah walked naked and barefoot for three years as a "sign" of judgment against the nations of Egypt and Ethiopia (Isa. 20:3). Similarly, in Ezekiel's prophecy, an iron pan is used as a sign to Israel (4:1–3). It is hard to argue that a naked old prophet and a common cooking vessel could qualify as miraculous or serve to create a "shock and awe" effect. So what is their purpose? They serve to authenticate the prophet in question as God's appointed and sent messenger to his people. Even the big-budget "signs and wonders" of the Exodus perform this function as they authenticate Moses' role as Yahweh's human servant to lead his people out of bondage in Egypt.

Signs in the Old Testament could be miraculous or mundane, but the common thread is that they were used by Yahweh to authenticate his human messengers whom he appointed to advance the story of redemptive history and to provide salvation to his people. It is very likely that John had this understanding in mind when, under the inspiration of the

Spirit, he authored his Gospel. Let's turn now to discerning the purpose of the signs in the Gospel of John.

The Signs of John's Gospel

Even a casual reader of the New Testament will quickly recognise how different John's Gospel is from those of Matthew, Mark, and Luke (the "Synoptic Gospels"). The content, literary structure, vocabulary, chronology, and theological emphases of John's Gospel are all unique in comparison with the Synoptics. The Gospel of John lacks many things that the Synoptic Gospels include, such as the nativity story, the temptation by Satan in the wilderness, the narrative parables, extensive teaching on the kingdom of the Father, the Sermon on the Mount, the Olivet Discourse, and a detailed account of the Lord's Supper. On the other hand, John includes things that the Synoptic Gospels lack, including the "I am" sayings of Jesus, the Farewell Discourse and the one that pertains most to our discussion the signs of Jesus. The signs of Jesus play a prominent role in the argument, theology, and structure of the Gospel of John. In order to understand these signs better, we will first identify the specific signs found in John's Gospel and then we will turn to understanding their purpose.

The Seven Signs of John's Gospel

Andreas J. Köstenberger (who currently serves as research professor at Midwestern Baptist Theological Seminary in Kansas City, Missouri) is perhaps the finest living conservative evangelical scholar working in the area of Johannine studies. Most of what I know about John's Gospel, and particularly the signs in it, is derived from Dr. Köstenberger's work.1 As he begins his discussion of these signs in his wonderful work *A Theology of John's Gospel and Letters*, 2 he notes an oddity about the scholarship pertaining to them. He points out that while studies on the signs are "legion," there is "no treatment of the exact number and identity of the Johannine signs."3 In other words, while there is a vast amount of extant academic literature on the Johannine signs, there is no consensus on how many there are!

While there is no consensus on the exact number, there is broad consensus regarding the identification of six particular signs. It is nearly universally accepted that the following qualify as Johannine signs:

1. Turning water into wine (2:1–11)
1. Healing the nobleman's son (4:46–54)
1. Healing the lame man (5:1–15)
1. Feeding the multitude (6:1–15)
1. Healing the blind man (9)
1. The raising of Lazarus (11)

Since scholars agree on these six signs, why don't we just stop there with this consensus position and say **there are six signs in John's Gospel**? Well, there is certainly a pattern in the Bible regarding the completeness and perfection of the **number seven**, and when one looks at that list it is one shy of the mark. It would be wrong, however, to simply suggest that those seeking **a seventh sign** are misguided by a wrong-headed biblical quest for this magic number of seven. There are sound exegetical reasons to seek **a seventh sign** in John's Gospel based on the revelation of the Gospel itself. Most prominent among these reasons, as Köstenberger notes, is the importance John places on the **number seven,** particularly in his purposeful recording of **seven** of Jesus' "I am" sayings. 4 Accordingly, there is good evidence to think that **a seventh sign** is present in the

Gospel of John. But how do we identify this **mysterious seventh sign?**

The best way to identify **the seventh sign** of John's Gospel is to act like a detective attempting to determine whether the same killer is responsible for a series of murders. This detective will look at the series of individual murders and then identify the common themes among them. We can use a similar methodology to identify the seventh sign of John's Gospel: all we need to do is to ascertain what the six consensus signs have in common. Köstenberger employed this methodology in his research and concluded that the six signs have the following three things in common:5

1. All six of the consensus signs represent *public actions* of Jesus;
1. All six of the consensus signs are *explicitly referred to as "signs"* in the text; and
1. All six of the consensus signs direct the reader's attention to the *glory of the Father revealed in Jesus Christ* and serve to *publicly authenticate Jesus* as the Father's chosen representative.

If we take these three criteria and use them to examine the "line-up" of potential suspects for the seventh sign, the one that best fits the profile is Jesus' cleansing of the temple in John 2:13–22.6

Clearly, the cleansing of the temple was a public act of Jesus, and it is also referred to as a sign in the account as recorded by John. Admittedly, this occurs indirectly in the text, but nonetheless the designation of the event as a sign is there, particularly in Jesus' exchange with the temple officials in 2:18–19, "So the Jews said to him, 'What *sign* do you show us for doing these things?' Jesus answered them, 'Destroy this temple, and in three days I will raise it up'" (emphasis mine). Finally, Jesus' cleansing of the temple and His words symbolically connecting the temple to his own body both point to his own death and resurrection. In John's Gospel, the glory of Jesus Christ is seen most vividly in his crucifixion. Thus the cleansing of the temple, like the other six signs, ultimately points to Jesus' glory and authenticates him as one who has authority over the Father's house. John even intrudes into the account as the narrator to remind us that, after Jesus' resurrection, the disciples grasped the true meaning of this sign: "When therefore he was raised from the dead, his disciples remembered that he had said this, and they believed the Scripture and the word that Jesus had spoken" (John 2:22).

The other main contender for the seventh sign among biblical scholars is the resurrection of Jesus. I remain unpersuaded by the arguments offered for this position, particularly because the resurrection is not a sign that points beyond itself, but rather is the destination to which all the other signs direct the reader. In other words, the resurrection of Jesus is not a means to an end, like the other signs, but is the end in itself.

If we accept the cleansing of the temple as the seventh sign, then this results in the raising of Lazarus being the final and culminating sign. That seems theologically and exegetically appropriate. First, this sign occurs in John 11 at the end of the first section of the Gospel (John 1–12), which many scholars refer to as the "book of signs." Essentially, the pivot of John's Gospel, from a structural perspective, occurs in John 12 as Jesus ends his public ministry and enters Jerusalem for his trial, crucifixion, and ultimate resurrection. Second, Jesus' raising of Lazarus unequivocally points to Jesus' own resurrection. Thus the culminating sign (the raising of

Lazarus) points to the culminating event in John's Gospel and all redemptive history (the resurrection of Jesus).

The Two Main Purposes of the Seven Signs

Having identified the seven signs, let's move to the more important question: What is the significance of these seven signs of John's Gospel? Why did John include them and make them central? What spiritual truths do we glean from them? What is their purpose? I am convinced that the seven signs serve two main purposes.

Purpose 1: To Authenticate the Ministry of Jesus and Reveal His Glory

This purpose brings us full circle to the purpose of signs in the Old Testament. Like the signs of the Old Testament, the signs of John's Gospel serve to authenticate the divine messianic ministry and message of Jesus. Earlier in this article, we briefly surveyed the signs in the Old Testament and learned that one major concentration occurred during the Exodus, the time of Moses. Moses was, of course, the mediator of the old covenant, and Yahweh used signs to authenticate his ministry. Accordingly, it should come as no surprise that signs would play a significant role to authenticate Jesus, the mediator of a new and better covenant. **Jesus is the promised prophet who is like Moses,** but who surpasses Moses in glory and greatness (Deut. 18:18).7

While the seven signs of John's Gospel share a similar purpose to the signs of the Old Testament, there is one stark and important difference between them: unlike the signs performed by Moses and the prophets, the signs Jesus performed not only testify to the divine authenticity of his message, but they also testify to the reality that Jesus *is* the divine message. The seven signs of Jesus in John's Gospel serve not only to verify that Jesus' spoken words are the very word of the Father but also to authenticate that Jesus is, ontologically and personally, the very divine Word of the Father (John 1:1). Thus, when Jesus performed his seven signs, he declared something about himself that Moses could never claim. By means of these signs, Jesus claimed his rightful title: the Son of the Father. Jesus used signs to authenticate his ministry and to reveal His glory.

When Jesus performed his signs, he consistently directed people not to focus on the sign itself but rather on what the sign signified. At Cana of Galilee, where he turned water into wine, the point wasn't to enjoy a good glass of wine but rather to see Jesus as the promised messiah—the one who brings joy and who will host his own wedding banquet with his bride. Jesus used these signs to signify who he is, what he had come to accomplish, and to demonstrate to the people their desperate need of him as their Saviour. Therefore, each of the seven signs serves the purpose of signifying something about the reality of who Jesus is and what he came to do. The chart below summarises the relationship between the things signified by each of the seven signs in the Gospel of John.

The Sign the Things Signified:

Turning water into wine (2:1–11) Jesus is the Messiah who inaugurates the new covenant order and brings joy. **Cleansing the temple (2:12–17)** Jesus is the Suffering Servant who builds the new temple of the church through his death and resurrection. **Healing the nobleman's son (4:46–54)** Jesus is the Son of the Father who grants life by the word of his power. **Healing the lame man (5:1–15)**

Jesus is the Son of the Father who renders people spiritually whole. **Feeding the multitude (6:1–15)** Jesus is the bread of life who is sovereign over the gift of eternal life. **Healing the blind man (9)** Jesus is the light of the world who gives sight to the spiritually blind. **The raising of Lazarus (11)** Jesus is the Son of the Father who rules over death and gives life to the spiritually dead.

One of the purposes of these seven signs is to authenticate the ministry of Jesus and to reveal his glory. Through these signs, Jesus Christ demonstrated who he is and what he came to do.

Purpose 2: To Persuade People to Believe in Jesus Christ

The second purpose of these seven signs relates to the field of apologetics. They have a persuasive purpose, which John explicitly acknowledges near the end. In 20:30, John reveals to his readers that he purposely selected a limited number of signs: "Now Jesus did many other signs in the presence of the disciples, which are not written in this book." Then, in the very next verse (20:31), John says, "But these are written so that you may believe that Jesus is the Christ, the Son of the Father, and that by believing you may have life in his name." John explicitly declares that he included "these" particular seven signs of Jesus so that the readers of his Gospel would "believe that Jesus is the Christ, the Son of the Father" and "have life in his name."

When Jesus performed these seven signs during his public ministry, he was making the case regarding the authenticity of his identity; and John, by recording these signs in the manner he did, makes a similar case to all who pick up and read his Gospel. Many scholars have noted the forensic and legal characteristics of this Gospel, which is replete with discourses that are meant to persuade the reader. In some ways, the Gospel of John is akin to a legal brief that sets forth an argument regarding why the reader should believe in Jesus Christ; at the center of that argument reside the seven signs. Like an able trial lawyer, John, under the inspiration of the Spirit, sifts through all the extant evidence (that is, all the many signs performed by Jesus) and selects for his argument those most persuasive for proving his case (these seven signs).

Carrying on with the legal analogy, John uses the seven signs as evidentiary building blocks with each subsequent sign adding to the cumulative weight of the evidence. The probative persuasiveness of these seven signs finds a crescendo in the final and seventh sign: the raising of Lazarus from the dead. This last sign serves as John's closing argument to the case he is making: that Jesus is the Christ, **the Son of Father.**

The Continuing Challenge of the <u>Seven Signs</u>

Although Jesus performed his seven signs over two millennia ago, they remain powerfully relevant and contemporary. Every time people read the Gospel of John, they are confronted anew with the power of these signs. Every time a preacher proclaims them from the pulpit, those in the pew are challenged by their enduring testimony. Even in our current age, whenever these signs are encountered water is again turned to wine, thousands are fed with the bread of life, and those dead in their trespasses and sins are raised to new life. **The seven signs of Jesus** memorialised in John's Gospel continue to serve as credible and persuasive witnesses, authenticating who Jesus is, revealing his glory, and challenging the reader (or hearer) to believe in Jesus Christ as **the Son of the Father.**

It is my hope that this article has deepened your appreciation for the **seven signs** and for the One to whom they point so powerfully. Most of all, I hope that the signs of John's Gospel will achieve their intended purpose in your life: "That you may believe that Jesus is the Christ, the **Son of the Father**, and that by believing you may have life in his name" (John 20:31

Matthew's Use of the Old Testament: A Preliminary Analysis

In the words of Lee Campbell, some contemporary evangelical scholars suggest that Matthew's use of the Old Testament is like the way rabbis of that period used it. For example, the Qumran community contemporized the Old Testament (a.k.a. *pesher*) by holding that Old Testament scriptures were predictive of their own situation. Many modern scholars would argue that Matthew also interprets the Old Testament using *pesher* when, for example, he applies Hosea 11:1 to Christ's sojourn in Egypt. If it is true that New Testament authors interpreted the Old Testament this way, then it is a little unsettling. The most pressing concern is that *pesher*, *peshat* and many later *misrash* techniques are fundamentally eisegetical. That is, these hermeneutical approaches are hostile to the notion of objective interpretation. If this is the case, then it brings into question the legitimacy of many critical NT uses of the OT. Ultimately, if NT authors did use rabbinical hermeneutics, then one must question the very authority of the New Testament in critical matters of faith.

A second, if lesser, concern is the contribution New Testament authors make to the study of scripture interpretation. Even if Matthew was not using *pesher* techniques, what interpretive approach was he taking? Can modern scholarship use his methods or was he exercising the insights of a prophet when he interpreted the Old Testament? If so, then contemporary interpreters can gain little assistance in their own hermeneutical tasks from Matthew. The purposes of this paper are twofold: to investigate whether Matthew was using *pesher* techniques in his use of Old Testament and, if not, to identify what interpretive approach to the Old Testament he was taking in his gospel.

What is Pesher?

Several approaches to scripture analysis may be discovered in first century Hebrew documents including literalistic, allegorical, *midras* and *pesher*. Longman doubts that these methods were distinguished from one another in the first century. Of these methods, *pesher* is of the greatest interest to this study, principally because Matthew does not lie under the accusation that he interprets the OT literalistically or allegorically but rather through *pesher*. Perhaps Matthew uses *midrashic* techniques, as many contend, but it can be argued that first century *midrash* could be very much akin to the manner in which Psalmists interpreted the Pentateuch. Early *midrash*, as defined by Hillel, is a fairly objective hermeneutical approach. It is the claim that Matthew is using *pesher* contemporisation of the OT, particularly in 'fulfilment' citations, that provides the most serious challenge to those holding to verbal, plenary inspiration.

The term *pesher* means, "to explain." In fact, however, *pesher* is an application of OT scripture with little to no concern for the context of the passage applied. *Pesher* may refer either to commentaries on the OT found amongst the Dead Sea scrolls or to the interpretive technique typical of these commentaries. *Pesher* interpreters assume that OT authors were speaking to the contemporary audience. This form of interpretation is tied to a word, text or OT allusion, which is then related to a present person, place or thing. The interpretations are generally aloof from the source context and appear to lack any coherent methodology. According to Lundberg, "This kind of commentary (*pesher*) is not an attempt to explain what the Bible meant when it was originally written, but rather what it means in the day and age of the commentator, particularly for his own community."

For instance, in the *pesher* Habakkuk the writers simply take Habakkuk's references to the Chaledeans and apply them to the Romans without any effort to justify the application. The context of Habakkuk seems to hold little interest for such interpreters. In the same commentary all the destructive activities described by Habakkuk are attributed to the 'wicked priest' while all the good things are attributed to the 'righteous teacher' – the antagonist and protagonist typical of Qumran *pesher* writing. Again, the interpreter shows little inclination to justify the wholesale substitution of the authorial intent for that of his community.

Was Matthew Using Pesher?

Clearly, Matthew is not a *pesher* commentary. Such texts are line-by-line analyses of an OT text and Matthew's gospel does not conform to this format. Rather, Matthew applies OT citations to his narrative of the life of Christ.

While Matthew cannot be construed as a *pesher* commentary, it could still be true that Matthew is using the *pesher* devise of OT contemporisation. Matthew's use of Hosea 11:1 seems so disinterested in its plain meaning that a cursory comparison of Hosea 11:1 with Matthew 2:15 certainly leaves the impression he is using this approach. However, there are several reasons to doubt that Matthew is using *pesher* techniques:

While both Matthew and *pesher* commentaries use citations from a variety of sources, it appears that many of Matthew's translations are his own and Matthew's citations do not show interpretive or selection bias typical of *pesher*.

The formal features of OT quotes in Matthew do not correspond to any such features in Qumran text.

Qumran applications were treated as identical to interpretations without regard to historic context - few such tendencies are found in NT use of the OT.

Matthew did not use many OT passages that conform to a fulfilment motif which is unexpected if he was simply grabbing proof-texts from the OT.

Many fulfilment passages used by Matthew do not conform to known messianic prophecy material advanced in Jewish circles. If Matthew wanted to make a case about Jesus claim to be messiah he should have taken better advantage of accepted messiah texts.

Some citations are so surprising that it is unreasonable to expect the NT author would have bent them to conform to the life of Christ (e.g. Jeremiah 31:15 for Matthew 2:16,18)

Even in the most radical examples of *pesher* used by the Qumran community, the authors do not modify their history to conform to an OT passage. Yet this is what a proponent of *pesher* Matthew must claim for him.

OT quotations in NT fall under a limited set of themes. This is much different than the piecemeal treatment in the DSS and in rabbinical writings. Motifs of NT citations of OT include the following:

1. **Jesus acts as YHWH**
2. Jesus is the predicted messiah
3. Jesus is the predicted servant of the Lord
4. Jesus is the son of man
5. Jesus culminates the prophetic line
6. Jesus is in a succession of OT righteous sufferers
7. Jesus fulfils the Davidic dynasty
8. **Jesus reverses the Adamic curse**
9. Jesus fulfils the Abrahamic covenant of universal blessing
10. Jesus recapitulates the history of Israel
11. The priesthood of Melchizedek & Aaron...the latter sometimes contrastingly anticipate the priesthood of Jesus
12. The Passover lamb and other sacrifices prefigure the substitutionary atonement of Christ and Christian service
13. Jesus & manna
14. The rock/living water
15. The serpent
16. The tabernacle/temple
17. John the Baptist & Elijah
18. The new covenant prophecy
19. Judas Iscariot
20. The law of Moses prefigured grace positively and negatively
21. The flood - last judgment/baptism

22. Red Sea/circumcision - baptism
23. Jerusalem - eternal city of Yahweh
24. Taking Canaan - spiritual rest

There are many reasons for doubting that Matthew is writing like an author of Qumran-*pesher* materials but particular OT citations do seem as careless of context as *pesher*. This requires an explanation of which Stendahl's failed *pesher* conclusion was an attempt to respond.

How was Matthew Interpreting the Old Testament?

Given that Matthew does not use *pesher* hermeneutics, what kind of interpretive approach is he applying and is it useful for contemporary interpreters?

It is important to realize that most of the time Matthew's use of the OT is so straightforward that it is not susceptible to the charge of OT misuse or misinterpretation. For instance, at times Christ utters language from the OT in ways that suggest he is calling forth the mood of the text he cites. This is entirely unsurprising for one steeped in the language and tone of the OT. At other times the OT is used by way of application. For example, Christ is recorded as using the OT for training when he frames OT narratives into question and answer sessions (e.g. 15:4; 19:4-7, 18-19). In other ways Christ draws particular applications out of OT narratives (e.g. Matthew 12:3-8, citing Isaiah 21:6; Leviticus 24:5,9; Numbers 28:9 to condemn Sabbath legalism). In these cases, however, Christ is generally using the OT the way OT authors used antecedent text. The psalmists often cited Pentateuchal narratives in order to draw out salient spiritual principles or theology. Even in those cases where Christ's application of the OT differs from the approach of OT authors, his use still is not at all like the approach seen in first century *midrash* because unlike much rabbinical *midrash*, Jesus works within the context of the citations he uses. When Jesus applies the OT differently from the psalmist application hermeneutic, he is speaking prophetically (e.g. "You've heard it said, but I say..."). In these ways he adds to earlier revelation, not in a way that disregards but rather extends the earlier revelation. This too is an interpretive role played by OT prophets in their use of antecedent and new revelation. In these uses of the Old Testament Christ, or Matthew as his biographer, are not guilty of interpreting the scripture in ways alien to how Old Testament authors interpreted the Old Testament.

Many of Matthew's citations are apologetic in nature, that is, Matthew cites the OT to show how Christ fulfilled OT scripture. It is because of this that Matthew is often charged with deriving from the OT meanings no competent OT scholar could ever develop independently. As a result of some of the more extraordinary examples of fulfilment citations Matthew is often held to be using *pesher* approaches to the OT. How is Matthew using the OT in these cases? How can modern interpreters make use of this approach?

As we saw earlier, a fairly common solution to this dilemma is to suggest that everybody was using the OT this way during the first century (i.e. *midrash pesher*). This not only appears unlikely but unsafe for the veracity of much of Matthew's gospel, to say nothing of the rest of the New Testament. Other scholars recognize the problem but suggest that careful analysis of the relevant OT citations would vindicate Matthew's interpretation. Some suggest that God's intent when he inspired the OT author was much more profound than the OT author himself realized. Still others say that Matthew was simply noting historically analogous situations for his audience with the suggestion that Christ completed the earlier motifs. Each of these attempted solutions to the problem of OT usage in NT fulfilment passages have provided some important insights into NT use of the OT but each also serves to raise critical questions about the appropriate use of the Old Testament. A few points must be considered before the question of Matthew's OT use can be fully addressed.

First, as many scholars have noted, Matthew's terminology pertaining to fulfilment is much richer than such words suggest to most readers. Matthew indicates 15 times that Christ fulfilled an OT scripture. The term *pleroo* and related terms have wider semantic range than simple predictive realization. These words can communicate the idea of 'completing', 'establishing' or 'filling up' as well as prediction-outcome. For Matthew to suggest that some aspect of the life of Christ fulfils some antecedent scripture could mean that an OT passage made a prediction and Christ expressed that precise prediction. But, fulfilment can also mean that Christ "filled to overflowing" or "completed" the antecedent scripture. This second sense is the way a reader can comprehend Christ's claim that he fulfilled the Law & Prophets in Matthew 5:17. Fulfilment quotations are infused with the concept of God's redemptive purpose in human history and so Matthew quotes texts that directly predict but also passages that have thematic significance that exceeds the OT author immediate meaning. This is different than *sensus plenior* because the NT author is not uncovering meaning hidden to the OT author. Instead, he is using the OT passage as an example of a broad theme of which the OT author was aware. Thus, some concerns over Matthew's use of the OT may be tempered by a better sense of what Matthew intended when he said Christ fulfilled a scripture.

Second, C. H. Dodd has shown that the NT use of the OT is not haphazard proof-texting but the use of a few text plots in the OT. For instance Isaiah 53 is cited 34 times in the NT. For the early church, it is likely that a limited citation served as a pointer to an entire theme of which the audience was well apprised:

Case Study: Matthew 2:15

In this citation, Matthew takes the MT approach of literally translating "son" rather than the LXX "His children." It is possible that Matthew may have intended to allude to the entire section through the use of a single citation (c.f. Hosea 11:1-11). It is difficult to concede that Matthew is using midrashic interpretive approaches for the reasons articulated above. On the other hand, efforts to find ways to argue that Matthew's use is an appropriate analysis of a prediction are also hard to concede.

Howard sees Matthew's use of Hosea as retrospective analogical correspondence rather than an effort on the Fsther's part to embed a projective type or prophecy about Christ in Hosea's words. That is, Matthew noted that Jesus was like Israel in that he also went to Egypt but that, unlike Israel, he was the son obedient to the covenant. When Israel left Egypt they dropped the ball. Whereas, when Christ left Egypt he was the son, in whom the Father was very pleased. In this way, Christ fulfilled (i.e. competed) all that the Father intended for Israel.

An alternative view is that the Exodus event was a prototype that was subsequently echoed when it was recalled for the purpose of instruction and that was repeated in the coming of Joshua to Palestine & Judah from the Babylonian exile.

The approach taken to the interpretation of this passage will include the following stages: 1. Analysis of the context of Matthew's citation of Hosea; 2. Analysis of the context of Hosea 11:1; 3. Assessment of the retrospective and projective function of Hosea's citation and 4. Assessment of Matthew's use of Hosea is an example of fulfilment.

The narrative passages before and after Matthew 2:13-15 appear to be arguments from the Torah that Jesus was the messiah and the fulfilment of the Abrahamic and Davidic covenants. The genealogy of chapter 1:1-17 is framed at the beginning and end with the claim that Jesus was the messiah. Chapter 1:18-25 is a reference to a passage that culminates in the promise of a God/king who would rule from the throne of David (Isaiah 7:14-9:7). Chapter 2:1-12 contain a reference to a messianic scripture that contains allusions to both the Davidic and Abrahamic covenants. After 2:13-15 Matthew cites Jeremiah 31:15 which is a clear reference to the mourning associated with the Babylonian captivity but is at the beginning of a long prediction of the restoration of Israel leading to a new covenant that will result in the laws of Yahweh being internalised by his people (c.f Isaiah 31:31-34). It is difficult to make definitive statements about Matthew 2:19-23 but many scholars believe it refers to prophecies concerning the 'branch' found in Isaiah 4:2, Zechariah 3:8,9 & 6:12. Finally, Matthew's citation of Isaiah 40:3 appears to be a pointer to a lengthy passage concerned with Yaweh's redemption of Israel through Cyrus and through the Servant of YHWH (Isa.42:1-7).

The context of Matthew 2:13-15 is the correlation of Jesus with significant OT scriptures that address the Father's redemptive activity toward Israel and toward Gentiles - scriptures that identify Jesus as messiah and the fulfilment of the covenants of Abraham and David. It would be expected, therefore, that Matthew's citation of Hosea 11:1 would also anticipate his role as redeemer or sovereign.

Hosea is citing the exodus in Hosea 11:1. This event was a critical one in the OT because it demonstrated Yahweh's remembrance and redemption of Israel. The expression "out of Egypt" appears several times in Hosea (e.g. 11:1. Hosea 11:1 is in the context of Yahweh's love for Israel. Hosea 12:9 speaks of Yahweh's discipline. Chapter 12:13 talks of how Yahweh used a prophet to redeem an ungrateful people. Hosea 13:4 uses the exodus to promise Yahweh will assert his sovereign rights over Israel once again. These passages and the core narrative of Hosea's redemption of Gomer make it clear that Hosea 11:1 is intensely focused on Yahweh's once and future redemption of Israel (Hosea 2:14 - 3:4).

The exodus account is a deferred hope in critical respects. Israel could have been a nation of priests (e.g. Exodus 19:4-6) but it chose not to satisfy the terms of the covenant. In this sense the exodus was incomplete. Hosea addresses the exodus to remind Israel of Yahweh's love, power and sovereignty and to anchor his promise for future redemption both from Assyria and ultimately from their own rebelliousness.

When Matthew cites Hosea 11:1 he is citing the entire redemptive context, not only of Hosea but of the rest of the Old Testament. Citation of Hosea 11:1 reminds Israel of their double redemption from Egypt & Assyria/Babylon but also anticipates their final redemption from themselves.

Assessment of Matthew 2:15's use of Hosea 11:1 as fulfilment

When Hosea records, *Out of Egypt I have called my son*, he is tapping into an exodus motif that was expressed in the original event; reiterated and extended to "the king" of Israel by Balaam (Nu.24:8); reiterated when Joshua entered Palestine; reiterated when the principle of redemption was applied repeatedly in OT didactic material; that would be reiterated later when Israel was restored after her impending discipline **(Hosea 6:1-3; 8:1-10:5) and again when Yahweh would permanently redeem his people. Matthew was simply noting something implicit in Hosea, namely, Christ was the ultimate fulfilment of Yahweh's promised redemption of Israel (Hosea 11:1-14:5). Hosea certainly understood that his recollection of the Exodus was anchored in Yahweh's past redemptive history** as well as his future promise of final redemption. And, this is exactly what Matthew did by pointing to its manifestation in Christ. Christ returned to Israel from Egypt, as an obedient son and also as Yahweh coming again to dwell in the tents of Shem. The resonance with the exodus motif is so remarkable that Matthew could say Christ 'filled up to overflowing' the entire theme. If we were contemporaries of Matthew we too could have anticipated a final redemption of Israel and rejoiced when we saw its penultimate fulfilment in the first advent of Christ and hoped in its ultimate fulfilment in his second advent.

Interestingly, Christ's *exodus* not only recapitulated the return of Israel to the land but also the advent of the Father dwelling with his people. For Christ's return to Israel was also the return of God dwelling in the tents of Shem. In these ways Christ *filled to overflowing* the exodus. And, in this sense, Hosea's recall of the exodus has a projective role because it is connected both to the past Exodus event and to the Father's redemptive commitment to Israel yet unrealized. When Matthew considers the words of Hosea he is not merely saying, "Gee, isn't this interesting how both Israel & Christ returned to the land from Egypt." What he is communicating must not merely be analogical correspondence. Isn't Matthew also saying, "What Hosea hoped for, the redemption of Israel from sin, was fully realised in Christ?"

Conclusion

What is clear from this preliminary study is that Matthew was not using *pesher*-like eisegetical techniques, when he used the Old Testament in his gospel. He apparently often used his own translations of Greek, Hebrew and Aramaic sources rather than isolating extant translations that fit an interpretive agenda. Significantly, his putative interpretations are not self-serving but correspond to interpretations found in Septuigental, Masoretic, Syrian and rabbinical materials from the same era. Similarly, his applications of the Old Testament to New Testament events do not have the tortured appearance of those found in the Dead Sea Scrolls. Even in some of the more challenging 'fulfilment' materials Matthew's use of the Old Testament does not correspond with *pesher* techniques used by the Qumran community.

What Matthew's fulfilment citations often appear to do is often show points of resonance with well developed redemptive themes in the OT of which Christ is the consummation. If this is true, Matthew may show us how to interpret the OT by indicating that earlier scriptures have both projective and retrospective functions as they reiterate the theology of an earlier motif or prototype and yet anticipate complete realisation in some future act of Yahweh/God.

Without prophetic authority we may have to hold conclusions drawn from such techniques more tentatively than Matthew does. Nonetheless, the use of interpretive methods consonant with those found in scripture substantially strengthens the confidence of modern interpreters who are committed to the kind of careful exegesis that honours the intent of the ultimate author.

These techniques included: *peshat* (i.e. literalistic), *midrash* (i.e. there is quite a bit of variance within this tradition), *pesher* (i.e. complete contemporisation of OT), apocalyptic (i.e. contemporisation of some OT passages) & allegorical. Longman suggests that individual interpreters may have used all four methods and may not have distinguished them as distinct approaches. This is not to say that *midrashic* approaches to interpretation were typically objective. Most rabbinical *midrash* used the OT as a springboard without concern for the context of the material cited. *Midrash* refers to a Hebrew method of citing, interpreting and then amplifying an OT passage. The term *midrash* also refers to the oral and then, later, the written collections of *midrash* expositions and applications. *Haggadah midrash* refers to the ethical and expository interpretation of non-legal materials from the Hebrew Bible. *Halakah midrash* applied the general principles of OT laws to specific situations.

Luke

Luke climactically ends his narrative with Jesus' departure into heaven (Luke 24:50–53; cf. Acts 1:9). The Third Gospel begins with Jesus' humble birth in a feeding trough (Luke 2:7) and ends with his exaltation to the Father's throne.

His exaltation is critical to the story. Jesus sits enthroned not in a subordinate role; he doesn't rule over the nations from an earthly, physical throne in Jerusalem. Instead, as Richard Bauckham argues, "Jesus was exalted to sit with the Father on this very throne of the cosmos. This makes Jesus sovereign over 'all things. His assumption to heaven demonstrates his incomparable rule over the universe, explaining why Luke has carefully woven Jesus' identity as Daniel's "Son of Man" and Israel's "Lord" into his narrative. Now that Jesus sits enthroned, he will pour out his Spirit on the church and empower his people to take the gospel to the "end of the earth" (Acts 1:8).

Luke penned his Gospel to convince Theophilus and Gentiles that Jesus is indeed the one whom the apostles proclaim and the one who fulfils the whole of the Old Testament. Two titles largely strike at the heart of Luke's presentation of Jesus' identity: the Son of the Father and the Son of David. As the Son of of the Father, Jesus is identified with Israel's Yahweh/God who redeems Israel from spiritual captivity in a second exodus. As the Son of David, Jesus inaugurates the long-awaited kingdom of Yahweh/God. Jesus not only faithfully adheres to the covenant, as a second Adam / true Israel figure, he also bears Yahweh/God's curse on behalf of the covenant community. Both forms of obedience, active and passive, establish the basis for the believer's justification.

How Should We Interpret the Old Testament?

Luke is thoroughly acquainted with the Old Testament. For Luke and the other Evangelists, the person of Jesus cannot be understood apart from Israel's Scriptures. Jesus doesn't simply fulfil one layer or stream of the Old Testament. He fulfils the whole of it. Related to the debate concerning the hermeneutical integrity of the apostles' use of the Old Testament is the question whether or not the church should follow suit. Should believers read and interpret the Old Testament like the apostles? Though many and perhaps the majority of commentators would answer in the negative, my contention is that the church today should interpret the Old Testament in accordance with the apostolic use of the Old Testament. The apostles learned to interpret and read the Old Testament through the Old Testament itself (the Old Testament prophets' use of antecedent revelation), the synagogue, family, and Jesus himself. Out of those four areas of instruction, Jesus is the primary resource. During his career and especially after his resurrection, he explained to the disciples how his ministry accords with the Old Testament and how Israel's Scriptures ultimately point to him. The question is, in reality, whether believers should interpret the Old Testament like Jesus. Since <u>Jesus is the perfect Adam and **Yahweh** incarnate,</u> his reading of the Old Testament is always valid and exemplary. If we should live like Jesus, we should also read like Jesus.

The First Christians

The first Christians were Jewish, so they still worshiped the same Yahweh/god that Christians worship (although Christians worship that god in two additional forms—Jesus Christ and the Holy Spirit).

The next wave of Christians were Romans and Hellenised Jews (Jews who had assimilated to Greek culture). They would have had particular gods in the Greek/Roman pantheon they paid particular homage to. That would have depended on their location and family tradition.

After that, the Romans adopted and adapted Christianity and spread it as they spread their empire. By the time the Roman empire collapsed, Christianity had already spread as far as Ireland. Various other states and shorter-lived empires emerged, continuing to enforce Christianity across Europe as they conquered the peoples that unfortunately are usually just labelled **"pagan."** Someone else can tell you more about pre-Christian groups in Africa and the Middle East.

The Summary

The pagan word god/God is a false spirit of Satan which had been worshipped by the ancient world with their religious groups. The individual pagans that worshipped gods include Terah, who is Abraham's father, Abraham himself who married his blood sister Sarah and had a son called Isaac with her. Other known pagans who worshipped pagan gods/Gods include Moses who was raised **in** Egypt, David who was physically anointed as King of Israel, Constantine and many others. Israelites worshipped many gods included Yahweh who became the head-god of their gods and also became their national pagan-god. This Yahweh, charged Moses to deliver the Israelites from Egypt murdered many people in Egypt including innocent first born children in the process. Whilst there are disputes among the biblical scholars about the true authorship of the 5 books of the Old Testament, it is claimed that, the Yahweh the elevated head-god of their many pagan-gods is claimed to be monotheistic and the creator of the world. But my research revealed that no pagan gods such as Yahweh, Brahma, Mazda ever created the world.

Unfortunately since Jesus Christ was born into the Abrahamic family whose mission was to reform the Jewish family for truth, forgiveness, peace and love, however He was rejected by the leadership of the Israelites, He was since been referred to as the Son of God/Yahweh. And all the Synoptic Gospel writers including Matthew, Mark, John and Luke quoted from the Old Testament referring to Jesus Christ not as the Father He taught them but rather as Father God. Another significant reason why Jesus is called God is due to the fact that He was born through the Holy Spirit by a human mother therefore, He was being equated by the Roman Catholic who also claim that their pagan god Jupiter was the king of their many different gods. He was the son of Saturn. Jupiter's wife is Juno and the queen of the gods. The Romans worshipped Jupiter who the Romans claimed was born on 25th December from a human mother Ops and Saturn the father they are all pagan gods named after the planets. All are pagan false spirits.

The word pagan-God of Satan is the false spirit and was worshipped by the individual pagans and their religious groups. These pagans include Terah, Abraham's father, Abraham who married his blood sister Sarah and had a son Isaac with her. Other known pagans include Moses, David, Constantine and many others. The Israelites national pagan-god Yahweh who charged Moses to deliver the Israelites from Egypt murdered many people including innocent first born children in the process. Whilst there are disputes among the biblical scholars about the true authorship of the 5 books of the Old Testament, it is claimed that, the Yahweh the elevated head-god of their many pagan-gods is claimed to be monotheistic and the creator of the world. But my research revealed that no pagan gods such as Yahweh, Brahma, Mazda ever created the world. Unfortunately since Jesus Christ was born into the Abrahamic family whose mission was to reform the Jewish family, He has since been referred to as Yahweh/God. *And all the Synoptic*

Gospel writers including Matthew, Mark, John and Luke quoted from the Old Testament referring to Jesus Christ not as the Father He taught them but rather as Father God. Another significant reason why Jesus is called God is due to the fact that He was born through the Holy Spirit by a human mother therefore, He was being equated by the Roman Catholic who also claim that their pagan god Jupiter was the king of their many different gods. He was the son of Saturn. Jupiter's wife is Juno and the queen of the gods. The Romans worshipped Jupiter who the Romans claimed was born on 25th December from a human mother Ops and Saturn the father they are all pagan gods named after the planets. All are pagan false spirits. Many of the planets in our solar system had been named after Roman deities. Romulus killed his brother Remus, and Romulus went on to name the city after himself, calling it Rome (or Roma).

BIBLIOGRAPHY

Alexander, D. and P. (eds) (1973). A Lion Handbook to the Bible. Lion Publishing. UK

Anan, G. J. (2011). The Organic Church: A practical approach to managing change. LANTERN TOWER – An Imprint of Melrose Press Limited Cambridgeshire. UK

Anan, G. J. (2015). The Illusive World of Love, Demystifying the Mindset of True Love in theological Perspectives. Author House; UK, Bloomington. IN USA

Anan, G. J. (2015). The Truth About Material Wealth, Is it God's Blessing in Disguise? Author House; UK. Bloomington. IN USA

Anan. G. J. (2016). Discerning The Prophetic Message: Knowing the Truth. New Generation Publishing. UK

Avis, P. D. L. (2nded) (2002). Anglicanism and The Christian Church: Theological Resources in Historical Perspective. T and T Clark Publishers. Edinburgh UK

Backhouse, R. (edt) (1993). Spiritual Life: The Life of St. Augustine. Hodder & Stoughton Publishers. UK

Baker, L. M. (1976-77). PEARS: Cyclopaedia, Pelham London UK

Ballard, P. & Pritchard J. (1996). Practical Theology in Action SPCK. London UK

Baldick, J (1997) Black God: The Afroasiatic Roots of the Jewish, Christian, and Muslim Religions. New York: Syracuse University Press.

Bleicher, J. (1990). Contemporary Hermeneutics as Method, Philosophy and Critique. Routledge. UK

Bonner, G. (1986). St Augustine of Hippo: Life and Controversies. Canterbury Press. UK

Briggs, J. (1990). Early English Baptists in, A Lion Hand Book The History of Christianity. Lion Publishing. UK

Brown, P. (2000). Augustine of Hippo. Faber and Faber. UK.

Bruce, F. F. (1989). Romans. Inter-varsity Press. UK

Bullock, A., Stallybrass, O., and Trombley, S. (eds.) (1977). Modern Thought. The Fontana Dictionary. Fontana Press.

Calvocoressi, P. (1987). Who's Who in the Bible? Viking Publishers. UK

Cole, Herbert Mbari. Art and Life among the Owerri Igbo (Bloomington: Indiana University press, 1982).

Comfort, P. W. (990). Early Manuscripts and Modern Translations of the New Testament Tyndale House Publishers, Inc. WHEATON, ILLINOIS. USA

Crofton, I. (1990) (1st edt.) The Guinness Encyclopaedia. The Guinness Publishing. UK

Davison, L. (1969) Sender and Sent. Epworth Press London UK

Doumbia, A. & Doumbia, N (2004) The Way of the Elders: West African Spirituality & Tradition. Saint Paul, MN: Llewellyn Publications.

Dowley, T. (ed.) (1990). A Lion Hand Book The History of Christianity. The Lion Publishing UK

Ehret, Christopher, (2002) The Civilizations of Africa: a History to 1800. Charlottesville: University Press of Virginia.

Ehret, Christopher, An African Classical Age: Eastern and Southern Africa in World History, 1000 B.C. to A.D. 400, page 159, University of Virginia Press, ISBN 0-8139-2057-4

Einstein, Carl. African Legends, First English Edition, Pandavia, Berlin 2021.

Erickson, M. J. (ed.) (1972). Readings in Christian Theology: the Living God. Barker and Baker. UK Hall, F. (3rd Ed. – 1967), The Fasting Prayer. Publisher: Frank Hall, Phoenix AZ. USA

Herbermann, C. G. (ed.) (2014). The Catholic Encyclopaedia: An International work of Reference on the Constitution, Doctrine, Discipline, History. ... Catholic Way Publishing (Kindle Edition). USA

Hermon, N. B. (ed.) (1974). The Encyclopaedia of World Methodism. Abington Press UK

Hill, G. E (1973) Who Jesus Is. Publishers: International Correspondence Institute. Belgium. Europe.

Horton, S. M. (1989). What the Bible Says About the Holy Spirit. Gospel Publishing House USA

Hunnex, M.D. (1968) Chronological and Thematic Charts of Philosophies and Phil osophers. Zondervan Publishing House, Grand Rapids, Michigan USA.

Mbiti, John African Religions and Philosophy (1969) African Writers Series, Heinemann

McKim, D.K. (ed.) (1998). Historical Handbook of Major Biblical Interpreters. Inter Varsity Press UK

Oates, W. J. (ed.) (1976). Basic Writings of SAINT Augustine: the city of God and On the Trinity. Baker Book House Grand Rapids, Michigan USA

Oates, W. J. (ed.) (1992). Basic Writings of SAINT Augustine: Confession & Twelve Treaties. Baker Book House, Grand Rapids, Michigan USA

Olson, R. E. (1999). The Story of Christian Theology: Twenty Centuries of Tradition and Reform. APOLO Inter-Varsity Press USA

Pitt-Rivers, G. (1966). The Riddle of 'Labarum' and the Origin of Christian

Rotelle, J. E. (1986). Augustine Day By Day. Catholic Book Publishing Co. New York. USA

Soyinka, Wole:, Myth, Literature and the African World (Cambridge University Press, 1976).

Stokes, P. (2004) Philosophy 100 Essential Thinkers. Index Books Ltd

Swinburne, R. (1999) Is There A God? Oxford University Press UK

Vardy, P. (1995). The Puzzle of God. Fount Paperbacks, an imprint of Harper Collins Religious Publishers. Great Britain

Vardy, P. (1992). The Puzzle of Evil. Fount Paperbacks, an imprint of Harper Collins Religious Publishers. Great Britain. UK

Weatherhead, L. D. (1936). It Happened in Palestine. Hodder & Stoughton Publishers. UK

Wilke, R. B. (1989) Sigs and Wonders: The Mighty Work of God in the Church. Abingdon Press NASHVILLE.

Wilson, I. (2001). Before The Flood: Dramatic New Evidence That the Biblical Flood was a Real-Life Event. Orion Books Ltd. UK

A NOTE ON THE AUTHOR

 The Revd Dr Gabriel J Anan was born and raised in Ghana where he received his primary and secondary education in the most challenging situation. He worked for the Ministry of Interior in Ghana for five years before leaving for Great Britain to study law, shipping and transport. His management training earned him the corporate membership of the professional bodies including Chartered Institute of Shipbrokers, Chartered Institute of Transport and the Institute of Export. He later worked as a manager and director for five years before engaging further in academic studies at the Greenwich University for his youth work qualification. He achieved a Master of Science **(MSc)** degree in Maritime Studies at the University of Somerset and a Master of Arts **(MA)** in Voluntary Sector Studies before gaining a Doctor of Philosophy **(PhD)** in the area of church leadership and management of change at the University of East London. Armed with authoritative knowledge of **"<u>MANAGING CHANGE</u>"**, has provided him the desire for seeking new ideas in **<u>any field</u>** of education for exploration.

After completing a programme for ministerial training course with a BA in Contextual Theology at the Middlesex University, he qualified as a Church of England clergy with

Roman Catholic background. In addition he studied for a BA Evangelical degree at Elim Bible College – now Regents Theological College. He had by then been appointed the **Honorary Professor of Contemporary Theology by the University of Europe**. His knowledge in Evangelism enables him to discern the theology of Paedobaptist and Credobaptist and many issues especially with regards to 'Born Again' Christian and infants Baptism.

The author has had several contacts with other traditional and African Praying Churches including Charismatic, Apostolic, Evangelical and Pentecostal and heir members, in the UK. These contacts gave him a firm grounding and insights for his understanding the gravity of the situation regarding prevailing issues affecting the followers in their churches.

He has vast practical experience in voluntary and charity organisations as he served as a chairman of Canning Town outlook, on the Board of Directors for Newham Credit Union and Vice Chair for Drew Primary School Governors for four years. He also worked as Youth Adviser for the London Borough of Newham for over ten years. Currently, he is a retired Associate Minister at the Church of England parish church of St George and St Ethelbert in East Ham London; but pursuing the direction of the Holy Spirit for the discernment of true Biblical **Sabbath**. He lives in Romford, Essex, UK with his family.

HERE IS THE SNOYPSIS OF THE BOOK, AND ALSO FOR THE BACK COVER OF THE BOOK

This book accesses the reasons why Jesus Christ the Saviour of humanity should be referred to or even called with the pagan word God which was in existence of worship in the ancient world before His coming 2000 years ago. Jesus Christ must be called the Christ the Saviour. This is because whether the word God/god is written with small or capital letter it still remains a pagan evil false spirit of Satan. Holding the thoughts has been the main focus of the text of this book which provides my final exegesis of revelation of the true nature of Jesus Christ the Redeemer of humanity which I began investigating and thus highlighting in my previous two books: WHO'S THE TRUE CREATOR OF THE WORLD and THE UNIQUENESS OF JESUS CHRIST THE SAVIOUR".

How the Spiritism began or started in the world

The true Holy Spirit is exposing many church leaders. It is undeniably fact that many Priests and Pastors are members of the evil secret societies such as Freemasons. Special attention must be drawn here due to the historical importance of how spiritism began in America and came into the world and spread like hot fire throughout the world. The fact is that there were three orphaned Fox sisters who were possessed by Satan and began communicating with the spirit in the early years of 1800AD. The phenomena continued and progressed from there and became a Spiritual church with their three older sisters Lelah, Marggeretta and Catherine Fox and other men praying and speaking in tongues through Satan influence. The church came to Gold Coast now Ghana in the year 1932 known as Kyire Bentuo church before some years later it adopted the New Testament name as Pentecostal Church.

The words to use by Pastors in order to invoke the spirit are the followings:

1. Ye ma ma ma ma san da lis: is the name for ma me water the sea gogddess
2. Mountain top for fasting
3. I am that I am is the another name of the spirit
4. da ka ta ya: is a demon spirit of miracle. This is the spirit of demons from shalia oriental
5. And many others…...

The first woman who Satan used to start speaking in the unknown tongues is Margaret McDonalds.

The church also became a Medium Spiritual Centre in 1846. As indicated earlier the creation of spiritism started in America by the three Fox sisters who were possessed by Satan and began speaking with the spirit in the early years of 1800AD. They continued communicating with the spirit in some more years before their elder sisters by name Leah, Margaretta and Catherine Fox and other men were instrumental in promoting the growth of the church with its centre at 312 Azusa street in Los Angeles USA. The church grew very quickly in popularity and spread like hot fire throughout the world and reached Gold Coast now Ghana in 1932. It has continued to grow ever since with praying and speaking in tongues or praying in unknown tongues.

Salvation is through Him alone

The true Holy Spirit is exposing many church leaders. It is undeniably fact that many Priests and Pastors are members of the evil secret societies such as Freemasons.

In many churches you can nowadays see many people including the Senior Pastors speaking in demonic tongues through the influence of Satan. Another demonic practice is where a Pastor will openly hold up

two Freemasonry swords in his two hands in prayer, whilst in other churches a Pastor will hold up a comb and a magic wand and would lift them up to pray to God for protection. These Pastors would raise the objects up and would ask the church members to also pray for their needs and protection to God as they focus on those idols in the name of Jesus, can the Light and Darkness co-exist?; would the Lord Jesus Christ answer such a prayer (1Peter 3:12-13)? Are they even worshipping Christ in the first place by praying to pagan God which is the false spirit of Satan? Can Jesus Christ who is the True and the Holy Spirit co-exist with the false spirit of Satan which is a pagan God? Of course not..? The word God/Satan was in existence and worshipped before the coming of Jesus Christ 2000 years ago, so Jesus is not a pagan God and must not be called or referred to as God which is of Satan. How can we justify that the church and members would be saved by the Saviour Jesus Christ? If these large churches are heavily involved in demonic worship instead of our Lord Jesus Christ the Saviour, what is the fate of salvation of those small churches?

The main issue is that according to many Bible verses, Satan is God and ruler of this world, before and even after Jesus Christ.

Well, Christ came to save everyone who will turn to Him as Jesus Christ whether as an individual or as a group especially families. So salvation is for all regardless of tribe or nation so long as one is adhered to the teachings of the Christ the Saviour.

Christ's message for salvation was spread throughout the world as **the Great Commission** by His Apostles and others. So, in order to highlight the truth of Christ's ministry, and to establish the genuineness of His undiluted divine words which His enemies have tried their hardest to dilute them, has been the reason to highlight the truth. For instance when Jesus said to His disciples "My Father in Heaven", some of them have added the word a God to it to become "my Father God in heaven". Another issue for instance is this, why is it that Jesus Christ who is the True Holy Spirit without sin, would be referred to or being called with the word of the pagan deity as "god/God" which is the false spirit of the Satan.

But Jesus Christ has been compared to various historical and mythological traditions within the Mediterranean Basin including Dionysus, Mithras, Sol Invictus, Osiris, Yahweh, Asclepius. Other pagan Gods include: the Greek, Roman, Egyptian, Celtic, Israelites, India and others. These pagan Gods are the false spirits of Satan worshipped by the ancient world before the coming of Jesus Christ 2000 years ago. These false spirits are still being worshipped by many religions and cultures.

These pagan Gods include: Gaia, Gera, Zeus, Junos, Jupiter, Neptune, Venus, Isis, Osiri, Horus, Morrigan, Danu, Lugh, Yahweh, Baal, Tetragrammaton, Brahma, Mazda and many others. But Jesus Christ is not a pagan God because He is NOT a false spirit of Satan but rather the True Holy Spirit Who has no sin.

Another query to highlight is of how these pagan gods/ Gods which had been worshipped by the ancient world and still being worshipped by many cultures and religions, could now be claimed to be the true almighty creator of the world. These are the Satan's major spirits such as Yahweh, Brahma, Mazda and Jupiter who had been deceiving the world and claiming to be almighty and monotheistic God who have created the world. And why should Jesus Christ who came to this world 2000 years ago as the true Holy

Spirit and the Saviour of humanity through Him that the Father Created the world, (Colossians 1: 16-17) to be called or referred to as a god/God? Is this not one of the reasons that Jesus refers to it as blasphemy in Mathew 12: 30-32 when Pharisees referred to Him as Beelzebul?

The truth is that if someone or a spirit is called or referred to as god/God, that person or thing is associated with the false spirit of Satan. So, when Jesus was referred to as Yahweh/God, He rebuked the leadership of Israel when they would not accept Him because He is the Truth and not like their god Yahweh which they wanted Him to be. He rebuked them saying His anointing and being a deity is not of the Kingdom of this world. This is because He is the Truth not a liar like their lying, evil spirit and a murderer like their god Yahweh from the beginning of the world, (John 8: 44-46).

So, to get some understanding of the issues raised, I resorted in employing primary and secondary research in order to obtain some ideas from people and the experts in their special fields. In so doing, it was revealed in this research that since the pagan god/God is spirit, even though this spirit is false spirit of Satan and whilst Jesus Christ is Holy and True Spirit, many people would not comprehend or see the difference and thus would take a lot of biblical exegesis, hence this book.

The Meaning of the Pagan Word god/God

The pagan word god/God is the Old English word derived from Proto-Germanic word which means a false spirit of Satan who is called or invoked on with libations such as beer or wine for pouring. This false spirit of Satan dwells in everywhere and in everything in the world such as in trees, rivers, rocks, lakes, planets in sky which are named by the Romans and Greeks after their gods/Gods, just as they have with the days, weeks and months after their gods/Gods. These demonic spirits of Satan had been worshipped by the ancient world both by the individuals and with their religious groups before the coming of Jesus Christ to redeem humanity 2000 years ago. The individual pagans that worshipped gods include Terah, he was a manufacturer of statues and idols and a worshipper of these idol/gods, he is Abraham's father. Abraham himself was an idol worshipper, who married his blood sister Sarah and had a son called Isaac with her. Other known individuals who worshipped pagan gods/Gods include Moses who was raised in Pharaoh idol/gods worshipping house in Egypt, David who was physically anointed for the worship of numerous gods of Israel was anointed as King of Israel, Constantine and many others. Israelites worshipped many gods included Yahweh who became the head-god of their gods and also became their national pagan-god. It was this Yahweh that charged Moses to deliver the Israelites from Egypt and murdered many people in Egypt including innocent first born children in the process. Whilst there are disputes among the biblical scholars about the true authorship of the 5 books of the Old Testament, it is claimed that, the Yahweh the elevated head-god of their many pagan-gods claimed to be monotheistic and also the Creator of the world. But my research revealed that no pagan gods such as Yaweh, Brahma, Mazda or Elohim created the world.

The Father in Heaven Created everything in the world through Jesus Christ, (Colossians 1:16-17), including Adam to be the father on this earth in order to be procreating with Eve. Hence men are fathers on the earth for procreation.

Although Christ was born into Abrahamic family, His purpose was to reform it through the teachings of truth, forgiveness of your enemies, love and peace in order for them to gain salvation through Him as a Saviour. This is because Jesus is the Way the Truth and Life. So, when the leadership of Israelites rejected the truth, Jesus rebuked and accused them. Jesus said to them that His kingdom is not of this earth, and that they belong to their father the devil Yahweh who is a liar and a murderer since the beginning of the earth, (John 8: 44-47).

The Birth of Jesus Christ is Unknown

Jesus Christ was not born on 25th December, yet the Catholic Church has enmeshed Him in their yearly pagan gods Christmas celebration on 25th December. *This research has revealed the truth about Jesus Christ that He is NOT a pagan God and thus should not be referred to or called god/God whether in worship or in prayer. It is deception in the use of a capital letter God in referring to Him as God. It is the same deception in disguising Him by Satan. Even many Pastors are worshipping Satan openly in their Churches by lifting up high the Magic wands, sticks, Combs and Freemasonry Swords in Churches and asking their members to focus on these idols whilst praying for protection in Christ's name. Will Jesus the Lord answer such a prayer? (see 1 Peter 3:12-13), of course not, yet there are many people with their mindset would insist on their stubbornness continue praying and referring to Jesus Christ as God. The truth has been revealed for your salvation, He is coming back soon for the judgement.*